12 Gifts from

JESUS CHRIST

Building Habits of Christlike Living

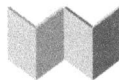

WINTERS
PUBLISHING GROUP

Published by Winters Publishing, LLC
2448 E. 81st St. Suite #4802 | Tulsa, Oklahoma 74137 USA

Published in the United States of America

ISBN: 978-0997612479

12 Gifts from Jesus Christ

*We dedicate this special book
to our Savior, Jesus Christ.*

*Each and every one of us is greatly blessed
by His love and sacrifice. And it is our hope and prayer
that we will all be inspired to live our lives embracing
each of the gifts Jesus came to earth to teach us.*

INTRODUCTION

Thank you for holding this book in your hand and reading the words on this page. We hope you will feel the love of our spirits touching your heart as you continue to read on. We expect that you will, because the entire process of creating the outline, gathering stories for each chapter, and the creative inspirations that came through us were guided by a higher power of LOVE. We speak about twelve GIFTS that Jesus gave to all of us when He lived on earth. We reflect on how we can each use these GIFTS in our daily lives, and how living this way will bring PEACE, JOY, a CONNECTION, LOVE and more. We are filled with HUMILITY and GRATITUDE to have gone through the experience of creating this book. It is just more proof and confirmation, that when we are following the promptings of the Holy Spirit and listening to the guidance, we will feel even greater blessings of the GIFTS. That sense of PEACE is so satisfying, and we think it's one of the best GIFTS in the world. Speaking of GIFTS, we began this project with the idea that this book would be one of those GIFTS that you can give to others, and it truly resonates with the heart and spirit of Christmas. For many people, the Christmas season is their favorite time of year, simply because there is so much LOVE and JOY in the air. Our book is full of stories because we wanted to follow how Jesus often taught concepts and truths, which was through using parables and stories. So we will share our first story with you right now.

We were sitting in a downtown restaurant about a month ago. We had just finished our lunch and were in the middle of making a list of things we had to get done in order to have our book available for this Christmas season. One of our plates had a large pickle left on it (Elizabeth Is allergic to pickles) and this charming, outgoing, funny man stopped at our table as he was walking by and made some silly comment about leaving the pickle on the plate. We joked back, and we started chatting. He had a positive energy about him and we liked his enthusiasm. One thing led to another, and he asked us what we were working on.

We told him about our book, 12 GIFTS FROM JESUS CHRIST, and how we were trying to get it to market before Christmas. (this was in October.) He reminded us that it was a little too close to Christmas for this, which we knew, but then we said how we were going to be looking for a "Print on Demand" printing company and coordinate with a fulfillment company for sending it out. These two steps were actually written on the list of "Things To Do" just five minutes earlier. We realized we were late in the process, but we told him how we had a strong prompting that we had to have it available for this Christmas., and we still felt it would possible.

This man's name by the way, is DeMarr, and he responded by saying, "This is no coincidence. This is meant to be. I am highly involved with a company that has a "Print on Demand" printing component, and we also have a fulfillment (shipping and handling) division in the company." We were amazed and we both just looked up, and felt strongly, that the Holy Spirit and Jesus wanted this book out this year, and they would help open doors for us. It was one of those moments where you realize that all things work together for good when you trust in the Lord.

DeMarr then told us the name of the company, which is SendOutCards. We met DeMarr on a Friday afternoon, and four days earlier, on Monday, one of us, (Janeen), had signed up to be a distributor for this company. And, believe it or not, my sister works for this company in customer service and has frequently told me about how amazing the company is. It is a brilliant business, built upon sincere intentions for helping people send messages, through cards and gifts, for all occasions. The back story of how and why this company was created, is an entire story, filled with hope and positivity. But the company concept began after a loss, involving promptings. The founder of the company, Kody Bateman, shares his entire story about how it all came to be for him, in an inspiring book, **PROMPTINGS: YOUR INNER GUIDE TO MAKING A DIFFERENCE**.

We felt like we were having a strong connection with DeMarr because we had listened to our promptings, and we opened up and told him all about our book. One of the reasons he loved the message of our book goes back to his own personal story. DeMarr told us the story of how one moment in time, when he was eighteen years old, he changed his behavior from that day forward, and it still continues today. When DeMarr was eighteen years old, his father made a comment that DeMarr would never forget. His father said, "I wish every day of the year could be Christmas. People are so nice and kind to each other. It would be nice to see this type of love every day." That moment caused DeMarr to do something every single DAY for **almost** three decades. (We are guessing at DeMarr's age, so we estimated the three decades. We are in our fifties, and just assumed... We sure hope this is not a deal breaker! Haha... Did you notice how we said, ..."almost three decades"?) Every single day, since he was eighteen years old, DeMarr has said, to at least one person a day, "Merry Christmas!" He does this because he wants to remind people to live the Christmas spirit every day of the year. DeMarr decided his father was right when he made that comment about living the Christmas spirit all year long. We loved his story!

And what another miracle! DeMarr's intentions were the same as ours, with the goal being that we all take the time to pay attention to the true GIFTS of Christmas, and practice living these GIFTS so they will become habits. Eventually, embracing these GIFTS as a way of living will cause each of us to become more Christlike year round. The spirit of Christmas is alive and well, and our goal is to help others ponder these same topics. It's easy to get caught up in the hustle and bustle of daily living. But it's also easy to make a decision to practice living each GIFT for one month, and then just see what miracles and PEACE come your way!

When we live each day, with the awareness that we are seeking to become more Christlike in all that we do, we will shift in how we do things. We know that we both did. When we live by our savior's example, we allow His light to beam through us, and people will feel His light. As we let the LOVE of Jesus Christ flow through us, we are letting Jesus LOVE others and touch the hearts of others. Sometimes, we don't know the words we should say to comfort someone, but when His light and LOVE are with us, the words will just flow. Trust in Jesus, and He will open the doors for you.

We wish you a beautiful Christmas season, and an amazing year of living the **12 GIFTS FROM JESUS CHRIST**. You will feel such PEACE and JOY as you do this. We pray that you will always seek His LOVE and guidance, that you will know He is always with you, and that you will feel it.

Merry Christmas!
To DeMarr and everyone!!
We love you!
Elizabeth and Janeen

DAILY REFLECTION

(Repetition is what creates new habit. Read this page daily as a reminder.)

Each chapter is meant to be read slowly,
Absorbing the deeper essence behind the words and stories.

This allows for continual reflection,
Prayer and listening for answers,
Which opens the door to
Greater insight and awareness of
The Gift of Life.

If we devote one month of the year,
To learning and living the Gift of Life,
Our awareness of the precious Gift of Life,
Will be spiritually heightened,
And our daily existence will emulate this awareness.

As we make this shift to mindful attentiveness to the Gift of Life,
We will be less likely to take for granted,
The beauty, the power, and the mystique of Life.
We will have developed a habit,
Which becomes part of who we are.

As we develop a new habit each month,
Based on a different Gift each month,
A Gift that Jesus came to earth to give each one of us,
We will become more like Jesus in the way we live.
As this happens,
We will be living a more Christlike life, every day.
As we do this,
We are expressing our deepest gratitude to Jesus
And our Heavenly Father.

As we share the 12 Gifts with others,
We cannot help but bring the same love and peace
To our own hearts and spirits.

— 1 —

The *Gift* of
LIFE

(and Returning Home) ETERNAL LIFE

As we began to pull our thoughts together for this special book, we pondered the gifts we have been blessed with by our Savior, Jesus Christ. We wanted to choose the gifts that mean the most to us – the gifts that have life-altering abilities – if we choose to allow them to change us. It is our desire that each of us begin to practice these gifts on a regular basis to help us become more like Jesus as we progress throughout our lives.

The idea of practicing is important because, as we have discussed many times, just because we are at the top of the chart in one area – maybe forgiveness – doesn't mean we are there to stay. Each of these gifts is something we must continually remind ourselves to keep working on – and we must put the effort into allowing them to elevate us to a higher level. We may have forgiven someone who wronged us, but down the road, those offenses may resurface or our ability to be kind to that person has wavered. Our constant attention and effort is required throughout our lives if we want to become more like Jesus Christ.

Why did we choose LIFE as the first gift?

"Then spake Jesus again unto them, saying, I am
the light of the world: he that followeth me shall not
walk in darkness, but shall have the light of life."
~ John 8:12 ~

We ultimately chose LIFE as the first gift because the incredible story of Jesus' earthly Life begins with his own birth to young Mary, a virgin, and her fiance, Joseph. The birth of Jesus changed the world.

From the moment Jesus was born, His Life was sought after – King Herod wanted Him dead and went to great lengths to try and make that happen. He ordered the deaths of all baby boys under the age of two in Bethlehem. But Jesus escaped death because His family listened when an angel told them to take Jesus and flee to Egypt.

Jesus' Life on earth was precious. He was sent here to fulfill a purpose, and nothing had power to stand in the way of that divine mission. Have you ever felt that way in your own Life? It seems as though things that are meant to be will find a way. I assume most of us have had moments where we felt that way at times during our lives. Jesus was protected by God and angels in order to fulfill the atonement and give us all not only the gift of everlasting Life, but the chance to gain eternal Life.

"And this is life eternal, that they might know thee, the
only true God and Jesus Christ, whom thou hast sent."
~ John 17:3 ~

According to the Bible and history, Jesus came to earth, not just for some of us, but for each and every one of us. He loves us all the same, and He paid the ultimate price so we could all have everlasting Life – not just some of us, but ALL of us. During His ministry, He taught us how to love and serve others. He suffered agony as He hung on the cross to atone for our sins. None of us is perfect. No matter how close we come in this Life, we cannot return to our Heavenly Father without our Savior Jesus Christ. It is only through Him we can be made perfect so we can one day stand in the presence of our Father in Heaven. He is the answer for each and every person who has ever lived. By repenting of our sins and taking advantage of that precious atonement, we are making Jesus' sacrifice worth the price He paid.

Never forget, He did it for YOU.

Jesus suffered so that we could live and so that we might not only have everlasting Life, but eternal Life – the blessing of living with our Father in Heaven and His Son, Jesus Christ, through eternity.

> *"Verily, verily, I say unto you, He that heareth*
> *my word, and believeth on him that sent me,*
> *hath everlasting life, and shall not come into*
> *condemnation; but is passed from death unto life."*
> *~ John 5:24 ~*

> *Jesus said, "For God so loved the world that He gave*
> *His only begotten Son, that whosoever believeth in*
> *Him should not perish, but have everlasting life."*
> *~ John 3:16 ~*

Life doesn't only pertain to us as human beings. It's about all living things – plants, animals, insects, ocean life, the environment. Even our very earth is a living organism. These are all creations of our Heavenly Father, and what a beautiful world we have been entrusted with – so much beauty and mystery.

"NATURE ALWAYS WEARS THE COLORS OF THE SPIRIT"
~ Ralph Waldo Emerson ~

Think about the times you have been blown away by nature and enjoyed the magic upon our incredible earth. Some of our special memories include:

- a fantastic thunderstorm,
- a breathtaking sunset,
- an ominous waterfall,
- a colorful bird,
- a thick forest or mountainside,
- a calm lake,
- the cool night air on a beautiful fall evening,
- the smell of grass after you mowed it,
- the fresh scent in the air after a rain,
- the beautiful white snow blanketing the earth,
- the beautiful flowers in your garden.

When we stop and think about all of the living things surrounding us in our beautiful world, it is hard to imagine how nature and humans could not co-exist. Imagine if we all protected each and every Life form as if it were just as precious to us as each of Heavenly Father's children are to Him, our world would be a more wonderful, beautiful place.

Our Life is a gift and we will hopefully learn to treat it as such every single day.

Go forth into the busy world and love it. Interest yourself in His life, mingle kindly with its joys and sorrow.
~ Ralph Waldo Emerson ~

When we think about Life and death, we might also contemplate closely-related words that help us to embrace a deeper meaning of Life. These words could include:

HEART, SOUL, DIVINE, BREATH, GROWTH, BEING, ESSENCE, PLANET, ENVIRONMENT, VITALITY, ENERGY

I chose to share the following story because it touched me so deeply that a woman so advanced in age could have such a positive outlook on Life and set aside her own grief to show respect for those dealing with the loss of a loved one.

"LET THEM LOVE YOU"
by Janeen

My good friend, Susan, was talking with me recently about the passing of her husband. He had died suddenly at the age of 58, and she was grieving and doing her best to work through a process of acceptance and understanding. Death of a loved one, especially a sudden death, can't ever be easy. It leaves behind so many unanswered questions and so much heartbreak. But Susan left early the morning after her husband's death to visit her husband's mother and tell her of the events that had just transpired. Her mother-in-law had some words of wisdom for her that I want to share with you because they were so incredibly insightful.

Here she was, a 93-year-old woman who had just lost her son, and these are the words she spoke to my friend, her daughter-in-law: "I know your first inclination is to go home, close all the blinds, climb into bed, and pull the covers up over your head. But don't do it. Instead, open all the blinds, and open your door to all of your friends and neighbors who want to help you, who want to bring food, who want to do things for you and take care of you and check on you. Let the world in to help you during this time. Let them love you. Do it for yourself and your family, and do it for them."

She was telling my friend, Susan, to go on living. She was telling her to celebrate Life and help her family and friends to do the same. Life is worth living, no matter what may happen to us along the way.

I was so moved by her words, I was speechless for a moment. This mother had just lost her very own son, but she was able to put her own grieving aside so she could help her grieving daughter-in-law find peace. The first words out of her mouth were to offer comfort to someone else.

How wonderful that a woman could be so selfless. Perhaps her years of wisdom have provided her with that ability. Perhaps the gift of Life has been precious to her. And perhaps the idea that her son was returning home gave her an incredible amount of insight.

"Let your light so shine before men, that they may see your good works, and glorify your Father which is in heaven."
~ Matthew 5:16 ~

"In him was life; and the life was the light of men."
~ John 1:4 ~

As we contemplate the gift of LIFE and what all the ins and outs of it really are, we thought it would be helpful to come up with some questions that would get our minds working. So see what you can come up with here. Really think about it before you answer:

What makes your heart leap?

_____

_____

_____

_____

_____

What did you savor today?

_____

_____

_____

_____

_____

What do you live for?

_____

_____

_____

_____

_____

_____

What makes you sing out loud in your car or the shower?

_____

_____

_____

_____

_____

What are your happiest memories?

_____

_____

_____

_____

_____

What takes your breath away?

_____

_____

_____

_____

_____

Jesus Christ came to this earth to show us, by example, how to live and how to treat others. Life is truly a gift. Our lives upon this earth serve a purpose, and it is up to each one of us individually to determine what our purpose is. If we believe that Life does not end with death, but continues on throughout eternity, this belief causes us to examine the depth of our own purpose on this earth.

So what is important in this Life? Have you ever seen anyone take their worldly possessions with them when they die? Do we have access to our bank accounts and our credit cards and our beautiful jewelry and clothes once we cross to the other side? The answer, of course, is no! I used to wish I could take those things with me when I was a kid... But now that I've lived quite a bit of Life, I realize the things I want are the people who are important to me, my experiences, and my Life lessons.

Fortunately for each of us, the things we DO get to take with us when we die are the relationships we have formed here, the lessons we have learned, and the wisdom we grew into as we became enlightened.

And we don't know, for sure, about some of the other things we might get to take – such as the awareness of all the love and kindness we shared with others. And what about our unhealthy relationships – do you suppose we might take with us the lessons we still need to learn from these relationships?

It makes sense doesn't it?

It is possible that a person who has an addiction that hasn't been resolved prior to their earthly death will take that struggle with them. They will be able to work on and resolve it after this Life. It makes sense that we will begin where we left off here on earth and continue to grow and learn and progress.
That offers us comfort because it gives us the assurance that if we do the very best we can in this Life, we have the opportunity to continue to work on our imperfections and improve once we have passed on.

We hope this offers you comfort as well as you ponder these ideas.

With that in mind, make it your GOAL this month as you ponder the Gift of Life to establish a new relationship or two, or repair one that needs some work.

Pick a topic you'd like to know more about and study it.

Come up with your own GOAL that you personally want to set as a way to improve in some area of your Life.

We would like you to begin your journey by thinking about what your impressions are about the gift of LIFE.

As you begin reading this chapter, write down a few thoughts you have as you contemplate the gift of Life. We will ask this question again at the end of the chapter after you have completed your study of the gift of Life.

_____

_____

_____

_____

_____

_____

_____

_____

_____

_____

_____

_____

_____

What did Jesus say about LIFE?

"He that findeth his life shall lose it: and he
that loseth his life for my sake shall find it."
~ Matthew 10:39 ~

Our Savior loves us. He wants us to be happy, and He wants us to do all we can to make our lives here on earth worthwhile. He expects us to take care of ourselves – to progress and learn and be productive. And He wants us to serve others – our families, our neighbors and people we don't know.

He wants us to believe in Him and rely on Him. He experienced our trials, our heartaches, our illnesses, our struggles, our fears, our worries. He carries our burdens so we don't have to. Even though Jesus may not have lived out specifically the Life experience each of us have, He understands, and He is there to love us through it.

We think one of the biggest tests of our faith lies in being able to turn our problems over to the Lord. It isn't easy to let go of the control we sometimes like to have over things, but if we can do it, hopefully we can begin to feel His hand in our Life. He will guide us, protect us and help us.

"And Jesus said unto them, I am the bread of
life: he that cometh to me shall never hunger;
and he that believeth on me shall never thirst..."
~ John 6:35 ~

Stories to help us reflect on the Gift of LIFE:

We are using stories as a means to discuss the gifts we are talking about in our book because one of Jesus' favorite strategies for teaching people was to speak in parables, which are symbolic stories that teach gospel truths by comparing them to earthly things.

Jesus spoke in parables to simultaneously teach his message to his disciples and conceal it from unbelievers. He let his disciples know that those who had ears that were listening for spiritual truth would find it in the stories he told, while those who were only interested in Jesus' celebrity would simply hear a good story.

When we listen to the stories of others, we can learn from example and find truth for ourselves. Stories are a compelling way to teach and impress on the mind things that may otherwise be forgotten.

We will share some of our own stories and the stories of others on the following pages to help you learn from some of the lessons we have learned in our own lives.

"LIVING WITH LOVE
AS WE APPROACH OUR DEATH"
by Elizabeth

I had a beautiful gift come into my Life about ten years ago. I met a feisty, happy, energetic and very spiritual woman whom I made a deep connection with. She was in her eighties and I was in my forties, so she had twice the Life wisdom that I had, and every now and then, she would remind me of this. She loved to make others laugh, smile and just warm their hearts. She often showed her love to others by being silly and funny and, of course, by telling many stories about her Life and lessons learned.

Her name was Adele. This is her true name because she is one person who would be upset if I DID change her name. She would want the story told correctly. I loved this about her. She was strong, opinionated, and she loved Jesus Christ with all of her heart. I noticed over the years that she would use her gift of humor to disarm people, and once everyone was relaxed, she would share her stories about her faith in Jesus and how God loves each and every one of us so much. People trusted Adele because she walked in truth and you could almost feel the presence of the Holy Spirit around her.

So therefore, It was easy to become friends with Adele because she knew how to love – her spirit was in tune with others, and she lived according to the promptings she felt from the Holy Spirit. Adele's husband, Max, had passed away many years before, and she missed him a lot. Many of my conversations with Adele somehow intertwined a story or two about the love of her life, Max. Adele was a great storyteller, and she loved telling the story about how she and Max met at a dance. They had both arrived with different dates. (If Adele was telling the story, there would be more details about a sister who had been asked out on a date by Max, but since I won't get the details right, I will give the brief version of the story.) But Adele and Max immediately noticed each other and, eventually they were married and had a beautiful son, loving daughter-in-law and grandchildren.

Even if I attempted to share one of Adele's stories, I would not do it justice. And when I tried to, Adele would remind me that I skipped a part, so that's why I will tell my version of what I recall. Mostly, with Adele, my memories were about love, laughter, and her hope for being reunited with her husband in heaven and meeting Jesus. She knew in her heart that Max would be waiting to help her cross over when it was her time. She spoke about Max on a daily basis to at least one person.

Many of my family members tell me, "Get to the point... Tell the story..." but I feel that I have to set the stage so that the reader or listener can understand the significance of the back story, and how it comes full circle to the end of the story. In this case, I believe you will understand why I had to provide such a long back story. But, in all fairness, my family members are accurate in how I can be very long winded, so I'm striving to find a balance. There is a balance.

Thank you Janeen, my very patient co-author, for letting me ramble at times, and then condensing many words into one paragraph! Janeen was an anchor for a TV station, and she was trained in how to get to the point in her college broadcasting classes, and she can take a 1,000 word story, and tell the same story in 100 words. Editing is another great gift, that some have and others desire. Yet, there is always something to hearing the reasoning and background of how a story came to be. Once the background is shared, the story makes more sense.

Here is the last part of my story with Adele on earth and how she made her transition to heaven. It is a sacred story, and I am sharing it now because I know that it can speak to others.

I have a strong prompting to share it, and I know Adele would want me to get the story correct. (If she can see, hear or watch this process, she is having a good laugh in heaven, because she knows that the details matter. Love you Adele!! Haha, and I still laugh when I think of our times together. Thank you.)

I'm sharing this partly because I know that many others have gone through a similar loss, and they might have worries about their own death process and crossing over. I believe that this story can take away many worries and fears. Adele would have wanted me to share her story, for this reason alone. She shared faith, hope and joy. She had a faith so strong that she knew she would see Max again when it was her time to cross over.

So here is what happened on a beautiful autumn day.

I was a busy professional keeping up with current research in my field, along with new emerging approaches for settling divorce cases. As a mediator and educator, I was very interested in learning more about this information. There was an important family law conference happening in my city, and I had arranged a meeting with the keynote speaker whom I had previously met at another national conference, and I was on my way to this meeting. I felt honored that he would take the time to meet me after he conducted his presentation.

I had prepared some questions and wanted to share some of the data from my program with him. I was looking forward to this, and it was clearly an important meeting. I was set to show up early for the meeting and be prepared and professional. Yet, there are times when the Holy Spirit is so strong that some meetings must be rescheduled. I learned later that this was indeed one of those times.

As I was leaving my neighborhood to go downtown to meet with him, I felt the strongest urge to drive down Adele's street and visit her. I had turned down her street many times and just popped in for a visit, and it was always wonderful. But this felt different. My logical mind tried to talk me out of visiting Adele, but I knew I had to stop. I am so grateful and glad that I listened to the promptings that day.

Preparing Adele for her Transition

I pulled into Adele's driveway, as I often did, and I went into her home. Adele had two friends from the neighborhood with her at the moment, one of whom was deaf and trying hard to communicate with me. She could hear loud words and read my mouth. Her name was Mary, and she was a dear friend and comfort to Adele. Another woman, also Mary, had stopped by to visit. She was trying to figure out what to do because Adele was either having a stroke or a heart attack. Adele could still speak and order us around (which I know she might chuckle about now) but she was also in great pain and having difficulty speaking. She was telling all three of us that she wanted to go back home to heaven and be with Max and be with Jesus. Adele had told all of us for years that she was excited about dying and going back home. So we all knew her wishes, as did her family members.

When I arrived at Adele's home, I felt Adele's concerns. She wanted to leave and meet up with Max, and be with Jesus, but she also knew she had some unfinished business on earth. She told me quickly what was happening with her. I assumed that she was having a stroke based on the look of her face (drooping on one side) and she was not able to lift her arm. She told me, "I can't move this side of my body," which often sounds like a stroke. So, as I was trying to recall my understanding of what to do for a stroke, I decided that an aspirin was the remedy, short term. I told Adele and she made me chop it up and put in water because she could not swallow. So I did. She sipped it down with a straw. I tried to give her another one, but she refused. The first aspirin helped.

I had been recalling the television commercials which suggested giving an aspirin to a patient who is having a heart attack prior to getting to the hospital. And, indeed, it was a heart attack that Adele was having and not a stroke. So, I felt like we had another little miracle in the midst of this stressful situation. As Adele described her inability to move one side of her body, and her face was drooping, many of us might guess that it was a stroke. Perhaps the medical field suggests taking an aspirin for a stroke, while waiting for medical attention – I'm not current about this or sure.

But what I do know is the doctors said that the aspirin helped Adele before she arrived at the hospital. I suggested the aspirin because I mixed up the medical condition. In the end, all of the people who intersected and assisted with Adele having an extra week on this earth provided the gift of Adele and her loved ones to have the necessary and tender personal closure of holding hands and expressing love. It was surely worth it for all family members and friends.

I knew that the other Mary (friend and neighbor) was on the phone calling Adele's son and daughter in-law, so I was busy talking to Adele. I also knew that Adele had told us NOT to call 911 because she was ready to go. She felt like this was her time. In the midst of her pain, she was still clear enough to inform us that we should NOT call 911. So as I was taking care of Adele, Mary went into another room and called Adele's son and daughter in law. They called 911 and the paramedics arrived quickly.

Adele was admitted to a hospital of her choice, and she learned that she was having a heart attack. She was offered a surgery to repair her heart, but she refused it. Her family tried to help her see her options, but they knew she was ready, and they also agreed. She fully understood her choices and was very aware of her outcome. She made it clear to everyone that she wanted to leave earth and make her transition to heaven. Several days later, Adele was moved to a lovely Hospice Care Center. Upon Adele's arrival, I visited. It was nice but she was tired. Several days later, I visited again. This time she wanted to talk. She asked me, "Why do you think the Lord did not take me that day at my home? I was ready to go."

I waited a few minutes, and I told her, "You have been telling everyone, for years, that you were ready to die and be with Max again, that it almost became routine. But your loved ones needed to have a chance to really say goodbye. If you had left on that day at your house, they would not have had the chance to hold your hand again and tell you how much they loved you. They needed more time, even if you did not." Adele agreed with me, and said that people had been coming by to visit.

I stopped by to hold Adele's hand and just share my love over the next few days. Usually, Adele was on the morphine drip to ease her pain, and she was not responsive. She did look at me when she woke up, but she drifted back to sleep. I was grateful that I had these moments with her. I knew she realized how much I loved her, and that made me feel great peace. I too, wanted her to be reunited with Max because he was the love of her life, and her eternal partner.

However, the day that Adele made her transition home to heaven I, once again, had a strong prompting to visit her in the hospice care center. It was in the morning about 10 am, and I was holding her hand and saying loving words to her. She opened her eyes and looked at me lovingly for about three minutes. I could feel her love. Then a nurse came into the room to check her vitals, and while she was doing this, Adele's eyes opened wide. Her eyes looked past both of us, and Adele looked towards the ceiling, and it was very obvious that Adele had just seen sprits from the other side. Adele's face just lit up, but she was not connecting with us. She was seeing the light from above. They were coming to get her and take her home. There was no doubt. The nurse even told me that I was lucky to experience this, and that she had seen it many times. But often, a patient will slip away quietly and others do not get to see the transition. This nurse said that it is a gift when you get to see how a person's eyes will find the light.

Adele was still with us, and I knew that her family needed to be with her. So I asked the nurse to get them, (they had allowed me to have a private moment with Adele) and then I left the center. I had received my closure and many blessings. Adele's family needed to sit with her, and they did. Adele made her transition later that afternoon with her family around her. I have never asked details about Adele's passing, because I already knew in my heart that she was back with Max and that she had met Jesus. I had all of the answers I would ever need. Adele was home again. Amen.

Thank you Adele for allowing me the gift of watching your eyes connect with the spirit world. I saw it and I felt it. I knew without a doubt that Max was there to help you cross over. I'm sure that your arrival in heaven was splendid and that you were able to meet Jesus. Your joy, laughter, and love touched many people on earth. I know that you get to take all of these loving memories with you to heaven. Thank you for your loving imprint on earth. Your love marks will ripple over and over again.

P.S. As fate and divine order would have it, the first firetruck that arrived on the scene did not have paramedics as part of the staff (they just happened to be nearby). The next firetruck had several paramedics on the crew. One of those paramedics was a former boyfriend of mine from college, whom I had never had closure with. He is a great person, has a wonderful family, and was very kind to me during this episode at Adele's house. I would guess that Adele might have had a hand in this opportunity for closure. I no longer wonder about anything and all is well, Adele. I have had the necessary closure about this past relationship, thanks to your heart attack. (Adele would laugh out loud about this, which is the only reason I am writing it this way.)

But thank you again, or other angels, if you had a hand in this special event with Adele and the paramedics. I love how life shows us many coincidental intersections about how divine order is really at work, if we are paying attention. We often call these moments, "miracles." Life is full of them. We just need to connect the dots and intersections, and we will feel God's hand in so many ways in our individual lives.

IT'S NOT YOUR TIME TO GO
by Janeen

Our lives on this earth are precious, and sometimes I don't think we understand just how thin the veil is between us and those who have passed on. I have a firm belief in the fact that the Spirit World is amongst us – that we are all very close. I have had friends experience things that have increased my faith in that knowledge. I'm sure each of us have had similar things happen or have had friends who have shared their stories with us.

I personally had never had a brush with the Spirit World until July of 2011 when my mother was in the hospital for an extended stay. I had been at my parents' home visiting early one afternoon because my mom hadn't been feeling well. She was in bed trying to rest, and when I woke her up I could see she wasn't doing well at all. Because I had been worried about mom for some time, I called my oldest daughter, Tia, to talk to her about it and she decided she was going to spend the night so she could keep an eye on her.

In the middle of the night, Tia woke up suddenly and so she climbed out of bed to check on things. She realized her grandmother wasn't breathing. She woke up her grandpa and they quickly called 911. But, by the time they arrived, she had been without oxygen for a dangerous amount of time. She spent the next six weeks in the hospital working to recover, and it was real touch and go for a long time. Each of us in the family would take turns spending a night at the hospital with her just to watch over her and make sure she knew someone was there – although she remembered nothing of that six weeks once it was over.

One night, my sister and I decided to stay the night together – kind of a slumber party on a Friday night – and a chance to talk and catch up. We were awakened in the middle of the night by mom talking loudly. We sat up and listened. It soon became apparent she was talking to her mother, her Aunt Ida Bell and her Uncle Bill, all of whom had passed on a few years earlier. She began crying and begging them to let her come with them. She was asking them, "Why can't I come with you?" and she was so adamant about going. They must have told her it was not her time yet, because she sobbed and sobbed.

My sister and I were heartbroken for her, but it was then that I knew for certainty she was going to pull through. She was not going to die – not now. It was not her time, and we knew it.

I know my grandmother, my great aunt and uncle were in the room that night. I did not see them or talk with them, but my mother did. It was a true and real experience.

When we told her about it once she recovered and returned home, she was so touched by it she began to cry.

Our Father in Heaven gave us the gift of Life, and He expects us to do something good with it. He expects us to help others, make life better for those around us, and contribute something.

I was so grateful that night to know my mother would be coming home and that we would have her awhile longer. When it finally was her time to go, we were all ready, and we had said and done the things we wanted to say and do before she left us.

The day she passed away, her precious Aunt Ida Bell came to take her home. I knew it with every fiber of my being as I watched mom look past me and say, with a sparkle in her eye, "Ida Bell is here." She looked around me to wave at her and seemed to be playing games with her. She waved at her a bit later as she looked over toward the window. I was so happy that it was finally time for her to go. She had lived a long Life, filled with much illness, and she needed relief. How wonderful it made us feel as a family to know that our angel, Aunt Ida Bell, had come for her and she was not leaving this world all alone.

She had fallen into a deep sleep when the monitors suddenly stopped and she slipped away quietly and peacefully. Her nurse looked at me with an almost excitement in her eyes as she told me, "She has passed over." I will never forget that. I too have always felt death is a blessing, because it gives us the opportunity to reunite with our Savior. For those of us left here on earth it seems sad because we will miss our loved one. But for them, it is a glorious day. It is a day when they return to their Savior and to their loved ones who have gone before. I never want to lose sight of that.

I feel now that my mother is my guardian angel – watching over my Life. I have felt her near many times and have even asked out loud if she was there with me. I look forward to the day when I will be reunited with her.

In the meantime, I learned from this experience to cherish my own Life and do my best to live it fully.

"I am the living bread which came down from heaven: if any man eat of this bread, he shall live for ever: and the bread that I will give is my flesh, which I will give for the life of the world."
~ John 6:51 ~

HOSPICE FOR PEOPLE WITHOUT A HOME
by Janeen

As we were in the process of writing this chapter, we came across a current story about a woman in Utah who is starting a new hospice for people without a home. The idea behind it is that all people - no matter their circumstance – deserve a comfortable place to die. What a beautiful thought. And how wonderful that there are people in this world who make it their Life's work to think of ways to help others. The hospice is a safe place for individuals to spend their final days, weeks or months and be helped and loved by people who care. It also plans to help reconnect patients with estranged family members, hold a community memorial service and place a marker in a memorial garden for each of them.

When we read this story, we felt a renewal of hope. The mission people were deeply touched. Everyone's life is meaningful. It's thought-provoking to realize that so many people in our world, and even so close to home, have such huge trials.

For someone to realize that everyone's Life is a gift and put the time and effort into creating a place of refuge that respects and honors that gift is an amazing thing.

LIFE, EARTH, BRIDGES AND CONNECTIONS
by Elizabeth

I have always loved the nostalgia and beauty of the old time wood bridges often found in the upstate mountains of New York and other east coast states where mountains, rivers and streams intersect. The autumn season in these beautifully created natural landscapes showcase a spectrum of colors that can be felt and experienced with all of our available senses. Walking through these areas with the breezy winds scattering the leaves in all directions, with just the right amount of warmth felt from the sun, is a breathtaking and truly humbling experience. These precious memories and other occasions when I have been in the midst of magnificent beauty here on earth, cause me to feel especially close to God as I quietly (and sometimes loudly) express my thanks and joy to heaven for the magic and beauty of earth.

To stand amongst the most beautiful mountains, rivers, canyons, meadows, and other gifts of nature, my gratitude meter is simply off the charts. First, that these places of beauty even exist on earth, and second, I have humble appreciation because I get to be a part of it and absorb it with my entire being. Our earth is a precious gift that we have been entrusted with to appreciate, enjoy, and preserve for future generations. As we mature in life, we tend to become more concerned with the legacy of what our generation will leave for future generations. As we contemplate long term planning issues, such as the building and restoration of bridges, it causes us to consider similar efforts from our ancestors.

When we reflect upon how our ancestors decided upon where to build the bridges, and how they would be built, it can captivate our true appreciation for the vision they had. Their work ethic, and the long term gift they were providing to future generations, was clearly evident in their planning. They recognized the importance of how a bridge could make necessary travels more efficient, along with how bridges connect people and communities.

Many of these amazing bridges have been maintained, restored, or rebuilt in a way to preserve the legacy and the foresight that our ancestors had worked so diligently on. When you stand on one of these beautiful bridges, if you are still enough, you can almost feel the vision and the hope that the builders had for the construction project. If you are fortunate enough to travel through the amazing landscapes of the beautiful United States, consider traveling through the northeast during an autumn season. These beautiful bridges are often situated in some of the most pristine areas of the countryside, and they often serve as the background for many famous movies and other amazing photographic moments, including thousands of postcards and paintings. The beauty of these areas upon our earth create feelings of comfort and reassurance that all is well in the universe. These feelings inspire other feelings of hope for the future and a sense of peace that God is in charge of our earth, and He will always provide for his children through our Savior, Jesus Christ. Nature on earth inspires people, and this made me start wondering about what animals and wildlife might also be feeling as they live in the outdoors, wandering through the beauty each day.

The beauty of our earth did not happen by accident. It was designed in heaven before we ever arrived here. You can read all about this in the Bible, and you can ponder the creation of earth. However, it's hard to not notice how amazing the full design and plan of earth, people and animals truly is.

We invite you, as the reader, to join us on this path of studying and practicing 12 gifts that each of us received from Jesus. One of the best ways to show our appreciation to a gift giver is to truly appreciate the gift, utilize it, and also enjoy the gift. If we accept that Jesus came to earth to teach us about these 12 Gifts, we can then show our gratitude to Jesus for His sacrifices and love as He shared the gifts with us. These gifts are part of the plan for how we can return to our Father in Heaven. It is hard to separate people from the planet earth because so much of our existence is intertwined and co-dependent in a healthy way. We believe that life on earth is so worth contemplating, and it is truly an individual journey worth exploring.

If you consider the possibility that individual spirits first exist in heaven, according to divine order, there is a time when each spirit departs heaven and takes a body on earth. During the soul's time on earth, there are many lessons to be learned and life is full of choices, challenges, and possibilities, along with, yes, those sometimes dreaded consequences. However, it is often through the consequences, positive and negative, that we learn our greatest lessons. If you consider that each life on earth is here to grow, learn, and evolve spiritually, then we understand that living and learning are a major part of our existence on earth.

We are sharing our back stories about this book project, along with our own personal stories of growth and insights, and some of our beliefs and philosophy. We are doing this because we want you, the reader, to be able to relate to us and feel that common connection that we all share. We all walk the same journey of life, with different life experiences and unique stories, but with common goals of living our lives with a spiritual purpose, and establishing and maintaining a strong relationship with our brother and Savior, Jesus.

It is our intention to invite you to join us on your own personal spiritual journey, and take the messages that inspire you, and put aside the messages that do not speak to you right now. One size does not fit all, and spiritual growth is a very personal and sacred process between a person and Jesus. We believe that it is through personal choice, desire, intention, and focused efforts that we each allow the Holy Spirit to work through us and with us. We are simply sharing our stories, our personal experiences, our understanding of specific biblical citations, as a way of prompting you as a child of this universe to seek a deeper connection to Jesus, and your own personal spiritual journey.

We know from our Life stories, faith, and our spiritual journey that Jesus is available to each of us, in good times and in difficult times. We might not always get the answer we are hoping for in prayer, but if we listen, during and after our prayers, we will often feel some comfort and guidance. We cannot predict exactly how this occurs. It is a spiritual journey that you, and only you, can awaken to when you are seeking the truth, the light, and the way. Jesus will be listening. Pay attention to the clues and listen. Your guidance will come. This can take time and some practice. Our book is about building habits that will bring us closer to Jesus as we live our daily lives.

I share all of this with you because I love Jesus, and I have had many promptings over the past ten years to write this book, along with many inspired messages. One of my challenges in life, among others, is day to day organization. I would get an inspiration, write it down and file it somewhere, and then spend much wasted time looking for it later. After many prayers about this, I finally met another author who was very organized and also strived to live her life in a Christ-like way. Janeen, my co-author, has become a great friend, and she has so many abilities and talents which compliment my creative talents and random indirection (or inspiration as I prefer to think of it), which often leads to a process of thinking "outside the box."

Between the two of us, we have been able to merge our gifts, talents and commitment to get this book into the hands of our readers. We know this book has been divinely guided, simply because of the many ideas and inspirations we were prompted to write about, and because of the many miracles that happened along the way. We have enough stories about the process that it might take a future website or another story to explain the details. (It's challenging enough to stay on focus with a clear topic, along with ADD interruptions, at least for one of us.) The story about the making of this book will come later.

We have learned that patience is one of the most time-tested life gifts that we can all learn. As most of us live our lives, we grow to understand the importance of patience. It is shown to us through typical Life moments, and our ability to pay attention to our spiritual "ah-hah moments". These precious and sacred "ah-hah moments" are the ones that we will share with you, our fellow life travelers and human beings, because we know that our journey here on earth is all about connecting with others and sharing stories about love. Between the two of us, we have over 100 hundreds years of living here on earth. (We have learned much about humility and honesty too.) Ten years ago, neither of us would have admitted our age. The older we get, we realize that as we grow older, we also grow in other areas as well, such as Life wisdom, confidence and security. This doesn't make us smarter or greater. The accumulation of years simply provides perspective about the past, wisdom about the things that really matter in Life, and a sense of desire to share things with others for our common good. We are all human, and we are all connected. This admission simply tells you that we have arrived at this point in our lives, and we are open to being honest, vulnerable, sharing, and caring about the important things in Life. Our book is motivated simply by love. It is the pure love of Jesus Christ that inspires us to do this.

We care about you and we love you. If our stories and messages can touch your heart, please embrace them. If not, we thank you for taking the time to read our words, and we hope that you find the peace and love in your heart that you might be seeking. We truly wish you all the best.

My Personal Story About The Gift of Life

So here is my very personal story about the gift of Life that I experienced when I was seventeen years old. I have not shared this story with any other person until now. I did not have a reason to share it before, simply because I found a spiritual way to resolve it and did not feel the need to tell others, until now. As I am co-writing this book, I feel a responsibility to be as honest and open as I can be as we share our journeys along our spiritual path to Jesus and with Jesus. Now there is a reason to share this private story from my past. As I recall that evening, I am humbled and grateful beyond words.

I was fortunate enough to grow up in a beautiful small town in upstate New York, with the Catskill Mountains on one side, and the Hudson River meandering on the other side of town. This town is charming, picturesque, and welcoming. Many NYC folks came up for the weekends just to absorb the amazing landscape and other landmarks throughout town.

I am writing this to speak to people of all ages, but especially to teenagers, who might experience a time like I did and possibly distort reality, which can lead to poor decision making. If my story can touch one, or many teenagers, helping to expand their present perspective and find the hope in tomorrow, then this is worth opening up and being vulnerable. Plus, I have to share it because I tried to pray my way out of it and each time I came up with a different story, I felt the prompting of the Holy Spirit, "Tell the story." We are all human, and I hope that you can feel the human connection here.

Many high schools have a dance where it is "girl's choice" to invite a boy, or partner, to the dance. My high school had one dance a year where the girl was expected to invite the boy.

I set my sets high and I invited a popular, very handsome guy to the dance. He said yes, and I was so excited and could not stop imagining how wonderful the date and dance would be. I was searching for the right dress and imagining all of the other details. I was just a few days into my bliss when I started to hear rumblings that this guy, my date who had said yes, was telling others that he did not want to go to the dance with me. Another girl had invited him after I did, and he had said yes to her. Of course I didn't believe it. He wouldn't or couldn't do that to me. Two days later, I realized it was true. He had asked one of my best friends to tell me that he was going with someone else. I should have known by then because everywhere I went in school, other students were looking at me. They were wondering if I had heard the bad news yet. It made sense later.

So of course, I was humiliated and embarrassed. Everyone else knew before I knew. But no one would tell me. They just stared at me and wondered. Can you imagine how hard it was to find out about this rejection later, after all of the rumors and gossip? I felt like the fool of the school. My way of coping with such sad news was to retreat into myself and play out the events in my mind over and over. I think that many teens today might still have similar ways of coping. At seventeen, I didn't have the verbal skills or emotional maturity to fully express my feelings and ask someone for help. I just knew going back to school and facing my peers after everyone knew that I had been told the truth – that this guy was going to the dance with someone else – could be the most humiliating day of my life. I knew I could not handle it.

So I thought about all of my options and nothing could possibly fix this. It felt like the end of the world for me at seventeen. So I asked my parents if I could use the one and only family car to go visit a friend that night. They said yes, and they had no clue about what happened that day at school. I was supposed to be home by 9:30. I did not go and visit a friend. I drove to a beautiful country bridge, parked the car, got out and sat on the ground and I cried my eyes out. I finally had a chance to release all of my pent up emotions. It felt great to cry it all out and finally get mad at him for doing this to me. But then I thought about going back to school and facing my peers. I wrote a note saying sorry and sharing my love for others.

Then I climbed up onto the bridge. My car was parked below, and I prayed to Jesus that He would take me and that heaven would be better than the pain I was facing. I was prepared to jump, thinking that I would die. But there was such a strong force of power not letting me jump. To this day, I cannot tell you if it was Jesus, guardian angels, perhaps a team of angels, or something else, but I could not jump. The force was so strong that when I tried to lean forward it pulled me backwards. Since I just prayed to Jesus, I concluded that He was telling me not to do it. I was still crying the last of my tears as I climbed back down to my car.

I wiped my tears back and decided that I was meant to live. Plus, I realized that my parents needed the car for work. I was a pretty responsible kid and I worried about them not having a car for work the next day. But at the time, the feelings to escape the pain were intense and real. I must tell anyone reading this who might ever have similar thoughts like I did, "This, too, shall pass." That saying has been around forever, but I can assure you it's true. Whatever crisis you might be facing at a moment where you are contemplating taking your own Life, I know for a fact things will get better. I am living proof of this. You have no idea of what God has in store for the rest of your Life. Please be curious enough about it to put off your suicide plans for a day, or a week, or a year. And then years will turn into decades and you will have endured many ups and downs. You will have grown so much wiser for it all. And, I promise, you will feel grateful for putting off your decision during your pain. Everything can wait a day, or two or more. And things will work out. Just pray to Jesus and listen for His love. It will come. I know this for a fact.

Please, please teenagers, NEVER even consider suicide as a solution. The pain left upon earth with your loved ones is Life changing, and your own Life has so many possibilities that cannot even be realized in the moment. I promise you that these negative dark thoughts are temporary, and the light will come again. There is always a way out of this, and these are temporary setbacks that will be overcome! I have so many other stories to share about this, but for now, please trust me. Suicide is not the way to solve a romantic teenage problem or young adult problem or frankly, any problem at all. There are so many other solutions. It's just that in the dark moments of despair, our mind and judgement get clouded and it's hard to see clearly. Take another day, at the very least, to think about it, pray about it, and reach out. I promise you that the light will come again and it will show you the way. Life is a beautiful gift from our Heavenly Father, and He wants us to live out our divine time on earth. His love will be with you to help you through your darkest hours. Just pray to Him through Jesus.

I am so grateful that I was prevented from jumping from the bridge that night. I thank God for this because it made me realize that each and every Life is so precious to our Savior, Jesus Christ. He will always be there to save us and love us, if we just give Him the chance, and trust that His peace will come. It will. Jesus gives us the amazing peace that cannot come from the world. His peace is so deep and still. Jesus knows each of our needs. He will share His peace as we open our hearts and trust His path.

Peace and trust go hand in hand. This has been my personal experience. The more I trust, the more I feel His peace. I imagine that He just smiles and wonders what I'm waiting for. But we all have our own divine paths to walk and Jesus knows this. Baby steps towards Jesus are much better than no steps at all. Jesus has a sense of humor, even when we don't get the joke. He loves us anyway, no matter what. He loves us in a way we cannot even comprehend. So just try and wrap your heart and brain around that. It's not easy to do, but that's why He is Jesus and we are on earth trying to become more Christ-like.

So now that I have shared one of my private stories with the world, and my family and friends, for the first time, I'm sure my family and friends are concerned. I promise everyone I have never had another thought about suicide since then. That evening changed me. The spiritual power with me that night told me no. I knew I could never consider this thought again. If you ever consider any thought about taking your own Life, please recall my story. It is not worth it. Life goes on. Problems get solved. Romance sadness is not worth the cost of your Life on earth. Everyone who loves deeply feels the devastating sadness of a break up. But we all have the capacity to get over it. Do not give anyone else that power over you to make you think that your Life is not worth it. EVERY LIFE MATTERS. We all have a purpose. Each and every Life comes to earth for a divine purpose. You might not have discovered your purpose yet, but with prayer and attention, I know Jesus will reveal it to you.

Patience and Gratitude are Necessary in Life

Patience is a gift that can also be developed. I know a teenager's despair and desperation at this type of moment is so real and overwhelming. These times could have the power to convince a teen there is no way out, and the best option is to just end it all and die. That was my plan on this very sad night, on this beautiful bridge that I loved so much. It was one of my favorite places to be during the autumn season. That would have been such a sad ending to my Life at seventeen. Now, at fifty six, my gratitude cup runs over. So much good has happened since then. I will share some of the wonderful stories of my Life throughout this book. My Life has had ups and downs, like most lives, but the positive always outweighs the negative, and lessons have been learned. Life can be a school as we have many spiritual lessons to learn while growing on earth.

I thank the angels, the Holy Spirit and Jesus. I felt the strongest sense of peace come over me as I stood on that bridge and wondered about how I would die. My thinking process was SO WRONG!!!! Please do NOT even entertain this inaccurate thinking. I think sometimes when we allow this negative thinking to come into our minds, we could open the door to be tempted to go along with bad thoughts. DO NOT even open the door. Just believe your Life is a gift, because it is. Healing will prevail and, in time, you will also realize how important your path in Life is to the universe.

I felt a pull for a reason. Over the decades, I knew I had a purpose and I truly felt a power so much stronger than myself. So I listened even when I struggled. My Life continued. I pursued my path. I married and started a family. Life was rearranged, as divorce does, but I was still a mother, a social worker, mediator, author, counselor, and more. The story of the bridge will come full circle.

Another Bridge, 31 Years Later

Thirty one years later, I encountered a scene that I could not ignore. I was picking up my teenage daughter and her friends from a local swimming pool, and the necessary road I drove crossed over a freeway bridge. On my way back to our neighborhood, I had an SUV full of kids (all buckled up), and I had to cross over this freeway bridge again. I noticed a person standing on the bridge, but many other cars had just driven by, making me think it was not a big deal. But I knew in my heart something was very wrong. Even though I had a carload of kids, I had to turn around, and I did.

When I parked, the woman standing on the side of the bridge looked like she was about to jump. I said a prayer as I exited my car to walk over to her. My prayer was simply asking for the guidance and wisdom to know what to say. I knew I could not approach her alone. I needed the gift of the Holy Spirit. But my heart was pounding, and I felt the pressure of the situation. There was not enough time to call 911 and I knew that. She appeared to be close to her decision. By the time that I had turned around and was walking towards her, another man (who turned out to be her husband) was next to her. As I walked up to them I simply said, "It looks like you might be feeling sad today and I wondered if I could stop by and help you." (I can't recall the exact words, but the words were certainly inspired, and I listened.")

The woman welcomed me as I approached. I told her I was a social worker, and I asked her how I could help her. She began crying. Her husband was distraught. She stated how sad she was feeling and how she didn't want to go on living. I told her how sorry I was that she was having a hard time. (It's important to validate the emotion of someone in this situation so you can make a connection and validate their pain, which is very real.) We talked for about 15 minutes on the bridge, the three of us, and I was so focused on helping her that I did not even think about calling 911. I assumed a person driving by might notice a woman standing on the upper level of the bridge and call 911. But no one did. As I talked with the woman and her husband, she agreed to step down and talk about her problems. She had five children and, she said she and her husband were having problems lately. As we talked, I listened to her comments enough that she began to trust me. She shared her concerns right in front of her husband, and she admitted she was depressed.

After she told me about her five young children, who were at the park across the street, I said some things that didn't even come from my mind; they were guided from above. Whatever those words were, it caused her to engage in a conversation seeking help. (I know the loving words that came through me were a direct answer to the prayer I said, as I exited my car and walked over to her. I will always remember that walk towards her, as I prayed to know what to say and do.) As we exited the bridge and crossed the street to walk back to the park where her five children were waiting for her, she walked ahead to go to her kids. Her husband stayed back to thank me for a minute. He told me he knew she was depressed, and he was worried when she started walking towards the bridge. He told me he had prayed for a counselor to intervene and come and help her. He said I was an answer to his prayers. He knew she was at risk for jumping off the bridge. The immediate problem was solved, but I was obligated to make a report to the appropriate authorities, which I did. She knew I would probably have to do this, and she seemed to be alright with it. She realized she needed some help.

This is one more story about why we all need to pay more attention to what is going on around us. I was very startled at how others were driving by, but did not stop and offer assistance or call 911. In my mind, it was obvious there was a risky situation at hand. Three people do not typically stand at the top of a freeway bridge to discuss the weather or the latest news. Something else was going on. We can all make a difference simply by noticing other people and our surroundings. Tuning in more to notice what is going on can change outcomes. We are all instruments for Jesus if we are in tune.

Listen for Promptings

Bridges can be a metaphor for how we embrace the connections we make with our fellow human beings as we travel along our individual Life paths. We know from experience that there have been many times where we each felt a prompting to speak up, reach out, or assist in a situation; but for so many reasons, we talked ourselves out of pursuing the prompting at the moment. A lesson we have learned along this journey is that it is difficult to go back and correct this misstep, because the window of opportunity has passed.

However, there is good news. As we embrace the lesson from a missed or foregone opening, we know the wisdom learned from a previous situation will usually prevent us from making a similar mistake again. There are always so many more opportunities to be embraced after we gain the wisdom from the missed ones. Just pay closer attention. These moments, or windows for listening, will present themselves in ways we don't typically expect. Tune in a little closer and you will notice them. Try not to let your logical mind talk you out of following a prompting.

We hope as you've read some of these stories, that you have thought of many of your own examples of people who have affected you in your Life in a positive way. Take some time to think of someone you would like to write a letter to and thank them for the way in which they helped you or made your Life better.

Now, pull out a beautiful card or piece of stationery, and begin writing a letter to that person. Once you have completed it – either mail it or hand deliver it. Not only will this help you appreciate their efforts more, it will fill that person with love and gratitude.

Here is a sample affirmation to say each day, to reinforce the commitment to living each day mindfully, while appreciating the gift of Life:

AFFIRMATION: I will seek and embrace moments of daily Life as opportunities to absorb the essence of each event. Whether simple or profound, there is meaning. It is often in the insignificant details of daily living that there is a chance to be used as an agent for a spiritual connection.

"Jesus said unto her, I am the resurrection, and the life: he that believeth in me, though he were dead, yet shall he live."
~ Matthew 11: 25 ~

Applying the gift of LIFE:

We thought it would be fun to come up with 75 ideas to help us appreciate the gift of Life – ways we can begin thinking about, feeling and acting on it. This is what forms the habit. We know from research that habits are powerful. They can emerge outside our consciousness – or they can be deliberate. They are a huge part of our lives and are so powerful, they can cause our brains to cling to them at the exclusion of everything else – including common sense.

- Common sense tells us not to smoke, yet sometimes people smoke.
- Common sense tells us to exercise for our health, yet some of us still sit on the couch instead.
- Common sense tells us to eat green veggies, yet some days we eat french fries and call it good.

Why do we forego common sense and do things that aren't good for us? Usually because it feels good or distracts us from something painful. It's easier to sit on the couch than lift weights, so why not do it just this once? Do it again tomorrow, and the next day, and, before long, we have formed a habit.

But good habits are also powerful and that is what we want to inspire in each of us – the ability to start thinking, feeling and acting in such a way as to make some changes to our behavior in a positive way.

Our goal is to help all of us begin to form DELIBERATE habits.

So here's our list of ideas to get us all started:

- Go to an animal shelter and talk to and pet the animals
- Get out in nature every day and notice the flowers, the trees, the rain - every living thing
- Hold a baby – your own, your grandchild, a friend's
- Lay on the grass, breathe in the fragrance, and look up at the clouds
- Visit an exhibit on the human body and study the intricacies and miracles of human life
- Hug your kids
- Hike to a waterfall
- Look for one new thing to appreciate about the life you are living
- Watch a hummingbird at a feeder
- Plant a garden and watch it grow
- Hold a sleeping puppy and watch it breathe
- Talk with an elderly person about one of their favorite life experiences
- Find a community garden and volunteer
- Go to an aquarium and be amazed by the dolphins and sharks and whales

- Go to an orchard and pick apples - eat one
- Volunteer at a homeless shelter and talk to some of the people about their life
- Make a contribution at a local hospice center
- Write letters to your parents thanking them for the sacrifices they made in your behalf
- Make a meal of only delicious vegetables once a week - notice how good you feel
- Go to the zoo and look at the amazing creations – the giraffes, the zebras
- Volunteer at an elementary school and appreciate the differences in the children
- Take fresh flowers to a nursing home and give them to someone who never gets flowers
- Mow your lawn and walk on it with bare feet
- Go to bethematch.org and sign up to be a bone marrow donor
- Watch a litter of kittens being born
- Feel a child kicking in her pregnant mom's belly
- Go to the ocean and swim in the water, snorkel, and watch the fish
- Talk about life and the beauty of it with friends
- Sit on your porch and listen to the sounds of the children in the neighborhood
- Visit a farmer's market and buy fresh fruit and vegetables - eat some in the park
- Find a bird's nest and watch the mama care for her eggs
- Hold hands with someone you love and feel the wonder in another human being
- Milk a cow
- Hold a baby chick
- Ride your bike along a river and enjoy the elements of nature
- Laugh out loud with your family and get to know what makes them happy

- Learn about a new culture and then visit the country to see how they live
- Take a meal to an elderly couple and visit with them
- Watch a grove of trees blow in the wind
- Keep a journal of your life experiences for your children to read when they're grown
- Spend a weekend in a cabin in the winter and watch the snow fall
- Go to a butterfly garden and take pictures
- Exercise every day to protect your body and improve your quality of life
- Walk out in a rainstorm without an umbrella
- Watch a documentary about our planet and all the wonderful life in existence
- Read about the creation in the Bible
- Listen to your children as they talk about what happened in their life today
- Pray to Heavenly Father for a life filled with gratitude
- Watch a spider spin its web
- Look into a dog's eyes and see how he connects and communicates with you
- Take pictures of your children and watch how they change over the years
- Paddle a canoe on a lake, enjoy the peace and quiet and watch for wildlife
- Lay in a hammock with your eyes closed and listen for sounds of life
- Write your life history
- Search information about your ancestors
- Donate blood
- Take a history class and learn about people who made a significant contribution
- Visit a military cemetery and pay tribute to those who gave their lives for our country
- Ride a horse and then feed him

- Go to a greenhouse and smell the wonderful flowers and soil
- Watch a lightning storm and enjoy the beauty
- Interview your grandparents and your parents and record their stories on tape
- Watch people when you are in an airport
- Sleep in the backyard under the stars one night
- Point out something positive to one person you meet today – validate them and their life
- Put fresh flowers by your bedside every so often and wake up to the beautiful fragrance
- Plant a tree
- Follow the Five Rs – refuse, reduce, reuse, recycle and rot (compost)
- Plant flower baskets for your porch and care for them all summer
- Take a nap under the shade of a beautiful tree
- Try a new vegetable every week for a month
- Go to a park and watch children play
- Find someone in your neighborhood you don't know very well and get to know them
- Adopt a pet from a shelter
- Go to a museum of natural history

Now, choose a few items from this list that you want to do right away. And DO THEM.

Being deliberate about having new experiences is necessary in order to get yourself out of your comfort zone and try something new. Once you have experienced a few new things – you will want to continue to experience more and more. Life is short, and we as co-authors have decided to do as much as we can while we're here and experience everything we possibly can. So make it a point to set aside some time each week to experience Life in a way you have not experienced it before.

We'd like you to actively work on some things as you go through this book that will help you begin to appreciate the gift of Life and the experiences you have had so far during your Life. So take a break from reading for a day or two and complete the activity below. Fill a couple of pages in your journal.

Think about a time in your Life when everything seemed to be going just right.

- Maybe it was when you were a child.
- Maybe you were just heading off to college.
- Maybe you had just given birth to your first child – or your fourth child.
- Maybe you had just started a career that you love.

Whatever that time in your Life was – write about it. Think of all the elements.

- Why was that time so good?
- What made it bring you joy?
- Who was close to you in your Life at the time?
- When was it in reference to your age?
- What are your emotions as you think back?

The purpose of this exercise is to get you thinking about the things that help you ENJOY and really LIVE your Life. Get yourself in tune with the things that make you HAPPY – with the things that make Life worth living.

At some point we will all be called to return home, and this is a new spiritual beginning; the expectation of everlasting Life.

Some food for thought: If we would each take the time to stop and think about it, there are times when most of us feel a little bit uncomfortable here on this earth. Do you find that to be true? It's perfectly normal, predictable and expected that as human beings, we will each feel a wide range of typical human emotions. Our lives on earth were not designed to have constant and continual bliss. Stress, anxiety, worry, loneliness, frustration and disappointment are common emotions. Yet they do not define who we are.

We may feel uneasy about meeting new people or having new experiences.

We may be treated unkindly or unfairly by others who have their free agency to make choices that sometimes affect us.

We may struggle with financial burdens or health conditions.

We never actually experience a constant outpouring of love and acceptance – we may, at times, have these feelings, but they are intertwined with feelings of sadness, doubt, uneasiness, fear, and any number of negative emotions.

Have you ever thought that the reason for this is because this earth is not our actual home? That we are in a temporary state here on this earth? That we are not actually home until our spirit leaves our body and returns to our pre-mortal existence? That is where we believe our true home is – where we can be free from the mortal ties and ills that affect us here in this earthly state, and be reunited with our loved ones who have gone on before.

"We sometimes congratulate ourselves at the moment of waking from a troubled dream... It may be so at the moment of death.
~ Nathaniel Hawthorne ~

We sometimes fear death because we don't completely understand the experience. But when we talk to others, read the experiences of those who have had near-death experiences, read the scriptures, and study what we believe to be true, there is great comfort and possibly even a longing to go home.

But while we are here, how wonderful it would be if we could make the absolute best of every day of our lives.

LIFE

By Mother Teresa

Life is an Opportunity, **BENEFIT FROM IT.**

Life is Beauty, **ADMIRE IT.**

Life is a Dream, **REALIZE IT.**

Life is a Challenge, **MEET IT.**

Life is a Duty, **COMPLETE IT.**

Life is a Game, **PLAY IT.**

Life is a Promise, **FULFILL IT.**

Life is Sorrow, **OVERCOME IT.**

Life is a Song, **SING IT.**

Life is a Struggle, **ACCEPT IT.**

Life is a Tragedy, **CONFRONT IT.**

Life is an Adventure, **DARE IT.**

Life is Luck, **MAKE IT.**

Life is too Precious, **DO NOT DESTROY IT.**

Life is Life, **FIGHT FOR IT.**

What are your thoughts and impressions now about the gift of Life? Has anything changed or come into your awareness that wasn't there before?

Jot down your thoughts now after 30 days of reflection:

_____

_____

_____

_____

_____

_____

_____

_____

_____

_____

_____

_____

_____

_____

"In the beginning was the Word, and the Word was with God, and the Word was God. The same was in the beginning with God. All things were made by Him, and without Him was not anything that was made. In Him was life; and the life was the light of men. And the light shineth in darkness, and the darkness comprehended it not."

~ John 1:1-5 ~

The Sea of Life
by Elizabeth Hickey

The sea of life
Brings many waves.
Some we ride on,
Others we break with.

But through it all,
We emerge.
We gasp for breath,
And we swim again.

The tide may change,
But the rhythm
Of the heart,
Always beats for Love.

Our life is a journey,
Of many ups and downs,
All divinely inspired
So that we can grow
In Love.

The more we love,
The more we honor
Our Savior Jesus Christ.
Life is about learning to Love.
Thank you Jesus for this Gift.

CONCLUSION:

Life is precious. We were each given a Life and our Father in Heaven wants us to do something meaningful with it. It is our choice whether to do something for good or bad. We hope this chapter about the gift of Life has inspired you to go beyond what you are already doing with your Life. I once heard someone on a radio program say something along the lines of "by the time we leave this Life, we should be so exhausted we can't possibly do anything more." That has stuck with me.

Experiencing as much as we can while we have the opportunity to do so is something to seriously ponder. Live your dreams. Take a few risks. Love unconditionally. Be happy. And live Life to the fullest. These are some of the things we think about when we think about living a full, meaningful Life.

If we can engage ourselves in doing good – serving others, making Life better for someone else, improving our attitudes, sharing our own experiences in order to help someone with a problem – whatever it might be, we will be able to look back on our lives as we near the end and say, "I have done all I could to live a Christ-like Life. I am at peace."

DAILY REFLECTION

(Repetition is what creates new habit. Read this page daily as a reminder.)

Each chapter is meant to be read slowly,
Absorbing the deeper essence behind the words and stories.

This allows for continual reflection,
Prayer and listening for answers,
Which opens the door to
Greater insight and awareness of
The Gift of Hope.

If we devote one month of the year,
To learning and living the Gift of Hope,
Our awareness of the precious Gift of Hope,
Will be spiritually heightened,
And our daily existence will emulate this awareness.

As we make this shift to mindful attentiveness to the Gift of Hope,
We will be less likely to take for granted,
The beauty, the power, and the mystique of Hope.
We will have developed a habit,
Which becomes part of who we are.

As we develop a new habit each month,
Based on a different Gift each month,
A Gift that Jesus came to earth to give each one of us,
We will become more like Jesus in the way we live.
As this happens,
We will be living a more Christlike life, every day.
As we do this,
We are expressing our deepest gratitude to Jesus
And our Heavenly Father.

As we share the 12 Gifts with others,
We cannot help but bring the same love and peace
To our own hearts and spirits.

---- 2 ----

The *Gift* of
HOPE

Think back on your life. Has there ever been a time when you felt Hopeless or lost? Most likely your answer is yes. Maybe you were depressed about a situation, or maybe you got off track in some area of your life that had you questioning the point of your existence. But feeling Hopeless for a period of time is very different from experiencing a devastating loss of Hope.

Having Hope in our Savior, Jesus Christ, is the blanket that encircles us and makes us feel safe. Practicing the gift of Hope is important because even though we may have a solid foundation of Hope in Jesus Christ, there are many things that can happen to us along the path of life that can make us waver and begin to doubt. Our constant attention and effort is required throughout our lives if we want to become more like Jesus Christ.

Why did we choose HOPE as the second gift?

"Blessed is the man that trusteth in the
Lord, and whose hope the Lord is."
~ Jeremiah 17:7 ~

We chose Hope because it is the foundation of our belief in Jesus Christ. Try to imagine a life without Hope. Our trials would not be looked upon as opportunities to grow, but rather hardships that bring us down. If we did not have Hope in our Savior, life would be meaningless. I remember an old saying that one of my friends used to jokingly say when she was frustrated – "Life is hard, and then you die." Imagine if that were true.

We think about all the small things we, as individuals, realize we Hope for on a daily basis – some of these might be:

- I Hope my daughter had a good day today;
- I Hope my puppies greet me at the door when I get home;
- I Hope I had a positive effect on someone's life today;
- I Hope I can make it home early to see my family;
- I Hope my goals are met this week;
- I Hope my dad feels better;
- I Hope there are tomatoes in my garden tonight;
- I Hope I get Friday off this week.

We Hope for things every day. Hope is a normal, natural part of our existence. And HOPE in Jesus Christ is a special gift that can help us each live a more fulfilling, much more meaningful life.

In your personal quest to become more Christ-like, or closer to Jesus, or closer to believing in Jesus, whatever it may be in your own personal life – may this chapter on HOPE help you get closer to your goal.

"Let thy mercy, O Lord, be upon
us, according as we hope in thee."
~ Psalms 33:22 ~

"Therefore my heart is glad, and my glory
rejoiceth: my flesh also shall rest in hope."
~ Psalms 16:9 ~

"May your choices reflect your hopes, not your fears."
~ Nelson Mandela ~

We have noticed lately there are some people out in the world saying they don't believe in God. We are not entirely clear on why this is happening, but know a few people who have bought into the notion that there is no God, only science. Maybe as you read this, you are saying to yourself – yes, I too have questioned the existence of God at some point. Maybe you have doubted, or wondered. Maybe you believe in God but have never truly felt that testimony of His existence. Maybe that's why you are reading this book – to help you in your quest to know Jesus Christ.

We were pondering this dilemma yesterday and asked ourselves, "How can someone go from knowing God and Jesus Christ and believing in them and praying to them – to turning their back on their very existence?" We can't personally understand it, but what we do know is that we are all on our own personal journey in this life, and each of us must arrive at the things we know and believe in our own time and in our own way. It is not for any of us to say what's right for another.

When we look back over our own lives, we see the hand of God intervening many times and in many circumstances to lead us to a better place or to a conclusion about something we may have been questioning. We believe those we love will receive their own manifestations and trials and experiences that will take them to the place they are trying to get to.

For us, a firm belief in God and Jesus Christ is what gives us HOPE and keeps us going in this sometimes crazy world we live in. If we did not believe in something better after this life, we are certain our perspective, values, ambitions, desires and priorities would be very different than what they are.

We pray if you are working to better your life or your relationship with you Savior, this book will help you – even if it's in some very small way – to reach your desired outcome.

"The wicked is driven away in his wickedness:
but the righteous hath hope in his death."
~ Proverbs 14;32 ~

"Hope is putting faith to work when doubting would be easier"
~ Thomas S. Monson ~

When we think about Hope, we might also contemplate closely-related words that help us to embrace a deeper meaning of Hope. These words could include:

ANTICIPATION, BELIEF, CONFIDENCE, EXPECTATION, OPTIMISM, RESILIENCE, FAITH, RELIANCE, ENDURANCE

I want to share the following story because it tells of one of the most difficult times in my life. Getting through it required me to rely on my Savior. I know if it weren't for Him, I would have gone to a place of bitterness and anger that I may never have recovered from.

"THIS IS JUST A TEMPORARY SETBACK"
by Janeen

About three years ago, the darkest, most stressful period of my life was beginning to unfold. I received a phone call from a woman who shattered my world. I spent many days crying and trying to rationalize how this could possibly be true. I was devastated and sad, and for a time I felt that denial we sometimes hold onto that will allow us to avoid facing things head on and making a decision. But eventually, I had to face reality and begin to make a plan to deal with the things before me and make a major change to my life and the life of my teenaged daughter. A few months later, other facts began to unfold that solidified the position I was taking and made me realize this was my new reality. Not long after, some devastating news was delivered to me by a close family member, and a few months after that, my mother passed away.

As I look back on this time, I am in awe at how much strength I had. I realize now that my strength came, not only from my upbringing, but from my faith in Jesus Christ.

My life has had many bumps in the road, but I have always tried to keep a positive spin on everything that has transpired. My mother used to ask me, "You have been through so much heartache – how do you stay so positive and so happy?" I would say to her, "Mom, this is just a temporary setback." She used to love it when I'd say that. It made her realize I was strong and that she didn't need to worry so much about me. But I am not strong on my own. I am strong because I rely on and believe in my Savior.

The things I have suffered have been my own experience and opportunity for growth. I'm certain everyone suffers their own pain to varying degrees. When compared to challenges others face, I realize my life has been a blessing, but for me, it has been what I needed to shape and mold me into the person I need to become. We all have our own trials and disappointments, and no one suffers any less than another. I believe our trials are given to us according to the things we need to learn.

We can all think of times in our lives when we felt like we couldn't go on, or when we felt like giving up on even trying, but somehow we pulled ourselves through. I think it's the gift of Hope that allows us to pick ourselves up and keep moving.Hope leads us to friends and family members who love us and help us see the light. I had many people in my life during my dark period that I could turn to – my dad, my brother and sister, my close friends, and others who had experienced similar things in their own lives.

Several of my friends would call and check on me. Many of them came to my mother's funeral to show their love and support for me. My family gathered around to help me see things from a different perspective so I wouldn't be so devastated about my family member who was making a choice that I didn't agree with.

Three years later, I am happy, healthy, relieved, moving on and stronger than ever. I owe that to my friends and family, and also to my Father in Heaven because I have felt Him near. I know I have been blessed with angels round about me who have lifted me up and given me Hope and direction in my life. I am ever so grateful for each one of them.

"For we are saved by hope: but hope that is seen is not hope: for what a man seeth, why doth he yet hope for? But if we hope for that we see not, then do we with patience wait for it."
~ Romans 8:24-25 ~

"Rejoicing in hope; patient in tribulation; continuing instant in prayer."
~ Romans 12:12 ~

The ability to feel Hopeful continuously is something some of us need to work at. Some of us are naturally positive, while others may have a more difficult time focusing in on their Hopes rather than their fears. Take some time to answer the following questions to get your brain wrapped around the idea of Hope:

What gets you feeling really excited?

_____

_____

_____

_____

_____

What inspires you?

_____

_____

_____

_____

_____

Think of a time when you worked hard and your dream came true... Write about it.

_____

_____

_____

_____

_____

Who is the person that can put you in a positive mood no matter what? Write about the last time you were with that person.

_____

_____

_____

_____

_____

When you hope for something to happen, what steps do you take to make it a reality?

_____

_____

_____

_____

Does your belief in Jesus Christ inspire you to have Hope? Explain.

_____

_____

_____

_____

_____

Without Hope, we are lost. Hope gives us joy and peace because we know there is something more – something beyond ourselves, something beyond this life. Try to imagine what it would be like to exist without Hope.

- Those who are ill would not believe they could get better;
- Those who are depressed would not see the possibility of a bright future;
- Those who have been betrayed could not imagine a new life;
- Those who may have lost a loved one would believe that relationship was over;
- Those who lost a job would not see the possibility of a better life.

The list goes on and on. When we break it down, we see that we experience the joy of Hope each and every day in our lives.

- We have Hope that tomorrow will be a new and better day;
- We have Hope that we are going to meet someone new;
- We have Hope that we will improve our health as we take the steps to do so;
- We have Hope that someone will love us regardless of our shortcomings;
- We have Hope that a child will change their life for the better.

We listened to a talk recently at a general gathering of faith. The speaker talked about this life we are in and asked a question similar to this:

"Do we really think this is as good as it gets?

We come to this life to suffer, experience trials, work hard to increase our talents and skills, feel the pain of losing loved ones, watch our bodies get old and sick, and then die. Is that really all there is?"

His answer was "Of course not!"

Because of Hope and because of faith, we know there is something more. Our common sense tells us so, and our Hope and faith keep us moving forward towards becoming better people. It makes sense to us that this life is a mere stepping stone to a better life, a better place.

Make it your GOAL this month as you study and ponder the Gift of Hope to decide on something you really want to change in your life – and then go after it – do what it takes to make the change happen.

What are your thoughts and impressions about the gift of HOPE? We want you to start thinking about this question as you begin your journey.

_____

_____

_____

_____

_____

_____

As you begin reading this chapter, write down a few thoughts you have as you contemplate the gift of Hope We will ask this question again at the end of the chapter after you have completed your study of the gift of Hope.

Just a thought – Instead of connecting through electronic devices, try connecting with your heart, warmth, and energy. See what a difference it makes by the end of the day.

What did Jesus say about HOPE?

*"Now the God of hope fill you with all joy
and peace in believing, that ye may abound in
hope, through the power of the Holy Ghost."*
~ Romans 15:13 ~

We love to hear about and read stories of Hope. Who doesn't? They're so inspiring and uplifting. They give us the courage to face difficult challenges in our own lives.

When we think of stories about Hope from the Bible, the one that comes to mind is when the disciples go quickly to the empty garden tomb after finding out that Jesus' body is no longer there. They were not worried, but rather excited to find out where Jesus is. They have Hope that He is risen.

We were reading over a talk recently that spoke of Hope. It talked about the "brightness of hope." While weak hope leaves us at the mercy of our moods and events, "brightness of hope" produces illuminated individuals. This kind of Hope allows us to press forward even when dark clouds hover. This is the Hope that is based in Jesus Christ – a strength that cannot be overlooked. We thought the following excerpt was particularly powerful:

"Just as doubt, despair, and desensitization go together, so do faith, hope and charity. The latter, however, must be carefully and constantly nurtured, whereas despair, like dandelions, needs so little encouragement to sprout and spread. Despair comes so naturally to the natural man!"

This goes right along with our belief that you have to constantly practice these gifts. There never comes a time when we have arrived. We may have significant Hope this year, and begin to waiver next year because of an event or a shift in attitude.

You've heard the saying, "It's a good thing we never quit on the same day," in reference to husbands and wives giving up on each other. Let's look at the 12 Gifts in the same way. Let's help each other in our practice of the gifts. When your husband is weak in his faith, maybe you can to help him see things differently or encourage experiences that will enlighten him. If your wife is struggling to forgive someone, maybe you can find it within yourself to show patience and compassion and help her see something she is missing. Perfection is not the goal.

Consistently working to be better is what we are striving for.

We both love to watch movies about Hope. When we need a boost, hearing someone else's story helps us put things in perspective.

Think of the books you have read over your life or the movies you have watched. Without a doubt, it's always the stories about people who have Hope – whether based on fact or fiction – to overcome some horrible circumstance or rise above a terrible tragedy, that bring us to tears and touch us at the very core of our souls. Some of the more recent movies that we think are truly inspiring are:

- **Unbroken** is the story of Louis Zamperini and the life threatening, unbelievable experiences he survives throughout his life.
- **Soul Surfer** is the story of Bethany Hamilton, who lost her arm in a shark attack and overcame all odds to become a surfing champion.
- **Castaway** is the story of Chuck Noland, a Fed Ex systems engineer whose life changes in an instant when a plane crash leaves him isolated on a remote island for more than four years.
- **The Impossible** is the story of a family vacationing in Thailand when the massive tsunami hits and leaves them each searching for their family members.
- **Captain Phillips** is the story of the 2009 hijacking of the Maersk Alabama by a crew of Somali pirates.
- **Schindler's List** is the story of one man's quest to use his wealth to save as many Jews as possible from the hands of Hitler.

These are stories that give us the inspiration to accomplish great things in our own lives.

Stories to help us reflect on the Gift of HOPE:

We would like to share with you a few of our stories of Hope, and we believe they will trigger thoughts of your own stories and experiences.

Sharing stories of Hope so we can learn from the experiences of others is a compelling way to impress the gift of Hope on those who are searching for it. So if you think of your own stories along the way, don't forget to write them down and let others learn from you.

"I CAN'T WAIT TO BE WITH YOU AGAIN"
by Janeen

I live in a neighborhood surrounded by wonderful people. I love my neighbors, and we all have a bond that lets each of us know we have help whenever we need it. I'm sure many of you can relate to this. There are people here in my neighborhood from all walks of life, and it makes me realize people who are different actually can get along. When we take the time to get to know people who are different, whether it be in their opinions, religion, race or circumstances, we often find we are all very similar. We are all just people who are trying to figure things out and do the very best we can with what we have.

When I told Elizabeth about the story I wanted to write, we began talking a lot about the circumstances of the situation this particular family was in. Before I relate the story, I want to say that as Elizabeth and I discussed this, we agreed, in the end, that ALL people deserve COMPASSION. ALL people, no matter what they've done, deserve FORGIVENESS, and ALL people deserve to have HOPE in their future. The man begging on the street for food to feed his family deserves compassion, and so does a man who bends the rules and ultimately breaks the law – but has taken responsibility, paid restitution, repented, turned his circumstances around and made things right with his family.

We are all on our own path in this life, and any person who makes a really big mistake – whether knowingly or unknowingly – deserves a second chance. Jesus Christ hung on that cross for each and every one of us – not for just a few of us.

We both believe people can get caught up in doing things sometimes they don't perceive as that big of a deal in the beginning, and we both believe people can change. A good friend of mine often says, "A person can change if they are motivated to do so by a spiritual or emotional experience." If that is true, this man stands every chance, because he has had both of these types of experiences over the past two years.

The family I want to tell you about are a close-knit, loving, faithful example of what a family ought to be. They are hard-working, kind and generous people. This man grew up and married his wife under very humble circumstances. They worked hard over the course of their marriage to become self sufficient and able to provide for their family.

They have a son who recently returned from Japan where he was serving a Christian mission for his church, and they also have three beautiful daughters who love each other, help each other, and have a deep respect for their parents.

These children grew up in a loving home and were raised to love their Heavenly Father and Jesus Christ. It is apparent they were taught to rely on their Savior under every circumstance, and trust in Him. The situation they found themselves in only solidifies their trust in the Lord. They have remained faithful, respectful and solid as the events unfolded and their lives were turned upside down.

So, here is the story. All families have their challenges, and this family is no different. The husband was a partner in a business and made a bad business decision, which seemed like a minor infraction at the time. The decision led to his arrest. He was sentenced to a prison term of two years.

I spoke extensively with this man and his wife about the events that took place. He admitted that, at first, he felt like he was thrown under the bus and treated extremely unfairly. After all, he wasn't doing anything that hadn't been done before by other companies. But, as time went on, he began to realize he had allowed himself to get caught up in deceiving himself to believe what he did was alright because everyone else was doing it. He started to see that he was wrong.

Sometimes we have to take a step back and remember what it is we are trying to accomplish in this life – to become like Jesus Christ. All of us, at times, have lost our way or done things contrary to what we believe, or to the way we have committed to living our lives. The important thing, in the end, is that we get ourselves back on track. This man is extremely sorry for what he did. He has taken responsibility for his actions and willingly served his prison term. He not only served it, but turned it into an opportunity to grow, help others, and work on his relationship with his Savior. He paid the ultimate price for his mistake – two years away from his family.

Most families would have crumbled having to face this most devastating experience and all the trials that accompany it, but not this family. It has been an inspiration to watch these people pull together, accept help from their loving neighbors, and continue to serve just as they did before. I have never seen a family more committed to each other.

One of my close friends recently visited this man in prison. She called me as soon as she left him to tell me how inspiring her visit had been. He greeted her with a huge smile, and she said he looked happy and healthy. She said his attitude was completely positive. She asked him how he had been able to not only cope, but almost thrive, as he has been serving his time. He spoke of his Savior, Jesus Christ, and told my friend the following story:

"I can handle anything this world hands to me. But the thought of leaving my wife and daughters alone for two years was tearing me apart. I simply did not know how they were going to survive. My wife has been able to stay at home and raise our children all these years, and our family has always been so incredibly close. I knew they were going to be heartbroken; but financially, I did not know how they could possibly do it. The mistakes I made have put our family in a position of having nearly everything taken away. We almost lost our home over it.

But the very first day I spent here in prison was life changing for me. I met a man who could see that I was unhappy, and he asked me what was bothering me so much. I told him the story of my family and expressed my concern and worry. He looked at me and said, 'Do you think for one minute that Jesus Christ loves your family any less than you do?' Those simple words changed my entire perspective. He was right. I knew from that very moment going forward that the Savior would provide for my family. And He has. That is how I have been able to thrive in here.

My family came to visit me this past month, and I have never seen my wife quite like this before. She has become a stronger, more outgoing woman. She is my rock. This experience has helped her grow in a way I would not have thought possible. I owe much gratitude to my Heavenly Father and His Son, Jesus Christ, and I have great hope for our future together."

His wife IS a rock. She is incredibly unselfish. She dresses modestly, does her own hair, doesn't spend money unnecessarily, and never has – even when she could. She works three part-time jobs in order to make the house payment, and has asked that her kids work to pay for their own expenses. She will tell you how grateful she is that Heavenly Father directed her to these sources of income so she could make it work, along with her family responsibilities. They have not only survived the past two years, they have become better – as individuals, and as a family unit. A lot of women may have taken the children and left the situation behind. But not this woman. She has Hope that her family will be stronger than ever because they all pulled together. And she knows, deep down, that her husband loves his Savior and his family.

My friend left the prison that day feeling inadequate. But she realized this man was filled, not only with gratitude, but with Hope – Hope for the future. The time he has given up with his family has been a mere drop in the bucket compared to the eternity he will get to spend with them, and he knows that. The gratitude and Hope that fill his heart are a true gift.

He will be reunited with his family again at Christmas. This family is a true example of living with Hope and letting it carry them through a difficult time. May we all look for examples of Hope in the people around us to inspire us to move forward with great strength.

REFLECTIONS ABOUT HOPE
by Elizabeth

Hope is one of those concepts and mysteries in life, where expert debaters would be able to discuss and debate for many hours. The word "Hope" is frequently used in casual conversation, with phrases like, "I Hope you have a great day!" and "I Hope your vacation is wonderful!" and many other expressions when our intention is to wish someone well. It is a lovely and kind thing to wish others well, and express our Hope for their joy and peace.

When we reflect deeper on Hope, and how it plays into our daily lives and beliefs, it becomes even more intriguing. During the writing of this book, Janeen and I have had many profound discussions that have challenged the way we have previously used words that we have selected as the 12 Gifts.

For instance, if a high school basketball player, who appears to have reached his full growth at the height of 5'5", has a dream of playing in the NBA, and he is asking for your support, it would be difficult to provide full support in an honest manner. The odds of making it in the NBA, with being under six feet, aren't good. So how could any of us sincerely extend our Hope and encouragement for a goal that does not seem realistic?

These ethical dilemmas prompt us to reconsider how and why we each extend and show feelings of Hope for ourselves and also for others. There has to be a realistic component to this as well. The more I pondered about Hope, the more I realized a valuable lesson. We put our Hope in Jesus Christ, and He will whisper, along with the Holy Spirit, the things that He wants us to Hope for. Our job is to pay attention and listen.

"BE STILL AND KNOW THAT I AM GOD"
by Janeen

I have been blessed to have a very close personal friend in my life, Cindy.

Cindy grew up in a very small town where she lived on a farm and loved life. Her father died when she and her siblings were quite young, leaving their mother to care for them and the farm by herself. They all learned to work hard and help each other. Cindy eventually married her childhood sweetheart and they had seven children together over the course of their marriage. But through the years, Cindy was controlled by her foul tempered husband who abused her and had jealous outrages that would manifest themselves when he had periods of uncontrolled doubt and insecurity. She knew he didn't want to be the way he was, but he was unable or unwilling to do what it took to control it.

She wanted to leave him many times over, but was always afraid that he would harm her or one of the children. Things grew continually worse, and she prayed often to Heavenly Father to help her leave him. She has spoken of it many times over the period of time I have known her. And she describes how each time she would pray, the thought would come to her, "Be still and know that I am God." She would always feel at peace and she had trust in the Lord that He would allow things to work out for her and her family the way they should.

So she continued to stay in her marriage.

One evening, she was driving home with her daughters in the car when she received a call from one of her sons. "Don't come home mom. Dad is in a particularly bad mood tonight." He was afraid for her and tried to get her to go stay over with grandma. But Cindy decided to drive home because she didn't want her boys alone with him either.

She arrived home and went into their bedroom where he was standing, holding a gun. She stopped dead in her tracks and tried to reason with him. She knew she could die in this moment and her children would be left without their mother. But as she prayed, she felt at peace. The words "Be still and know that I am God" kept running through her mind. She began to walk toward her husband and, as she did so, he turned the gun on himself and took his life.

It was a horrible, devastating event that changed the lives of my friend and her children forever. But they were saved. Cindy was torn apart beyond words, but at the same time she was grateful that they were free now. And she began to have Hope for her future and for her children's futures.

They had much healing to do, and the journey has not been easy. But one by one, each has gone on with their life and worked through things in their own way and their own time. They have faith in the Lord, Jesus Christ. And they have been given the gift of Hope.

PRAY AND LISTEN FOR GUIDANCE OF HOPE
by Elizabeth

I have a close family member who struggled with addictions. They began in her teenage years and ultimately lasted for nearly thirty years. There was so much drama with all of the problems related to drug and alcohol addiction that most family members and extended family members eventually gave up Hope. Many of them encouraged me to give up also. A few of them, with sincerity in their hearts, said, "You are wasting your time." But I just knew that I wasn't supposed to give up, and I didn't. I was the last hold out, and I kept praying for a miracle.

I had many memories of this relative where I saw a glimpse into her soul, her joy, her kindness, and her innocent way of trusting others. I felt protective towards her. Of course, it broke my heart to see and learn of some of the things she had done and was still doing – behaviors that accompany drug addiction and the lifestyle it creates. But there was a strong pull inside of me to not give up on her. I held onto spiritual Hope. I prayed often, and I prayed with conviction. There were children involved, and these children needed to see a few miracles in their lives.

I was the only one who made the unpleasant visits to the jails and prison and put money in her account for simple necessities. I accepted the collect phone calls from prison and listened, and I shared how much Jesus loved her. I told her many things to encourage her to seek a spiritual path. I am so grateful I did all of this, because by the grace of God, there we can all go. I learned a valuable lesson about not judging according to the typical ways of responding, but to listen to the promptings of the Holy Spirit. When we are hearing and feeling the promptings from the Holy Spirit, all of the jargon and other typical slogans just go out the window.

Many other relatives had reached the point of using the "Tough Love" approach, which works for many individuals and has been extremely beneficial to millions of families, as they seek to turn a loved one towards rehabilitation and Hope. But I am a strong believer in the idea that "one size does not fit all, or work for everyone." There are always exceptions. It is difficult to know when we, as helpers or "hopers," might be enabling a person with their addiction. Learning about and understanding these patterns of behavior is so useful and important because it allows us to understand more deeply how the addictive patterns take hold in a person's life. This understanding truly does influence how we can interact with a loved one who is addicted, in a positive way, without enabling the addict to use our kindness as a means to support their addiction and lifestyle.

But Jesus has His own unique gift of Hope and a divine plan that, along with others on earth who are willing to assist Him and follow through with the promptings of the Holy Spirit, can make miracles happen. I know this to be true in this personal story that I am sharing. Many professionals in the field had said something similar to, "She is a long time addict, and her lifestyle is ingrained within her. She can't change after decades of living this way."

I will always believe in the power of prayer and Hope and how it can and will be the conduit for miracles on earth. I will always have Hope in my heart and soul, for a person or a cause, if I discern that Jesus and the Holy Spirit are leading me in this direction. This is why we need to pray often, so we are able to discern divine messages from above. If we have Hope and faith, but cannot hear or discern where to share these gifts, these gifts might not be utilized to their fullest extent.

To conclude the story of my relative, the only reason I held onto Hope for my relative was because Jesus gave me this Hope. I know He was the one who joined me when I walked into the jails for visits, when I had so many other things I needed to be doing. But Jesus made me feel this was the most important thing I could be doing. I felt His presence. He loved me through it all, and it was a secure and beautiful love. I never doubted that it was the right thing to do, because I felt His Love through it.

Thirteen years later this relative is now a fully functioning, contributing member to society – and a born again Christian, who knows more about the Bible and biblical history than I ever will. She has been clean and sober for over thirteen years now, after an almost thirty year addiction, and she credits the love of Jesus for her recovery and her transformation. She lives the message of loving others, and she shares the Hope of Jesus with others whenever she is prompted to. She wanted to give back and help others, so she began a difficult process of facing her past.

She followed through with the many necessary steps to demonstrate to the state that she is worthy of being able to visit others in jail and prison and share messages of Hope. She was approved, and she now volunteers and does ministry work to individuals who are in jail or prison. She shares her personal story, along with how Hope and the Love of Jesus changed everything for her.

She has stayed true to her belief and her personal conviction in Jesus Christ, and she strives every day to share His love to others through her. I can see and feel that she is doing this with grace and kindness. Those she works with have shared stories about how loving and kind she is. Family members have all made beautiful and positive comments about how she has overcome so many challenges, and how she has such a strong faith in Jesus. This message of Hope has been manifested in beautiful ways in her life. She is a walking example of Hope. Her life transformation is a true reflection of the Hope of Jesus Christ on earth, in one individual life at a time. That's how Jesus listens and works – one person at a time. His love is individual love.

Her story is an example and a reason why we should not give up on Hope for others. However, this does not mean that I am suggesting that you do what I did. I followed through with the promptings that I felt. Each and every situation is unique and special to our Savior, Jesus Christ. As you pray about your specific concern of a loved one, possibly one who is living a similar addictive lifestyle, you can be assured that your prayers will be answered. Wait with patience and faith, and the message of Hope about what you could or should do will be revealed to you through promptings from the Holy Spirit. It can take time (thirty years took some patience, faith, and great Hope), but you will know and feel it when your answer to prayer comes to you.

Be careful so you don't mix up what you Hope to hear, with the message of what is really coming though, which might be a little more difficult to digest. (I struggled with this for a time, and I finally let go of trying to control the outcome. It was actually a great feeling of relief). We all have those moments where we need to reconcile the truth in comparison with what we were Hoping to hear. We eventually learn and know that Jesus knows best, and He only shares His guidance with us because He loves us so much. Jesus loves us more than we can comprehend, and when we are given guidance from Him which doesn't necessarily fit into our plans, it's time to pray again. The truth will surface when we are seeking His wisdom and guidance. Peace and wisdom will also come from this process of letting go and letting Jesus guide us. He will whisper His love, and it will be stronger than any whisper you ever felt before. As we Hope, we are fortifying our faith in Jesus Christ.

We wish you Hope, and we know that by choosing Hope we are all strengthening our faith, which creates more peace, trust, and calmness in our lives. When we are calm and still, we can also hear the messages from the Holy Spirit more clearly. It's a win-win all the way around when we start with Hope!

As an adult, I've learned that none of us get to have an easy, breezy life where everything goes well and we feel joy and peace each and every day. Life on earth is more about learning the lessons that could help us evolve to higher states of awareness, which lead us to love. We have both hinted at this throughout the book, with the stories we've shared. We believe that our lives are about being in the school of life. There are many classrooms where specific lessons are learned, and we refer to these lessons as gifts. But it is through these gifts we are able to rise higher and higher in the evolution of our lives.

As we grow and rise above previous life lessons, we learn from new lessons. We are always growing and we are always rising in life. It is part of the divine plan to live and love on earth, and embrace the lessons we need. If we agree with this, then we should be willing to accept some of the losses, changes, and unexpected life turns, which bring upon more twists and turns in the story of our lives.

TRUSTING IN LIFE,
AN EAGLE SOARS.
AND SO WILL I
WHEN I TRUST.
by Elizabeth

I agree with this philosophy now, but when I was in in the deep despair of one of the most painful emotional times in my life, my divorce, I might not have listened to anyone who said the above words. I might have been a bit cynical and skeptical about finding any thread of positivity, just because my pain was so raw and deep.

However, as a professional in the field of divorce, (educator, mediator, author, child custody evaluator) I can assure any reader that the process of divorce is a powerful emotional experience, and then the legal, financial, logistical and other matters, layer on top of the emotions. I learned first-hand, that it is only through dealing with the deep emotions associate with the pain of loss and change, that we can grow into the future and feel a sense of hope again. If we repress our pain, and refuse to deal with the emotional side of it, we simply get to carry that baggage into our future relationships. So I knew that I had to heal from the pain, but I wasn't sure how to do it.

As I was still struggling to find a sense a peace through my divorce, I resorted back to one of my favorite pastimes, which was running. Many studies have shown that there is a hormone, a positive endorphin, that creates a feeling of bliss and joy, after we run several miles, and after we complete the run. I know about this experience very well. I used running as my main method to cope and heal from the pain of my divorce. After one autumn run, along a beautiful countryside of mountains, streams, and native landscape, I fell to the ground, as I began crying from my pain. As I did, I prayed and asked God how I was going to get through these hard times. After I fell, I rolled around as I cried in pain. After several minutes of deep and loud crying, in a quiet and isolated area of this mountain area, I had a feeling to turn over and lay on my back. So I did.

I saw a beautiful eagle flying through the sky, right above me, soaring beautifully and naturally through the sunlight sky, seemingly without a care in the world. This eagle seemed to know that it was destined to fly, and it was capable and soared with this incredible sense of strength and Hope.

I must admit, I try to avoid using the word "jealousy" in my life, because I know we all have different gifts for various reasons, but if there was ever a day I could admit to feeling jealous of another, it was that day. As I watched this beautiful eagle soar around with such confidence and beauty, it truly lifted me with

Hope. This eagle clearly felt comfortable in its identity, and was simply soaring around enjoying the gift of the day. This eagle reminded me that I had not been soaring lately, not at all. I missed it. I had soared before, but not like this eagle. I felt like I wanted to fly again, and reach above my situation, and achieve my goals, and let go of my pain. The eagle motivated me to spread my wings again, really wide, and soar above the confusion and the pain.

After this experience, I was inspired to write the following poem. It is based on watching this powerful eagle fly above the sadness and enjoy the flight of power, while allowing the current and winds to lift its wings and carry him higher and higher. Watching this eagle fly caused me to lift out of my despair and sorrow. I wanted to be like the eagle, and find a way to soar again, and I did. I soared like an eagle in certain areas of my life, and I grew with caution, in other areas of life. I remembered how great it felt to soar again. However, I might always have a bit of jealousy for the complete joy that this eagle was enjoying that day. I saw it and I felt it. It was a gift. It was awe inspiring and simply beautiful.

This eagle taught me great wisdom, so here is the poem from that experience:

The Eagle's Wisdom

I looked and saw an eagle soaring through a stormy sky
It didn't stop or hesitate or pause to wonder why.
It simply flew upon the winds as every eagle must
And moved about the air with confidence and trust.

The eagle's flight inspires my hope
I know that I can always cope.
When storm clouds come and winds blow fast
My faith can lift me 'till they're past.

I felt myself uplifted to new heights again today
I rose up and stayed much longer than I did just yesterday.
Gliding high above the forest, I could see across the trees
And get a larger vision of all the possibilities.

Starting in my center it traveled on and through.
I could feel contentment and power as it grew.
The strength of peace and trusting in life's gentle helping hand
Lifts and guides me to a better path across the land.

The eagle didn't fight the storm. He spread his mighty wings.
He let its fury lift him up in every rising rings.
High above the lightning, the thunder and the cold
The sunlight touched his feathers and turned them into gold.

We Hope you have remembered many stories from your life that have inspired you as you've taken the time to read our stories here. We'd like you to put some thought into completing the following activity. So get your journal out and start writing.

Isn't it amazing to read about people who have such amazing strength. They are the ones who give us all Hope. Think about someone in your life who has given you Hope when you felt you were ready to give up on someone or something.

Now, pull out a nice card and write a note to that person expressing your gratitude for the time they helped you turn your thoughts around and created an opportunity for you to choose Hope over despair. It's nice to let people know they influenced you in a positive way and helped you change the direction of your life.

Let us all work to be that person who changes the life of another.

When we slow down enough to feel the soul of a stranger, we are getting a glimpse of how Jesus loves this person, and then our attitude can shift. This is when love can change another. A glimpse of love, felt in both directions, provides Hope. When love is felt again, the door to Hope is opened again. When Hope is felt, the door to faith can be restored. Love, Hope and faith provide the reassurance of personal connection – something most of us seek in the world. It begins with personal, human connections every day.

Here is a sample affirmation to say each day, to reinforce the commitment to living each day mindfully, while appreciating the gift of Hope.

AFFIRMATION: I will stay the course – no matter what I am trying to accomplish. Because in my heart I know that good things are going to happen. I won't let worry or fear overtake me. I will it take one day at a time and know that there is Hope.

Applying the gift of HOPE:

Without Hope, we can experience depression, fear, anxiety and other negative emotions that can drag us down. We want each of you (including Elizabeth and me) to practice ways of bringing Hope into your lives. Here are 75 ideas to get you on the road to beginning to appreciate the gift of Hope – our plan is to throw these ideas out there so you can begin to think about, feel and act on Hope.

See if you can come up with your own ideas and add to the list we have provided you with, and get started on learning more about Hope and how to use it and apply it in your life each and every day:

- Keep a positive attitude about the future
- Smile often
- Let others see your excitement
- Express your gratitude to Heavenly Father
- Write down your goals and work toward them
- Remember "when things look like they're falling apart - they may just be falling into place"
- Plan trips far out in advance
- Express hope even when you don't feel it
- Talk about hope in your daily activities
- Surround yourself with hopeful people
- Read quotations about hope
- Make statements that affirm your belief in yourself
- Know that you will get better from an illness
- Know you can recover from an addiction, work toward it
- Know that life does get better after divorce
- Call a supportive friend and talk for a few minutes

- Have courage
- Spend time with someone who has a debilitating illness
- Do something you are afraid of
- Volunteer on a suicide prevention hotline and talk to people who need help
- Find a new job
- Learn something new that interests you
- Get out of bed each day
- Think of the things that make you happy and focus on them
- Get hopeful input from family members and friends
- Read from the scriptures every day
- Step outside your comfort zone
- Invest in something
- NEVER lose hope
- Give a few dollars to a beggar
- Notice the stars in the dark sky
- Read books about someone's courageous life story (Helen Keller)
- Watch movies that indicate hope (Schindler's List)
- Pray to have your dreams realized
- Remember that good things are going to happen
- Let others know you believe in their abilities
- When you feel like crying, laugh instead
- Find the positive spin on something in your life that's difficult
- Have a prayer in your heart at all times
- Look for people who need a boost and give them a word of encouragement
- Study the account of the Savior's life
- Do what it takes to have a soft heart
- Endure your hardships – they are shaping your future
- Remember that "hope is the only thing stronger than fear"
- Keep your eyes focused on the light at the end of the tunnel
- Teach your children to always have hope

- Let your story inspire others
- Make a plan for your future
- Hope for things you can't see
- Watch the sunrise every morning
- Practice patience – believe things will get better
- Remember that life has a funny way of working out
- Have hope even when things seem hopeless
- H.O.P.E. = Hold On, Pain Ends
- Remember, you never know what tomorrow will bring
- HOPE whispers maybe when it seems all you're hearing is NO
- Inspire someone you love to NEVER give up
- Remember, the most amazing things often happen right at the moment you're about to give up
- Let doors close in your life – know there are others waiting to open
- When you experience change, think of it as a fresh start
- So – never be afraid of change
- Never stop believing in your own abilities
- Visit terminally ill patients
- Read stories of inspiration
- Talk to your neighbors – everyone has a story of hope
- Laugh as often as possible
- Have a close friend you can call for an uplifting conversation
- Don't carry around regrets – your experiences ultimately shape the person you will become
- Speak inspiring things to those you know are struggling
- Help someone in need
- Talk to someone who is living in a homeless shelter
- Smile at someone who looks down and out
- Encourage your children to reach for the stars
- Sing loud with some of your favorite songs when you are feeling sad
- Hold hands with your loved one

Choose three or four things from the list that you can get to work on right now. And then DO THEM.

Having Hope does not come as easy for some as for others. Listening to the stories and experiences of others can help you realize you have control over your attitude, and that one thing can bring you around to the idea of Hope. So get to work and try turning any negativity you might be allowing in your life – into positivity and Hope.

"The Lord also shall roar out of Zion, and utter his voice from Jerusalem; and the heavens and the earth shall shake: but the Lord will be the hope of his people, and the strength of the children of Israel."
~ Joel 3:16 ~

Hope and Faith Connected

Hope is an expression of Faith.
When your Faith is your foundation,
It causes you to have a sense of optimism,
In daily living and for the future.

Hope is an attitude of expectancy,
That things will work together for a higher purpose.
Even if we Hope for something,
And it doesn't work out that we wanted,
We can find out way back to Faith,
And our Hope will be restored again,
(after we grieve the loss or situation we had hoped for).

When we have a strong conviction in our Faith,
We carry a sense of Hope in our hearts.
As we do this, we must reconcile,
That simply because we have Hope and Faith,
We cannot "will our plan into existence"

Part of what we need to reconcile,
Is that it is "Our Father's will and Divine Order"
Where we put our Faith and Hope.
He knows so much better about all things,
And how the veil is in place on earth for a reason.
This is a way for each of us to exercise
Our Faith and Hope on a daily basis.

As we remember this, we can say out loud, frequently,

"Not my will or way, but our Father in heaven, Through
my Savior Jesus Christ, As I dwell in my Faith,
and put my Hope in Him. His will be done. Amen."
~ by Elizabeth ~

Without a feeling of Hope, it's difficult to get out of bed in the morning and share our kindness and optimism for the day. Therefore, it is a worthy goal and habit to pray each morning for an attitude of Hope and goodness. This type of prayer also reinforces the positive goodness that we try and reinforce. The more we expect good, the more we will see it, and vice versa for the negative thoughts we let come in.

It is also important for us to stay close with people who make us feel positive. It is easier to experience the power of Hope when those around us are experiencing it too. Some people are just naturally optimistic, and it's a joy to be around them, so seek out those people in your life.

Think back in your life about a time when someone or something turned your disappointment into Hope.

- Think about what was disappointing you.
- Describe the way you were feeling at that time in your life.
- Remember who the person or thing was that became the turning point.
- Begin to realize what changes began to happen at that time.

Now, write about the experience and be as detailed as you possibly can.

The purpose of this activity is to get you thinking about the triggers and the transitions that created this entire experience for you. If you can, start thinking about what it would take to get yourself in that place where you begin to feel Hope no matter what is going on in your life. And, hopefully, you will be able to inspire others to change their way of thinking as well.

Patience is required to practice Hope.

Faith creates patience.

So when faith becomes full trust, you can know that things might not go your way, but you can trust the process. This creates patience and a willingness to wait. It isn't always easy, but if what you are Hoping for is right – things will begin to fall into place.

Sometimes we Hope for things that should not be. It's possible to force our Hope onto something we want, that isn't right for us. Have you ever wanted something so bad, you were determined to "will" it to happen? The ending of that story is usually not a good one. Looking back, we typically see why we should have listened.

If we truly believe God has a plan for each one of us, it may become easier for us to learn to listen. One of the biggest challenges in life is learning to trust and let things work out on their own after all we have done.

The same principle applies to the Hope of eternal life. Living a life that is pleasing to our Savior, Jesus Christ, generates a deep soul satisfaction that is rooted in true peace. So, after all we can do, we have Hope.

The Old Testament speaks of the Messiah. Hope paved the way for Jesus' birth because people knew He was coming. They waited for Him and looked forward to His arrival. Jesus' birth was highly anticipated because He provided an open door to God.

Hope in everlasting and even eternal life is the foundation of our existence on this earth.

> **The heart holds healing plans**
> **Waiting for our permission**
> > **to release**
> > **to mourn**
> > **to lift**
> **To higher places**
> **Where eagles fly.**

"Keep the faith. The most amazing things in life tend to happen right at the moment you're about to give up hope."

What are your thoughts and impressions now about the gift of Hope?

Has anything changed for you or become more clear to you? Jot down your thoughts now after 30 days of reflection:

_____

_____

_____

_____

_____

_____

_____

_____

_____

_____

_____

_____

_____

_____

"Which hope we have as an anchor of the soul, both sure and stedfast, and which entereth into that within the veil."
~ Hebrews 6:19 ~

CONCLUSION:

Hope is what keeps us moving forward in this life. It is Hope that compels us to keep hanging on and never give up. Hope in our Savior, Jesus Christ, leads us to want to do better – to BE better. Without Hope, we would all be lost – we would all give up. But with Hope in our hearts, we are unstoppable.

Hope is the foundation of our belief in Jesus Christ. And as we practice Hope on a regular basis, our outlook on life becomes more and more positive. When we keep a positive attitude toward our challenges, our hardships, even our routine daily lives, we will be happier and more content.

If we can spread Hope to reach and touch the lives of all who know us, think of the shift that can occur. People in general will be more productive, more focused, more committed to working on the things that truly matter. We will treat our families with more respect because we are Hopeful about the future.

The scripture above talks about Hope being an anchor of the soul. Cultivate Hope in Jesus Christ, and you have created an immoveable foundation.

DAILY REFLECTION

Each chapter is meant to be read slowly,
Absorbing the deeper essence behind the words and stories.

This allows for continual reflection,
Prayer and listening for answers,
Which opens the door to
Greater insight and awareness of
The Gift of Faith.

If we devote one month of the year,
To learning and living the Gift of Faith,
Our awareness of the precious Gift of Faith,
Will be spiritually heightened,
And our daily existence will emulate this awareness.

As we make this shift to mindful attentiveness to the Gift of Faith,
We will be less likely to take for granted,
The beauty, the power, and the mystique of Faith.
We will have developed a habit,
Which becomes part of who we are.

As we develop a new habit each month,
Based on a different Gift each month,
A Gift that Jesus came to earth to give each one of us,
We will become more like Jesus in the way we live.
As this happens,
We will be living a more Christlike life, every day.
As we do this,
We are expressing our deepest gratitude to Jesus
And our Heavenly Father.

As we share the 12 Gifts with others,
We cannot help but bring the same love and peace
To our own hearts and spirits.

3

The *Gift* of

FAITH

One of the most compelling gifts we have been blessed with, we believe, is Faith. There are many things in this life that require great Faith. Just coming here to this earth to live life is a test of our Faith. There are so many trials and sacrifices and hardships. It can be easy to lose sight of our real purpose if we allow our Faith in our Savior, Jesus Christ to waiver.

Keeping our Faith strong and staying grounded by a knowledge of Jesus Christ is what we believe makes it possible for us to accomplish great things in our earthly life. If we stop and think about it, praying to Heavenly Father is a big act of Faith. We are saying we know He is there. Many of us know from experience that prayers are effective. Think of the times you have prayed for something or someone, and through Faith, have had your prayers answered. They may not always be answered exactly the way we want them to be, but that is a huge part of Faith. We have to let go and know that the Lord will handle things as He sees fit.

Keep in mind as you study this chapter on Faith, that our constant attention and effort is required throughout our lives if we want to become more like Jesus Christ.

Why did we choose FAITH as the third gift?

"And the apostles said unto the Lord, Increase our faith."
~ Luke 17:5 ~

We chose Faith as the third gift because we feel strongly that it is having Faith in our Savior Jesus Christ that makes all things possible.

We love this quote by KP Kelly:

"When God places a purpose upon you,
when he makes his will clear to you,
when he tugs at and guides your heart,
no matter how difficult or how uncomfortable it may be,
stay the course.
His plan is better than yours and your faith will be rewarded."

We both recently came through experiences that we are reminded of when we read that quote. Looking back, it is difficult to overlook the hand of God in the decisions each of us have made over the past several months. It is not always so easy to see that you are actually being guided until you look back one day and realize there is no other explanation. You are right where you should be at this moment in time.

Our personal lesson from our experiences is to LISTEN. Listen with a clear mind and a pure heart to the promptings that are being given. If you can do this, we believe you will land where you are supposed to land. It is these kinds of experiences that strengthen our own Faith in our Heavenly Father and our Savior, Jesus Christ.

"And the Lord said, If ye had faith as a grain of mustard seed, ye might say unto this sycamine tree, Be thou plucked up by the root, and be thou planted in the sea; and it should obey you."
~ Luke 17:6 ~

When we think about Faith, we might also contemplate closely-related words that help us to embrace a deeper meaning of Faith. These words could include: BELIEF, CONVICTION, LOYALTY, HOPE, CONFIDENCE, ASSURANCE, CERTAINTY, ACCEPTANCE

"And he said unto them, Where is your faith? And they being afraid wondered, saying one to another, What manner of man is this for he commandeth even the winds and water, and they obey him."
~ Luke 8:25 ~

I want to share the following story because this experience increased my ability to rely on Faith. It's so amazing to look back at things you've gone through and realize how much you learned, how much you benefitted.

"OUT OF THE BLUE"
by Janeen

There have been many times in my life when I was required to have Faith and leave things in the Lord's hands. Over the years, this has become easier for me to do because of the experiences I have had where I have turned things over to my Heavenly Father and been blessed greatly for doing so. I'm certain each of you can relate.

There was one particular time where I found myself alone, with two teenagers and a small toddler. I had no job at the time, and had just closed on a brand new house without the equity I had expected to receive from my former home because of a divorce.

I was scared!

I was working hard trying to get a business up and running plus trying to take care of my kids, and had almost no income. I prayed very diligently during these three months and asked my Father in Heaven to help me figure out a way to earn enough money to stay afloat, and be able to be at home with my two-year-old daughter as much as possible.

I had been in my new home for just about a month when I received a call – out of the blue – from someone I didn't know very well, asking me if I would come in and talk about some work. I was overcome with gratitude as I walked into their offices and left with an opportunity to earn the income I was desperately in need of. I sold and produced commercial spots for the next two years on a freelance basis so I could have the freedom I needed with my daughter AND pay the bills.

It was a miracle sent from heaven – a tender mercy I was desperately in need of. And I have never doubted the hand of the Lord in what transpired that day.

The people who brought me under their wing have remained good friends, and we continue to have a working relationship on a freelance basis. They have been good to me.

I was greatly blessed for having enough Faith to allow the Lord to intervene and send angels to guide me and help me during a very difficult time in my life. That experience helped me develop great trust in my Heavenly Father and my Savior, Jesus Christ. I have learned to rely on them in hard times – and there have been many.

"And he said unto them, Why are ye so fearful? how is it that ye have no faith?"
~ Mark 4:40 ~

To get each of us thinking more about FAITH and what it means to us personally, we want to present the following questions for you to consider and think about carefully. Answer the questions when you're ready – remember this is personal. There are no right or wrong answers:

When was the last time you displayed significant faith in someone or something?

_____

_____

_____

_____

_____

_____

_____

What makes you feel invincible?

_____

_____

_____

_____

_____

Who do you trust more than anyone in the world – and why?

_____

_____

_____

_____

_____

What experiences have you had in your life that required great faith?

_____

_____

_____

_____

_____

Recall how one of those experiences turned out and write about it.

_____

_____

_____

_____

_____

What does it mean to have Faith in Jesus Christ? We believe having Faith in Jesus Christ means we are relying on Him completely, trusting His infinite power and love. It could also mean we believe His teachings. We may not always understand, but we have Faith that Jesus Christ does understand because He experienced all of our pains, both physically and emotionally. He knows how to help us rise above our difficulties. Jesus Christ overcame the world and made it possible for us to achieve eternal life.

The Apostle Paul taught that:

"Faith is the substance of things hoped
for, the evidence of things not seen"
~ Hebrews 11:1 ~

And Alma taught something similar:

"If ye have faith ye hope for things
which are not seen, which are true"
~ Alma 32:21 ~

Faith is a principle of action. You've heard the saying, "Faith without works is dead." Well, If we are working toward a goal in order to accomplish something, we are exercising Faith – we are hoping for something we cannot see yet, but we know if we work hard and stay diligent, it will come to be. But it will not come without our efforts.

If we plant a garden, we have Faith that it will grow, but if we forget to water it, the plants will die. It's a simple concept, but one that we sometimes need to be reminded of. At times, we may have a tendency to sit and hope for a certain outcome, but if we don't do everything we can, our Faith is useless. "Faith without works is dead."

We might also want to consider that doing things to increase our Faith will help us become stronger. The more we see that having Faith paid off, the more we will exercise our Faith. But Faith most definitely requires patience, and that is something we could all use a little more of.

One of the things we notice when we exercise our Faith and combine that with hard work, is that we feel a sense of calm knowing things will come together. It's a great feeling to know you are receiving Divine help when working toward something worthwhile.

Faith
It's all about BELIEVING.

You don't know
how it will happen,
But you know it will.

We have both had that kind of Faith at times in our lives – just knowing that things were going to work themselves out. I'm sure each of you have had similar experiences. People often say things like:

- Life truly does have a way of working out;
- If it's meant to be, it will be;
- If it's supposed to happen, things will fall into place.

But we believe it isn't by chance. What we are really saying when we make statements like that is that things will come together because we believe the hand of the Lord is in everything we do. We are saying we have FAITH.

With this in mind, make it your GOAL this month
as you ponder the Gift of Faith
to consider a problem you might be having
and find the Faith to turn it over to God.
Keep a journal about your experience.

Come up with your own GOAL that you personally
want to set as a way to improve in some
are regarding your personal Faith.

What are your thoughts and impressions about the gift of FAITH?

As you begin reading this chapter, write down a few thoughts you have as you contemplate the gift of Faith. We will ask this question again at the end of the chapter after you have completed your study of the gift of Faith.

_____

_____

_____

_____

_____

_____

_____

_____

_____

_____

_____

_____

"I believe in Christ like I believe in the sun. Not
because I can see it, but by it I can see everything else."
~ C S Lewis ~

What did Jesus say about FAITH?

"But Jesus turned him about, and when he saw her, he said,
Daughter, be of good comfort; thy faith hath made thee
whole. And the woman was made whole from that hour."
~ Matthew 9:22 ~

There are many instances in this life where our Faith is tested. Think about the times you have been on an airplane and experienced turbulence. For some, it is difficult to sit back, relax and have Faith that the plane will land safely. Many things in this life are out of our own hands. We are at the mercy of others, and we are at the mercy of our Savior.

It is a natural response to become frightened or worried over things we have no control over – the weather, for example, can wreak havoc at times. We don't welcome interferences and challenges, especially big things like natural disasters, but in Faith we trust that God is in charge and He will help us all to handle things that come our way.

Most of us have flown in a storm at one time or another and have experienced the uneasiness it brings. Or maybe you have been on a boat when a storm rocked you to the point of fear, or possibly you have been trapped outdoors during a lightning storm. Most of us pray harder and longer than we ever have before when we find ourselves in a situation like these. Our prayers seem to come easily when things are rough.

But there are many things that cause turmoil in this life besides the forces of nature. Our family members can cause us to worry because of the choices they might make. Co-workers and neighbors and people in general can discourage us or push us to become angry. People we love can hurt us in unintentional ways. We have to constantly remind ourselves that what other people do is out of our control just as much as the weather is out of our control.

Attitudes and behaviors of others can often be a bigger test of our Faith than almost anything else. But what we do have control over is our response. And if we choose to have Faith that all will be well, that the Lord will take care of things, that things will work out – then we can be at peace.

It is also important to keep in mind that we all have times when we, too, may be the ones causing the worry or discouragement to others. We want compassion, patience and understanding from others when we are in difficult places in our lives. It is only right that we offer those things back to those who are testing our Faith.

When we talk about Faith – the kind of Faith that can move mountains – we are speaking of something far greater than just have Faith in a general sense. We are talking about Faith in our Savior, Jesus Christ.

We found this on-line and thought it was appropriate to share because it speaks so well to Faith. Make the comparisons in your own life and think about the times you have fostered Faith rather than fear. What a difference having Faith can make in every instance in your life.

GOD'S VOICE	SATAN'S VOICE
CALMS	OBSESSES
COMFORTS	WORRIES
CONVICTS	CONDEMNS
ENCOURAGES	DISCOURAGES
ENLIGHTENS	CONFUSES
LEADS	PUSHES
REASSURES	FRIGHTENS
STILLS	RUSHES

"Where there is HOPE, there is FAITH. Where there is FAITH, MIRACLES happen."

Stories to help us reflect on the Gift of FAITH:

One of the greatest stories of Faith is told in the Bible. Abraham and his wife, Sara, conceived a child when Sara was well past the age of being able to bear children. They were able to do so because of their great Faith, and they named their son Isaac.

But Abraham's Faith was tested in a significant way. He was asked by God to take his son to the base of Mount Moriah, a three-day journey from their home, where he would be required to sacrifice Isaac upon an altar.

Think about that for a moment.

How is it possible that Abraham could have such great Faith, that, not only was he willing to do as the Lord commanded, but he could walk side by side with his son for three days to a destination where he knew he was going to have to kill him?

Many mundane tasks had to be completed in order for Abraham to carry out his Father's will:

- They had to carry wood up the mountain to build a fire;
- They had to build the altar;
- Isaac had to be bound and laid upon the altar;
- Abraham had to explain to Isaac at some point that he would be the sacrifice;
- Abraham actually lifted the knife to slay his son.

We're not so sure any of us in this day and age could equal Abraham in his Faith, but we can certainly take his example and do our best.

The happy ending to the story of Abraham, as we know, is that the Lord was testing Abraham to see just how Faithful he could be. And, in the end, an angel called out from heaven and stopped Abraham from sacrificing his son.

When Abraham demonstrated unwavering Faith, God rescued him.

We, as co-authors of this book, believe if we demonstrate Faith by doing our best to be obedient to God's commandments, we too can be rescued ultimately by living in the presence of God and Jesus Christ in eternity.

We also believe prayer is the ultimate proof of our Faith in God and Jesus Christ. When we communicate with Heavenly Father through prayer, we are letting Him know we believe He is there and we trust Him to help us through any situation.

FAITH IN PRAYER
by Elizabeth

I think most of us can relate to the times in our life when we send up the desperate prayer in a crisis situation, or when we are struggling with an issue. I believe these prayers are heard immediately because our hearts are so sincere and we are praying for truth, guidance and direction.

Many years ago I read the enormous bestselling book **Embraced By the Light** by Betty Eadie and I still recall an image that has stuck with me throughout the years. Ms. Eadie described how, in the afterlife, she saw that there were many angels who waited for those urgent, desperate type of prayers, and they carried those prayers quickly to heaven. I remember getting the sense that no prayer is said in vain, and that when we are very challenged, or in a crisis, the intensity of our prayers are felt in heaven. I will share a story below where I know this happened for me, as my car was heading into an accident situation. My daughter and I prayed out loud, and our prayers were answered. The accident was avoided. (It's a story worth reading!)

Based on my own experiences, I am guessing that many people send up prayers before they take a road trip, or even before they drive on freeways, or perhaps, just getting into the car! I must admit, the older I get, I recognize that there are more distracted drivers on the road. Cars have so many features that can easily distract drivers, yet these new systems can also increase efficiency in our lives. Drivers need to recognize that there is a balance. No meeting is too important if it causes a car crash. So I pray a lot more than I used to when I'm driving. I pray whenever I see a situation where a person is at risk on the road; I pray for safety and divine guidance for all in the situation. (These are times when someone is speeding excessively, weaving in and out of traffic, or perhaps on the side of the freeway with a disabled car or truck. These prayers are heard. We can all do this. I have Faith and Hope that angels will assist and prevent problems, and perhaps teach a lesson while preventing a tragedy.

The loved ones who have suffered pain and/or loss due to a distracted driving accident would tell you, without a doubt, that there is no text, conversation, or anything else in the car that could make up for the heartache, pain, and loss that others suffer from the choice of distracted driving. Please reflect about this each and every time you get in a car. Remind yourself, if you are the driver, many lives depend on your full attention and focus on the road. Accidents can happen. There are times when our poor choices contribute to the cause of an accident. Slow down. Help prevent these sad times. Pray more often in your car, and make a choice to become less distracted.

Unfortunate things happen because drivers are not paying attention to driving. Please pay attention and remember that all, or most, communication, can wait. Faith in the universe, and in God, tells us so. Embrace your Faith. Driving is one of the most important times in our lives to remember that all will be fine, even if we don't answer our phones. Ninety-nine percent of our communications are probably not life threatening, and the conversations can and will wait, if we just remember to have Faith in the big picture. Faith creates patience. But picking up that phone, can cause an incident that might be regretted forever.

The larger message about distracted driving, is to find a place of peace in your heart, that all communication can wait. There are very few life threatening situations that cannot wait a little extra time for some type of resolution. This is where a strong sense of Faith can come into play, to change our behaviors. When we have Faith, we just know in our hearts, that all will be well. Faith reassures us that nothing is that urgent, that it can't wait for a safe moment to take the call or view the text. That sense of urgency that tells us, "You must pick up, see what is happening…" while you are driving, is simply not that important. The distractions that checking the phone can cause, are not in accordance with the sense of Hope and Faith that you are seeking and cultivating in your hearts, souls, and lives.

Connecting with your heart, presence, spirit, and love when you arrive at your destination, with loved ones, is much more important than a text message trying to explain when you will arrive, especially if you don't arrive. Common sense goes hand in hand with Faith and Hope. Strong Faith in your heart will remind you that most communications can wait. Our society needs to build habits that focus more on the importance of relationships that we cherish, instead of speed and making good time on the road. (What time did we really save by getting there an hour earlier? An extra story or two from Great Aunt Adelaide, who couldn't remember who was in the story from the start?)

IT HAPPENED OVERNIGHT
by Janeen

One of my dearest, most trusted, most loving and genuine friends shared a story with me not long ago about how having Faith at a critical time in her life changed everything for her.

When she graduated from high school, Cindy lived for a time in San Francisco and then decided to move to Hawaii with one of her friends. She was in a place where she wanted to enjoy life just a little too much, and she led a fun and adventurous lifestyle that eventually led her to begin some unhealthy habits which included smoking. Cindy actually became a chain smoker, smoking two packs a day for several years. She knew it was unhealthy, but it fit in with the environment she had been hanging around in, and she just didn't think all that much about it.

The time came when she met her future husband and they married. Cindy was married for a short time, and during that marriage gave birth to a beautiful son, who, at 18 years of age was in a fatal motorcycle accident. She had lost her only son and felt completely alone and devastated. She felt such a great loss and sadness, and longed for more in her life – something that would bring her joy and lead her to relief from the pain.

It wasn't too long after that she met a wonderful man who was a member of a Christian church. He fell in love with my friend, Cindy, and married her believing she was such an amazing person, she would one day turn to her Savior and change her life. He was right. They had been married about five years when she decided she wanted to join the church because she truly wanted to change her life and accept the Savior and the atonement.

This particular church lives by a health code, and in order to be a Faithful member, she wanted to do what was required of her –

she knew she had to give up smoking. This wasn't going to be easy - two packs a day is not usually something that can be given up overnight. But that's exactly what she did! The very night before her baptism, she sat down and smoked what she knew was going to be her very last cigarette.

She was baptized the following morning and has never touched a cigarette since. That was many years ago.

When I asked her how she had possibly accomplished something so difficult, she replied, "I prayed to my Heavenly Father and asked for the strength to quit. I had the Faith that it would happen - that He would bless me with the ability to set aside my addiction so that I could have something much greater in my life. And he did."

I admired her before I knew this story, but hearing this increased my respect for her a hundred-fold. The most wonderful part of this story is the knowledge that if we only have Faith, we can accomplish great things.

Her life since then has been wonderful. She is happy. She is at peace. And she knows, through her Faith in Jesus Christ, she will be reunited with her son one day.

LIVING OUR FAITH
by Elizabeth

As we said in the title and introduction of this book, one of the goals is to assist in building habits of Christlike living. That can sound like a tall order, and it could cause some people to hesitate, not knowing where and how to begin. This is why we've organized the book into 12 chapters of Gifts, which all represent the teachings of Jesus Christ. If we each select one Gift per month to study, ponder, pray about, and then practice living, it's a lot easier to do. Of course, this is all a personal choice. No one should be forcing another person to follow this program, because at the heart of this is a true desire to WANT to live a more Christlike life.

So given this, I thought of many stories I could share about Faith in action, and there are some amazing stories out there from big public ones, to the very private ones we have from living our personal journeys. Every story is amazing because they lead us to strengthening our Faith in Jesus Christ. Please, never think that one of your stories is not big enough, or dramatic enough, because Jesus sees every single story. He is pleased when we are willing to share a story that could help another person to grow. As we listen to stories about other lives, they trigger feelings from our experiences, and this is what leads us to growth and a stronger conviction in our Faith.

Dr. Martin Luther King, Jr. Used FAITH to Create Change and Propel a Movement

There have been many books written about the life and legacy of Dr. Martin Luther King, Jr., and rightly so. What Dr. King did to create a movement of change in our country was based on his Faith and his love of Jesus Christ, which increased his love for his fellow human beings. There is no way to summarize

Dr. King's commitment for change and equality in just a few
paragraphs, so I do hope, by reading these few paragraphs, it
might motivate some readers to read a few of the books about
Dr. King, or books that Dr. King wrote.

He was a powerful speaker, with great charisma and the ability
to captivate millions of people. He was strong, knowledgeable,
compassionate, hopeful, loving, forgiving, honest, humble, and
a great teacher. He lived his life with passion, and he was truly
a Christlike person. He embraced at least these 12 Gifts of Jesus
Christ in the book and many more. However, he understood
that all have made mistakes, except for Jesus, and Dr. King
had compassion and forgiveness for others, because he knew
Jesus Christ. His Faith in Jesus, allowed his heart to be
humble, because we knew we were all here on earth to learn
and grow.

When I spoke with young adults about Dr. Martin Luther
King, Jr., many of them did not realize Dr. King had a Ph.D. in
Theology, (it was actually a Ph.D. in Systematic Theology). I
knew his degree was in Theology, but I looked it up to be sure,
and then I learned it was Systematic Theology. (Thanks Janeen
for checking that!) My mind immediately went to, "Of course,
Dr. King's mission was about change and yet, he had this strong
Faith, so this degree was a natural fit for him. I plan to read more
about this because I find it so intriguing. This would actually be
another thing to pursue in the course of the month for Faith.

When we go back and study the life of Dr. King, and the choices
he made, and how he was influenced by his Faith in Jesus
Christ, it becomes clear how he had the strength, conviction, and
determination to do what he was lead to do, because he didn't
just believe – he knew he had Jesus with him as he marched
and spoke. He also felt many inspirations from the Holy Spirit
because he prayed often and asked to be guided to make the
decisions that would lead to change and equality. I am grateful

this wonderful, Faith-filled man devoted his life to the causes he did. Thank you Dr. King. Your example of Faith in action is everlasting.

As I was reading the bestselling book, **"The Power of Habit: Why We Do What We Do In Life and Business,"** by Charles Duhigg, I read a powerful summary about Dr. King. It has stuck with me. I will paraphrase slightly, but then quote from this book, what Dr. King said.

Dr. King had been preaching at the church when he learned that a bomb had exploded at his house while his wife and daughter were inside. King rushed home, and he was grateful to realize no one was injured, but the bomb left a crater in his porch, and windows were shattered. It was obvious that if family members had been in the front room of his house, they would have been killed. Of course, there were high emotions, and the police were on the scene. And then Dr. King said the following words, partly because he recognized that violence could erupt:

"We must love our white brothers, no matter what they do to us. We must make them know that we love them. Jesus still cries out in words that echo across the centuries: 'Love your enemies; bless them that curse you; pray for them that despitefully use you.'"

This was the message of non-violence Dr. King had been preaching about. Dr. King had a persuasive way of settling down the anger and desire for revenge. He later said, "We must meet hate with love." Dr. King continued, "If I am stopped, our work will not stop. For what we are doing is right. What we are doing is just. And God is with us." Perhaps the Holy Spirit had been whispering warnings to him, but he knew his purpose, and he walked forward in Faith.

Dr. King was clearly using his Faith in Jesus, and the teachings of Jesus, to get the people on board on both sides of the conflict. Even the white police officers acknowledged how Dr. King's statements probably saved their lives that night.

Racial tensions in our country are still present, and there are many issues to discuss and changes to come. Working from peace, hope and Faith are the ways to create change for good. I sincerely hope and pray that we can follow in the example of Dr. Martin Luther King, Jr. and remember that non-violence is what Dr. King preached, because it is what Jesus Christ preached, and Dr. King followed the teachings of Jesus Christ.

It was Dr. King's FAITH that caused him to preach the teachings of Jesus. What a strong example Dr. King is for FAITH in action. Thank you for your amazing demonstration of Faith.

Faith is not containable.

It pours out of our souls.

It ignites the hearts of others

Causing them to seek, pray, and grow

Even without words.

Faith in action is one of the best ways

To let your LOVE for Jesus Christ shine forth.

Live your FAITH in Jesus,

Even when you can't find the words to share it.

Trust that Jesus will do the rest.

HERE IS ANOTHER STORY ABOUT FAITH, FROM A FAMILY PERSPECTIVE
By Elizabeth, but this is about Elizabeth Smart

My family lives about five miles from where Elizabeth Smart and her family lived when she was kidnapped from her bed, at age 14, at knife point, while her younger sister watched in horror. Elizabeth was about to embark upon a journey that could have been soul shattering. She had to find a way to cope through all of her ordeals and, in the end, Faith was the reason why Elizabeth was found and also the reason for Elizabeth's recovery. Her story is for her to tell, and I will not even begin to tell it for her. But living in the same city, which is a community that cares, there were many updates about her ordeal.

If you read Elizabeth's book, **"My Story: Elizabeth Smart,"** in her words, you will also see how Faith held her family together with hope, believing that they would find her again. Faith created reasons why Elizabeth was noticed with her kidnappers. Elizabeth's family hired a sketch artist to create an image of what the kidnapper looked like, based on the memories of Elizabeth's younger sister. Obviously, Elizabeth's younger sister was traumatized from the ordeal and was threatened also, which can cause a time lapse in details. But when Elizabeth's sister recalled the image of the man who took Elizabeth, the family wasted no time in sharing this information with the public. Signs were posted, the media helped, and the word was spread.

Elizabeth's family had Faith that she would be found. They prayed and they believed. I wonder if they ever wavered in this, because most people would. It was Elizabeth's family who insisted the images of the kidnapper be circulated, and this insistence came from their Faith. Elizabeth's father, Ed Smart, was very vocal and persuasive in asking the community to come forth if they had any clues about where Elizabeth was and who the kidnapper could be. He spread the images of the kidnapper everywhere. He was bold because he believed in his younger daughter, who had seen this man, and he knew she was telling the truth. He was also very bold because he had Faith they would be reunited. Their entire family had Faith, but it is also a heart wrenching time when a child has been kidnapped. None of us can predict how we would act if this happened within our family, or extended family. Some people are quick to judge and speculate, but until facts and truth surface – prayer, support, and search efforts are more helpful.

Eventually, a couple at a bus stop in a suburb of our city noticed a group of three people and, based on the images of the sketches from Elizabeth's younger sister, the couple suspected the young girl with this couple was Elizabeth Smart. They alerted the authorities, and the police quickly moved in.

You can read the details about this in Elizabeth Smart's book.

The main point of highlighting Elizabeth Smart's story is that our city and community came together in Faith to share, pray, search and find a way to solve the mystery of Elizabeth's kidnapping. And, Elizabeth was brought home to be reunited with her family. Her family had a strong Faith, and they never gave up hope. It seemed, in the end, that it was the Faith of the family to fully believe in the image of the person which Elizabeth's younger sister conveyed during the kidnapping. Without this strong conviction of Faith within the family, the posters might not have been hung up, which caused the bus bystanders to recognize Elizabeth and her kidnappers.

Elizabeth would be the first to say she was fortunate and blessed to be reunited with her family. There are so many kidnapping stories with sad endings. There is no way to compare one story with another. It is never due to a lack of Faith or worthiness. None of us can question the details of why some children are reunited and others are not. Every child and every family deserves to be reunited. When this does not happen, we need to come together in Faith for the loved ones who are mourning. This is when our Faith is truly tested and challenged. Finding a way to trust in Jesus when things are so devastating can be very hard.

Watching for miracles along the way is one of the best ways. They might come gradually, or obviously. But paying attention to grief, and knowing that the mourning process happens over time, will help. Letting others love you through it will also help. Jesus will be there, as your loved ones comfort you. Nothing makes it easy, but love will be there. We truly pray for the families who have suffered loss, and we pray that you will find a sense of hope, Faith and peace again, if you haven't already.

There are no easy answers. But it can't hurt to try Faith and love and see how it feels. We sincerely wish you all the best if you are still going through grief and loss. Jesus is there and available through prayer. Much love to you.

"And he said to the woman, Thy
faith hath saved thee; go in peace."
~ Luke 7:50 ~

"And he said unto her, Daughter, be of good comfort:
thy faith hath made thee whole; go in peace."
~ Luke 8:48 ~

We know as you've read some of these stories, you've been able to contemplate your own Faith and how you have grown in your own life by the examples of others, and by having Faith that carried you through a difficult situation.

Get your journal and write a few pages about a time you had an opportunity to experience great Faith. Think about what happened, what you were feeling, who you turned to, where you decided to put your efforts, what you said and what you thought. Write it all down and, most importantly, write about the outcome. Figure out how that experience brought you to where you are today.

> *"There isn't enough room in your mind for both worry and faith. You must decide which one will live there."*
> *~ Anonymous ~*

Alma taught the Zoramites about Faith in God. He told them that asking for a sign from heaven so they could believe – is NOT having Faith. Faith is believing what is TRUE without seeing it or without having proof.

You would probably agree that if God appeared to each of us, we would believe. The problem though is that we wouldn't be required to have Faith. And having Faith is what helps us to grow stronger and receive blessings from God.

Faith isn't only about trusting in God.

- It's about believing in the people you love;
- It's about being loyal in a committed relationship;
- It's about having trust;
- It's about believing that there is good in all of us;
- It's about acting on your instincts and trusting yourself.

Have you ever noticed how when you are working so hard to achieve something good – it seems everything is against you at times?

Have you realized that you have to keep looking ahead and moving forward and working even harder to achieve your goals?

Have you been at that place where you know you can do it, but at times it seems like you will never make it?

It requires great Faith to keep going.

One of our favorite inspirational quotes is the following:

"God is up to something
or the devil wouldn't be fighting you this hard.
You're going to win!"

Isn't this SO true? Have you ever experienced this very thing? Have you ever spoken of it out loud to someone who understood what you were going through? As we worked on this book, we said this very same thing many times. We mentioned early on that we had many things working on us during this period of time making it very difficult to complete our task. But we both had Faith and persevered so we could finish the book and share it with all those who want to improve their relationship with their Savior.

When we do good, we are tried and tested. Faith is required to get us through and push us to the finish line. We never, ever want to give up on something that is pure, something that is positive, something that can benefit mankind.

Here is a sample affirmation to say each day, to reinforce the commitment to living each day mindfully, while appreciating the gift of Faith:

AFFIRMATION: I will do my best not to think, not to worry, not to obsess. I will just breathe, and have Faith that things will come together and work out for the best.

"And Jesus said unto him, Go they way; thy faith hath made thee whole. And immediately he received his sight, and followed Jesus in the way."
~ *Mark 10:52* ~

Applying the gift of FAITH:

We can increase our Faith by participating in activities that will influence us for good and allow the Spirit to be comfortable in our presence. The more we do to act on our Faith, the more we will begin to see that our Faith will grow in leaps and bounds. There is something so amazingly peaceful about your life when you are relying on Faith every single day.

We want to help you increase your Faith, so we're getting you started with 75 ideas that will help you appreciate the gift of Faith – we want you to get inspired and start thinking about, feeling and acting on Faith.

Our hope is that you will add to this list as you read it, finding things that will help you learn to apply Faith in your life each day.

- Remember Faith and fear can't co-exist
- Show your Faith in the Lord by turning a problem you have over to Him
- Talk to someone about a time when your Faith healed you
- Write about the times in your life when you experienced great Faith
- Take a leap of Faith and do something you've been afraid of
- Get out of your comfort zone and try something new
- Ponder what God has created you to do – why are you on this earth
- Figure out what your gifts and talents are – then use them
- Never give up
- Pray to Heavenly Father to bless you with other gifts
- Be obedient and have Faith that your obedience will bless your life
- Pray for help with something
- Read books about Faith
- Commit yourself to the things that are important
- Vow to make a difference and then dig in and do something
- Tell yourself you can accomplish something great
- Watch an animal give birth
- Keep pushing toward your dream
- Believe in the unbelievable
- Realize that fear is not of God
- Serve others believing you will be blessed
- Plant a garden and watch it grow
- Talk to your children about what it means to have Faith
- Pray for a loved one to be healed from an illness
- Believe that you will heal from your pain
- You can't have Faith and worry at the same time – stop worrying

- Keep a FAITH notebook
- Put all your trust in God
- Let go of things you can't change
- Remember Faith makes all things possible
- Know that better things are coming
- Keep trying
- When you know you have something good – stay the course
- Pray often
- Take one step closer to something you've been wanting to do
- Put your Faith in the people you love and care about
- Watch the sunrise
- Look through a telescope at the stars and planets
- Believe that something you are waiting for is about to happen
- Have Faith that someone you love will change for the better
- Share your thoughts about Faith with someone
- Plant flowers and water and tend to them everyday
- Know that God will guide you if you let him
- Believe that you can handle anything that comes your way
- Remember, with God, all things are possible
- Let go of the things in your life that have caused you pain
- Read from your scriptures daily
- Work hard and believe your efforts will pay off
- Keep in mind that Faith won't exempt you from difficulties
- Believe in miracles
- Understand that God has a plan for you
- Don't get discouraged – discouragement is Satan's greatest tool
- Laugh a lot
- If a door closes, know you are headed to a better place
- Smile and know that things are working out
- Watch for special people to come into your life

- Let your Faith inspire others
- Don't let anxiety creep into your life
- Enjoy the adventure of life each and every day
- Never stop moving forward
- Remember that God wants you to win – he is there to help you do it
- Fly in an airplane
- Believe in people and know there is good in them
- Let others share their stories of Faith with you
- Believe you can do something and then go do it
- Keep a positive attitude at all times
- Hold a baby
- Pray expecting to receive an answer
- Be patient
- Be grateful
- Change your attitude and you will change your future
- Light a match and build a fire
- Take a risk
- Let the Lord use you for good
- After you say your prayers – listen

Choose a handful of things from this list that you would like to do right now. And DO THEM.

Make it a point in your life to set aside some time each week to put your Faith to the test and do things that will help it grow. Do things you have not done before. Stay positive and keep working on it.

Remember, being deliberate about having new experiences is necessary for growth. As you begin to incorporate Faith promoting activities into your life, your Faith will increase. And as you practice Faith on a daily basis, you will begin to form habits that will strengthen you throughout your life.

The following activity is something we'd like you to do for a few moments every day for one entire week.

You are going to keep a log in your journal.

Think back on some of the "tender mercies" you have experienced that happened during a time you were required to have a lot of Faith. For example, with some huge changes happening in both of our lives, we began to notice all the little things that started happening that made our lives easier – extra work, people offering help, a lot of little things that really added up.

Keep a log of these "tender mercies" for a week, and then work on keeping track of these tender mercies throughout your life. Write them down and you will begin to notice that God is watching over you.

The purpose of this exercise is to get you to begin building your Faith by paying attention to what's going on in your life on a daily basis.

"Wherefore, if God so clothe the grass of the field,
which to day is, and to morrow is cast into the oven,
shall he not much more clothe you, O ye of little faith?"
~ Matthew 6:30 ~

Faith in Jesus Christ is a Gift that comes to us as we choose to believe in our Savior, and as we seek it and do those things that will allow us to keep it.

Faith doesn't just fall on us by chance. It is something we work at. At all times throughout our lives, our Faith is either becoming stronger or it is becoming weaker. The condition of our Faith is by choice.

I, Janeen, was acquainted with a young family a few years ago who lived very modestly in a loving home. The parents had three children who were all very close in age, and their mom had struggled for a long time to care for her children and also hold a full-time job in order to make ends meet. When the kids were teenagers, the son was diagnosed with a severe form of cancer. He was not expected to live very long.

This family was devastated, but not about to give up on their son. I observed this family's Faith, as all of their neighbors did, as the health of this boy was at risk. The family called on friends for prayers in his behalf. They did all they could between doctors, diet and other conditions that might help this boy. They called upon the priesthood to bless their son. They had great Faith that their situation would work out for the best – in the way the Lord wanted it to.

Miraculously, their son's cancer went into remission. His ten-year anniversary recently passed, and he is still cancer free.

This family was greatly blessed because of their Faith in their Savior. And their Faith has increased significantly because of their experience.

Having Faith requires letting go. It requires us to leave everything in the Lord's hands after we have done everything we can. It is trusting in our Savior, Jesus Christ.

> *"Accept what is, let go of what was,*
> *and have faith in what will be."*

> *"Faith is not believing that God can,*
> *it's knowing that He will."*

What are your thoughts and impressions now about the gift of FAITH?

Has anything changed or come into your awareness that wasn't there before?
Jot down your thoughts now after 30 days of reflection:

_____

_____

_____

_____

_____

_____

_____

_____

_____

_____

_____

_____

_____

*"I tell you that he will avenge them speedily, Nevertheless
when the Son of man cometh, shall he find faith on the earth?"*
~ Luke 18:8 ~

CONCLUSION:

Faith is letting go and knowing in your heart that everything will work out the way it should. For some, that may come easy. For most of us, it requires continual effort to grow our Faith and to even be calm in the face of adversity.

When our Faith is tested, we sometimes want to run away, or at least have a good cry accompanied by a healthy temper tantrum. But, once we come through the trial, we can look back and know it was for our good.

We hope this chapter about the gift of Faith has inspired you to get out of your comfort zone and work to become stronger in many areas of your life. If we can engage ourselves in Faith-promoting activities, we give ourselves a better chance at not only surviving the hardships that come to us – but surviving them WELL.

DAILY REFLECTION

(Repetition is what creates new habit. Read this page daily as a reminder.)

Each chapter is meant to be read slowly,
Absorbing the deeper essence behind the words and stories.

This allows for continual reflection,
Prayer and listening for answers,
Which opens the door to
Greater insight and awareness of
The Gift of Forgiveness.

If we devote one month of the year,
To learning and living the Gift of Forgiveness,
Our awareness of the precious Gift of Forgiveness,
Will be spiritually heightened,
And our daily existence will emulate this awareness.

As we make this shift to mindful attentiveness to the Gift of Forgive-
ness,
We will be less likely to take for granted,
The beauty, the power, and the mystique of Forgiveness.
We will have developed a habit,
Which becomes part of who we are.

As we develop a new habit each month,
Based on a different Gift each month,
A Gift that Jesus came to earth to give each one of us,
We will become more like Jesus in the way we live.
As this happens,
We will be living a more Christlike life, every day.
As we do this,
We are expressing our deepest gratitude to Jesus
And our Heavenly Father.

As we share the 12 Gifts with others,
We cannot help but bring the same love and peace
To our own hearts and spirits.

4

The *Gift* of FORGIVENESS

The ability to Forgive when we have been deeply wronged is not only a gift, but an ability that requires divine intervention at times. Have you ever carried the burden of anger or resentment towards someone? How does it make you feel – tired - run down - weak - angry? Holding onto anger is very draining and exhausting.

I, Janeen, once had someone ask me how on earth I was able to Forgive a particular person, and why would I even give them the satisfaction of knowing I was over it. I was disappointed at the attitude he held – believing that holding a grudge and closing the person out was a much more "satisfying" way to deal with the situation.

Forgiveness is a difficult thing sometimes. And just when we think we've done it – something else happens to possibly reopen the wound, and we find ourselves having to begin again. Just as with each of the gifts, we must continually remind ourselves to keep working on our efforts. Our constant attention is required if we want to become more like Jesus Christ.

Why did we choose FORGIVENESS as the fourth gift?

"Wherefore I say unto thee, Her sins, which are many, are forgiven; for she loved much: but to whom little is forgiven, the same loveth little. And he said unto her, Thy sins are forgiven."
~ Luke 7:47-48 ~

According to the Mayo Clinic, Forgiveness can lead to:

- Healthier relationships
- Greater spiritual and psychological well-being
- Lower blood pressure
- Less stress, anxiety and hostility
- Fewer symptoms of depression
- A stronger immune system
- Improved heart health
- A higher self-esteem

Forgiveness is an act of the will. It is a decision we make – whether to Forgive or not. Forgiveness requires a humble heart and that is not something that comes easy to many of us. It also requires that we let go of the idea that we need to punish the other person – the one who wronged us.

We have often thought that holding onto a grudge is about being in control. Most of us like being in that position of control, even if it is hurting our relationships. And when Forgiveness is required, many of us would rather hold onto our pride and forget about Forgiving. It's interesting how we think that if we hold onto the bitterness, we will be punishing the person we think deserves to be punished. But the truth is, we are only punishing ourselves.

We have all been in that position where we were hurt, betrayed or wronged in some way. Think about how you felt when you did not want to let go of your anger or your bitterness. Think about the quality of your own life during that period of time. Were you happy and content? Were you at peace? The answer is always NO.

We've all heard it said that Forgiveness is not for the other person, but rather it is for us. We are giving ourselves that gift of freedom when we choose to Forgive, and I for one would rather feel at peace and know that I can move forward in a positive direction.

It's interesting to note that when we freely Forgive – whether it be our spouse, our family member, friend, co-worker, neighbor, or whoever it may be – others will more freely Forgive us for any wrongdoing we may have done. It is required of us by our Heavenly Father to Forgive all men. If we do not Forgive, we will not be Forgiven by Him. That puts it into perspective doesn't it?

*'Then came Peter to him, and said, Lord, how oft
shall my brother sin against me, and I forgive him?
till seven times? Jesus saith unto him, I say not unto
thee, Until seven times: but, Until seventy times seven."*
~ Matthew 18:21-22 ~

One of our favorite books is "Believing Christ" by Stephen E. Robinson. Here is a paragraph from the beginning of his book.

"We have all done things that shame us, and we have felt the horrid weight of guilt and remorse and self-reproach. There are sins that maim us spiritually; sins that may not kill us outright but will fester and will not heal; sins that make us feel as though we've drunk raw sewage or contracted some loathsome disease, as if we can wash but can never get clean. In the grip of such sins and in the midst of guilt and despair, in our terrible aloneness, cut off from God, we raise our eyes to heaven and cry out, 'Oh, Father, isn't there any way we can ever be friends again?' The answer of all the prophets and all the scriptures to the question of the Great Dilemma is a resounding 'YES!'"

If we will do our part, Heavenly Father will Forgive us of all of our sins, no matter how serious they are. Why then, would we not chose to do the same for those who wrong us, no matter how great the pain they cause?

Forgiveness will make us whole again – in the eyes of God, in the eyes of our fellowman, and within ourselves. What a beautiful concept!

And don't forget to Forgive YOURSELF as well. Sometimes that is the most difficult thing we ever have to do.

> *"And when ye stand praying, forgive, if ye have*
> *ought against any: that your Father also which* •
> *is in heaven may forgive you your trespasses."*
> ~ *Mark 11:25* ~

When we think about Forgiveness, we might also contemplate closely-related words that help us to embrace a deeper meaning. These words could include: ABSOLUTION, COMPASSION, GRACE, MERCY, REMISSION, REPRIEVE

I want to share the following story because I am fortunate to be close friends with one of the most Forgiving people I know. She has taught me to work harder to love people, no matter what. It isn't always easy. We believe it's helpful to listen to the stories of others for inspiration.

FORGIVENESS - A DELIBERATE DECISION
by Janeen

I have a dear friend, Sherry, who understands the true spirit of Forgiveness beyond anything I have ever seen in another human being. She was betrayed on the deepest level by her husband of twenty-two years. She did all she could to work things out and remain in the marriage, but, in the end, he left her for someone else.

Watching her go through this experience was an inspiration to me. I never saw her get angry, and I never heard her say one negative thing towards the other woman. As we are extremely close, it would have made total sense for her to vent to me and at least express her feelings of loss and resentment. And in all honesty – she had every right. But she never did. She had the deepest sense of giving everyone the benefit of the doubt and working to understand the situation from every angle. She realized she had done all she could and made the decision to move forward with Forgiveness and a positive attitude.

To this day, she continues to express gratitude that this person who entered her life in such a tragic way is always very kind to her children. She found the positive and continues to focus on that. Her own life has moved forward to a happier place. And she continues to practice Forgiveness in her everyday life. She has truly been blessed for it.

I wanted to have Sherry speak to her ability to Forgive so freely, so I sat down with her and asked her a few questions:

Question: How have you been able to keep such a positive outlook?

"Because of my faith and knowing Heavenly Father has a plan for me. My life is so good now and so full. I wouldn't trade my experiences for anything."

Forgiveness is for the person who has been wronged. It is not for the person who needs to be Forgiven. It is the only way we can truly come to the peace that will transform us, and hope for a better life.

Question: Did the process of Forgiveness begin with a deliberate decision?

"Absolutely! You have to decide the anger and resentment aren't worth it. I didn't want to live that way. I asked Heavenly Father to take that away and replace it with charity and love for my ex-husband and his new wife. I would rather have love for them and have the peace rather than live with continued anger and resentment. Charity is a spiritual gift.

We read about charity in I Corinthians. It says in 14:1 'Follow after charity, and desire spiritual gifts, but rather that ye may prophesy.' We can ask for our Heavenly Father to give us charity, so that's what I did.

The anger creeps in from time to time because I am human, but because I made that deliberate decision, I have been truly blessed."

Question: You still care for your ex-husband to some degree. How has that been possible?

"It hasn't been hard at all because his intent is never to hurt me. I know and believe that even though he has hurt me more than anyone else in the world. Things happened but I know he didn't want me to suffer.

My life is so good. I am grateful for what I have now and for what I have learned through this whole process. I have a wonderful husband and a wonderful life. It really comes down to gratitude and expressing it everyday. I don't regret all those years of marriage because I have four beautiful children and even grandchildren now. My life is different now, but it comes down to being grateful everyday for the new life I have been given."

Forgiveness is truly a blessing in each of our lives.

"Then said Jesus, Father, forgive them; for they know not what they do. And they parted his raiment, and cast lots."
~ Luke 23:34 ~

"But if ye forgive not men their trespasses, neither will your Father forgive your trespasses."
~ Matthew 6:15 ~

Let's start thinking about Forgiveness and how it can help us. We've come up with a few questions we want you to thoughtfully answer. So see what you come up with. Spend some time thinking about them before diving in:

What emotions do you experience when someone has done something to hurt you unintentionally?

_____

_____

_____

_____

_____

If you did something that unintentionally hurt someone you love, how would you want them to respond to you?

_____

_____

_____

_____

_____

Think of a time when you reached a point of Forgiving someone. What did you say to them and how did you feel afterward?

_____

_____

_____

_____

_____

Remember when someone who means a lot to you Forgave you for something you may have done. Express your gratitude here for that gift.

_____

_____

_____

_____

_____

What are the things that start to soften your own heart when you begin to reach a point of being able to Forgive someone?

_____

_____

_____

_____

Have you ever known someone who could not Forgive and lived their life holding onto that grudge? Write here about how that person was affected by their inability to Forgive.

_____

_____

_____

_____

_____

_____

_____

_____

When we practice the gift of Forgiveness, we are honoring Jesus Christ and our Heavenly Father. We are reaching deeper into our hearts and souls, and asking for the Lord's help to Forgive a painful wrong. We all know it is not easy to Forgive deep wounds, but it is necessary. We can ask for help through prayer. If we are unable to Forgive a person, situation or event, our spirits will hold onto the bitterness and pain. We will continue to feel it. To release the negative memories or feelings, we ultimately need to Forgive. It is in the process of Forgiving that we also give ourselves a gift – that gift is freedom.

As we Forgive, and sometimes we must repeat the process before it is truly cemented into our souls, our spirits become free of the pain, and we can fly again. Remaining attached to the wound and event does just that – it binds us to it like rubber cement. Staying bound up to a painful memory causes us to re-live it over and over in our subconscious. Eventually, the repetition of these negative emotions affects our bodies, our minds and our souls. People get sick from this. Many people choose to stay angry because the pain was "unforgivable." Jesus was in enormous pain as they nailed Him to the cross and crucified Him. Yet, He knew beneath His physical pain that He needed to ask His Father to Forgive them, for they truly did not know what they were doing. They knew they were physically torturing Him, but they did not have the same spiritual understanding that Jesus had. They did not know the bigger picture of how hurting another person in this way was completely wrong, let alone it was our Savior.

In a way, Jesus was trying to tell us that when people do evil things to others, they cannot possibly understand why they are doing, or they would not be doing it. Therefore, He was asking His Father to Forgive them due to their complete lack of understanding. This is something we can think about when we are struggling with our ability to Forgive a person or circumstance. If they truly knew how wrong it was to condemn and hurt another, they would not be doing it.

We can become more Christlike simply by doing what Jesus did in His extremely painful situation. Ask your Father in Heaven to Forgive them, because you are having a tough time doing it. As you do this, you may immediately, or gradually feel the burden of the wound and memory lifted from you. When it is too heavy for us to carry a burden, our Heavenly Father, through Jesus, can assist you with the gift of Forgiveness and take it from you. Then you are free to fly again. When you experience this, you will never want to be unforgiving again.

At times, people become confused with the phrase, "Forgive and Forget." Just because you Forgave, does not mean that you will ever forget. In fact, it is the memory of the circumstance that propels many individuals to use their pain to create advance causes or create solutions to problems.

Forgiveness can lead to feelings of understanding, empathy and compassion for the one who hurt you. But Forgiveness doesn't mean that you deny the other person's responsibility for hurting you, and it doesn't minimize or justify the wrong. You can Forgive the person without excusing the act.

Now that the gift of Forgiveness is on your mind, make it your GOAL this month as you ponder this gift to think of one person you need to Forgive and take the steps to do so.

And figure out a way to take any pain you are feeling from an event and turn it into a positive, or create a solution to some problem you are experiencing.

We want you to begin your journey by thinking about your impressions of the gift of Forgiveness.

As you begin reading this chapter, write down a few thoughts you have as you contemplate the gift of Forgiveness. We will ask this question again at the end of the chapter after you have completed your study of the gift of Forgiveness.

_____

_____

_____

_____

_____

_____

_____

_____

_____

_____

What did Jesus say about FORGIVENESS?

"Judge not,and ye shall not be judged: condemn not, and ye shall not be condemned: forgive, and ye shall be forgiven."
~ Luke 6:37 ~

"Take heed to yourselves: If thy brother trespass against thee, rebuke him; and if he repent, forgive him."
~ Luke 17:3 ~

Forgiveness is one of the most necessary things we must do in this life. Every one of us has done things that require us to be Forgiven – both by those here on earth who love us, and by our Savior.

All of us need Forgiveness, and all of us need to Forgive. That's a lot of Forgiveness going on in the world on a continual basis. Think about a time when you wanted someone to Forgive you. The things we do don't seem like such a big deal to us, but they can deeply wound another person. We may not realize that fact until we are deeply hurt by someone else. And then things come into perspective pretty quickly.

Think back on how good it felt to have someone truly Forgive you. What did that feel like? If we truly Forgive someone, it means we treat them the way we treated them BEFORE the offense. Depending on the nature of the offense, this can feel nearly impossible. In fact, it probably IS impossible without the help of our Savior.

Stories to help us reflect on the Gift of FORGIVENESS:

We love stories about Forgiveness. We all have them, and we all share them with those we care about. As we share some of our stories and the stories of others, think of your own stories and write about them so the next time you are working to Forgive someone, you can remember the wonderful healing that took place.

We want to begin with a current event because the timing is so interesting. Elizabeth was so touched by it that she wanted to include it here:

TRAGEDY IN SOUTH CAROLINA
by Elizabeth

I am writing this portion of the Forgiveness chapter on Sunday June 21, 2015. Four days earlier, on Wednesday, June 17, 2015, our country, the United States of America, suffered a terrible tragedy. A twenty one year old Caucasian man, who has since admitted to the crime, walked into the Emanuel African Methodist Episcopal Church in Charleston, South Carolina, and was welcomed into a Bible study group by the others.

The members had come together to study the Bible and share in their faith, with their devoted and beloved pastor leading the Bible study.

According to news reports so far, the white male sat among the black church members for at least an hour before he pulled out his gun and began shooting the devout Christian church members, as he began by shooting the pastor first.

These Christian individuals had gathered together to share in their love for Jesus and God, and study scriptures as they lived, learned and grew in their faith. This was a Christ centered meeting, seeking greater love and light in their hearts and lives. I can only imagine what a beautiful experience it was, to be among a Bible study group of such strong Christian believers, and to have the strong leadership of such a loving, kind, and wise pastor. Love and light were surely present in that sacred place of worship, study and prayer.

Given this beautiful atmosphere, focused on the pure love of Jesus Christ, it is difficult to understand how this male shooter could have sat among these loving and faithful individuals and not have allowed the love of the group permeate into his heart and change his premeditated plan. This is a mystery that can only be speculated about here on earth, and it should be pondered and talked about. This is how we learn and grow from awful events, and thereby, gain wisdom and insight on how we prevent this type of event from happening again. Lessons must be learned from this, and policies and awareness will change.

Coming Together For Change

There are events that happen in life that are so difficult to comprehend, and our earthly minds will never be able to fully understand the motives of another person. But this should not stop the masses of many great minds and compassionate individuals to seek greater understanding of the issues that could cause a person to turn against other innocent people, and to harbor such hatred in their hearts for other people whom they have never even met. There are reasons for a person to shift towards hate, revenge, violence, and cruelty. The more we learn about these reasons, the more we can all do collectively in society to notice, pay attention, and share information if, and when, it is necessary.

Going even further upstream towards prevention of these issues is to pay much closer attention to children and teens who seem to be withdrawing from society and a connection to others, and possibly be developing angry attitudes towards society and groups of people. Along with the many benefits of the internet and social media come the opportunities for individuals who might feel isolated to listen, stalk, and create a sense of generalized unfairness in the world.

One lesson that is common sense about this, even in the early days of healing from this ordeal as a country, is that it should prompt all of us to pay closer attention to other people and notice what they are saying, feeling and hinting at. In hindsight, there are often signs that an individual is heading down a negative, dark and angry path. Sharing these insights with appropriate people, and passing laws, policies, and rules that allow for the protection of others and society, are worthwhile endeavors.

Coming together in society with a motive for solving problems and preventing future problems with meaningful discussions, I believe we can address these issues. Part of creating solutions would most likely involve checking any political agendas and egos at the door before entering and truly focusing on the best interests and safety issues of individuals and society. When intelligent individuals come to the table to solve a problem with the focus being on sincere, practical and necessary solutions, amazing things can happen. Outside agendas and other issues often hamper and stifle the process and ultimately perpetuate the previous problems. When intelligent individuals come to the table to solve a problem, AND they have a respect for the type of Gifts that we are referring to in this book, whether they practice a belief in a higher power or not, even more amazing things can happen.

Forgiveness Is Often A Miracle

An appreciation for the gifts of Life, Love, Compassion, Connection, and many more, should be guiding principles for creating laws and policies that help govern a civilized society. However, the reason for sharing the story of the murders in this beautiful, devoted and historical church in Charleston, South Carolina, is to use the experience as a way of opening the discussion about Forgiveness in our modern day society.

Many people would say that the ability to Forgive another person in the midst of a horrible tragedy is a miracle and, most likely, a divinely appointed event. This may be true, or partially true. But again, it is one of those life mysteries that our earthly minds cannot prove or disprove. Since there is no way to intellectually argue for either side, it is worth putting that point aside to ponder the other ways of more fully understanding the gift and act of Forgiveness.

(We decided to capitalize the name of the gift that we are writing about, throughout the book, to reinforce the importance of the gift, and to make an emphasis upon the twelve sacred gifts that Jesus lived while on earth.)

These lessons were truly "gifts" and we agreed that each gift is profound enough on it's own to deserve capitalization, but collectively, these twelve gifts are why Jesus made the decision to come to earth and teach us. He came to teach us all about how we should live our lives and about our Father in Heaven, God, along with the eternal love they both have for each and every soul.

Ultimately, Jesus taught us about one of the greatest gifts that will help us stay close to Him and to God. Although Jesus spoke about Forgiveness throughout his thirty three years of living on earth and teaching, we believe that one of the most lasting lessons, that lingers in millions of hearts around the world, is how He could possibly say, "Father forgive them, for they know not what they do." During the many hours of torture inflicted upon Jesus, as He was lead to His crucifixion, and then again as He endured more extreme torture in an earthly body, He still found the words in his heart and mind to say, "Father, forgive them, for they know not what they do."

We know it is recorded in the Bible that "Faith, Hope and Charity" are three of the greatest gifts we can learn and live.

And Charity is the greatest gift of all:

1 Corinthians 13:13 "And now abideth faith, hope, charity, these three; but the greatest of these is charity."

1 Corinthians 13:8 "Charity never faileth: but whether there be prophecies, they shall fail; whether there be tongues, they shall cease; whether there be knowledge, it shall vanish away."

We believe this and know it as a scripture. However, if we each want to be able to live these three gifts to the fullest in our hearts, minds, souls and bodies, we also need to examine the gift of Forgiveness more deeply. Especially in our modern society with so many methods for hearing the opinions of other people, it would be easy to build up a grudge towards another person if we don't agree with their opinion or perspective. Relationships and the heartfelt disappointment that comes along with the parting of ways are another very familiar way for individuals to harbor resentment and pain. In today's society, it is very easy to be offended by others, especially if we linger on it and choose to see it as an attack.

This is why it is so interesting to explore how, why, when, what, and who it is that Forgive others as they take this journey of Forgiveness. It is worth studying the hearts, minds and beliefs of those who are able to Forgive to learn more about this special gift.

"I Forgive You"

Four days after the murder of nine Bible studying Christian children of God, we are learning stories about Forgiveness all across America – in the church where the brutal murders occurred and throughout churches across the country.

It seemed to begin with the adult daughter who spoke about her deceased mother, who was one of the victims, at the first court hearing of the man who was arrested. She cried as she told this young man how his actions hurt her, her family and many others, but she also said, "I forgive you." Clearly she was in the midst of grieving the loss of her deceased mother, but through her words, it is clear that she made a deliberate decision to Forgive the offender. Otherwise, she could not have said those words. A person who is still consumed with rage and anger would not be able to let those words flow from their mouth. The act of saying, "I forgive you..." shows the intent of a person's heart and mind. They have made a decision to move in the direction of Forgiveness.

As an observer, it seems from this situation, and many others, that the act of Forgiveness begins with a very decisive intention. Unless there is a profound and divine miracle that enables a person to Forgive a very horrible offense, (which happens and people have spoken about this) the act of Forgiveness is usually a process that takes time and a strong commitment to move in this direction. True Forgiveness does not happen right after a person decides to Forgive another. Studies and research have shown that most humans go through various grieving stages or cycles to work through the pain of loss and bereavement. The same body of research indicates that it is healthy and expected to go through the emotions of grief, and it is through experiencing the grief and many related emotions that we are able to move through the pain.

After going through the roller coaster of emotions with honesty and openness, we can allow ourselves to resolve the pain in a way that suits our individual way of coping and grief. There is no exact formula for grief. There are just guidelines and stages of what a person can expect, partially, to normalize the process so that a person opens up to the process instead of resisting it.

"HOW SIMPLE IT WAS TO FORGIVE"
by Janeen

The story we just read required more Forgiveness than most of us will ever be required to give in our lifetime. There have been so many tragedies in the world lately – school shootings, bombings, trafficking, drunk drivers and so many other crimes that have left people and families devastated.

But most of us will only be required to Forgive people we love for hurting us when they didn't intend for their actions to spill over to others.

When I think back on my life, it has been my family members or close friends who have asked for my Forgiveness or needed me to ask for Forgiveness, and even though the things that can happen in relationships are small in comparison to a devastating mass murder, they are still heartbreaking and require us to dig deep to move past it and go forward.

Several years ago, I was living in another state close to a family member who asked to borrow money at one point for something that wasn't necessary. I didn't have the money, but offered my credit card, thinking I would be paid back almost immediately. The short story is my credit card was tied up for several months.

I was very young at the time and not capable of being reasonable, so I became angry at my family member and caused a rift between us that didn't heal for several months. I was upset with him, and he was upset with me, so we didn't speak for awhile and the resentment started to build.

Luckily, my older family member decided one day to ask my Forgiveness for taking advantage of me. His apology melted my heart, and we made amends and moved on. But I learned something that day. He taught me how simple it was to Forgive, and I was blessed to learn a lesson from his attitude. In return, I told him I too was sorry for treating him the way I did. I will always remember what a relief it was to put that issue behind us.

"LET IT GO"
by Elizabeth

Holding onto to resentments and anger limits our ability to Love like Christ as we strive for this goal in our lives. We know that we cannot compare ourselves to living a life like Jesus did, but just having the awareness and focus of being more Christ-like propels us in this worthy direction.

However, as we will share in this next story about a father who lost four members of his family, including his wife who was six months pregnant, there are times when God speaks loudly and clearly. This father, Chris Williams, heard it loud and clear moments after a horrific car accident when his family car was hit head on by a teenage driver who was charged with a DUI. He describes that his experience of hearing the words, "Let it Go" were so strong that he didn't have a choice. He was being told in the moments after, from heaven, that he needed to "Let it Go," and he did.

He wrote a book about his experience, and a movie based on the story was recently released called "Just Let Go."

Just imagine for a second. .

You are a father of four, taking your family out for ice cream with your devoted loving wife next to you – while six months pregnant with your next baby – and a tragic car accident occurs.

Imagine that this tragedy ends up killing your wife and unborn child, along with two of your other children, (a teenager was not in the car that night), how you might react as you endured this ordeal and witnessed the suffering, pain and loss.

It is very difficult to imagine, let alone think about the pain and anger, that most of us would experience as we watched our family members depart this earth, all so suddenly, simply because we all went out for ice cream.

It is a horrible thing to even ask you as a reader to ponder and consider. However, we share this story with you because, by his own accounts and his personal story, Chris Williams lived this experience. He wrote about his personal story in his own book, "Let It Go," (published by Shadow Mountain, July 30, 2012) and he tells the vivid story about how he heard the words "Let it go" come to him as he got out of his car and went to the other driver who had caused the car accident.

Chris Williams shares with his readers how he knew at that moment that the words were coming from a higher power, (get exact words and quote him) … and that he knew at that moment that he was not to act in anger, but with Forgiveness. This is within minutes of watching three of his family members suffer and die. The only way he can explain it is through his faith and his connection to our Father in Heaven. On his own, he would not have been able to even consider the possibility of Forgiveness.

It is definitely a topic that can't be proven with science. Learning about the many stories surrounding a person's ability to Forgive another will certainly increase our life wisdom and teach us, once again, through story telling. Stories are so powerful. Underneath an amazing story is often a miracle waiting to be discovered.

We know as you've read these stories, you have thought about Forgiveness maybe in ways you had not thought of before. We have noticed in our own lives that doing something kind for the person you are trying to forgive or feel better towards can bring about a change in our hearts.

We'd like you to take the time this week to perform three random acts of kindness – anonymously – for one person or three different people, if you prefer. Do these acts for people you either need to Forgive or who you need to apologize to. The kind acts will hopefully move you closer to your goal of full Forgiveness.

Write about your experience in a journal.

Here is a sample affirmation to say each day so you can reinforce the commitment of living each day mindfully, while appreciating the gift of Forgiveness:

AFFIRMATION: I will reach deep inside myself to remember that no one is perfect – we all make mistakes – we all deserve to be Forgiven. I will Forgive others so that I may experience complete Forgiveness from my Father in Heaven.

"Whether is it easier to say to the sick of the palsy, Thy sins be forgiven thee; or to say, Arise, and take up thy bed, and walk? But that ye may know that the Son of man hath power on earth to forgive sins, (he saith to the sick of the palsy,) I say unto thee, Arise and take up thy bed, and go thy way into thine house."
~ Mark 2:9-10 ~

Applying the gift of FORGIVENESS:

We have provided you with a list of 75 ideas to help in beginning to appreciate the gift of Forgiveness – these will help us begin thinking about, feeling and acting on this most precious gift. Add to this list if you think of personal things you need to do in your own life to aid you in your quest to be more sincere in your efforts to Forgive.

- Do something kind for someone who hurt you
- Say you're sorry for something small
- Read The Miracle of Forgiveness
- Look up scriptures about forgiveness
- Ask Heavenly Father for forgiveness for a wrong you committed
- Teach a child about the importance of forgiveness
- Smile at someone you haven't forgiven yet
- Think of someone you need to forgive and write down 3 positive things about them
- Spend 5 minutes thinking about why you are angry with someone

- Spend 15 minutes thinking about why you should let your anger go – write it down
- Talk to someone about how your life changed when you forgave
- Write down 10 positives of forgiveness
- Take a deep breath and let it go for today
- Ask someone you have hurt to forgive you
- Ask someone who hurt YOU to forgive you – feel the power
- Be kind to someone who irritates you
- Put your judgements aside and treat everyone you meet with fairness
- If you misunderstand someone, ask questions and work to become their friend
- Don't jump to conclusions about anyone
- Get ALL of the facts before rushing to judgement
- Hug someone who's hurting
- Read books about forgiveness
- Write about how you felt when someone forgave you
- Give people the benefit of the doubt
- Convince a friend to see the wisdom in forgiveness
- If you know someone who's holding a grudge, ask them to seek help in letting it go
- Don't be afraid to seek therapy, if needed
- Always give someone a second chance
- Consider the value of forgiveness and its importance in your life
- Move away from your role as a victim and release the power you have let your offender have over you
- Consider your health and well-being and what you can do to make it better
- Figure out how to have compassion for hurtful people
- Don't dwell on the past – look forward to your future
- Write an apology letter to someone – practice saying it until you can do it in person

- Remember – forgiveness is something we do for ourselves to get well and move on
- Speak to your clergy about the power of forgiveness
- Read other people's stories of forgiveness
- Let yourself cry to rid yourself of the hurt you feel so you can forgive more freely
- If you need to forgive yourself, stand in front of a mirror each day and say "I forgive   you."
- Pray to Heavenly Father to help you forgive someone
- Remember - you would want to be forgiven of the things you have done
- Meditate and try to understand why people do hurtful things – are they themselves   hurting?
- Write down your thoughts about forgiveness
- Remember forgiveness can improve your health
- If you are dealing with someone particularly difficult, remind yourself it is not your job to   fix them – just to do your best to forgive them
- Ask a friend to tell you of a time they forgave someone and the impact it had
- Send a nice card in the mail with a handwritten note to someone you need to forgive
- Remember, forgiveness is not an event – it is an ongoing process throughout our lives
- Practice being kind to everyone so that forgiveness is required less often
- Ask someone to tell you how they felt when they had been forgiven by someone
- Read the book, "Believing Christ" by Stephen E. Robinson
- When you feel upset with someone, take a step back and try to understand things from their perspective
- Talk to your children about forgiveness
- Find a reason to love someone you might otherwise have issues with

- Go out of your way today to treat someone with respect
- Work hard to understand what true forgiveness can do for you
- Practice forgiving small offenses every day
- Remember none of us are perfect – we all make mistakes so be more tolerant
- Focus on the positive attributes of your loved ones rather than the negative
- Keep in mind everyone needs to be forgiven and everyone needs to forgive
- Meditate and think about ways in which you can forgive
- Be kind to someone you misunderstand
- Make a list of the people you want to have greater forgiveness for
- Work on your list - one person at a time - and do some of the things suggested here to help you move on
- Don't be difficult on yourself if you are struggling to forgive someone – keep working
- Write down some of the lessons you learned as you have forgiven people – use them to   help you be better at forgiveness
- If you need to be forgiven, don't wait – take the necessary steps to put it behind you
- Be an example to your children of someone who is forgiving
- Be quick to let things go if you have been offended – most don't realize they have offended someone
- Be open minded about those who are different than you
- Live what you know to be true and accept others for what they believe
- Be slow to anger and quick to forgive those you love
- Never make someone feel worse about something they've done
- Be loving and gentle with others
- Keep working on forgiveness – it takes time

Choose a few items from this list that you can do NOW. And then do them.

Keep in mind that if you are deliberate about the way you practice Forgiveness, it may become easier for you. Forgiveness is a choice. It is a decision we make. Do what you can to work at it throughout your life.

Forgiveness can be difficult. Sometimes we find it easier to hold on to an offense or wrongdoing than to willingly Forgive someone.

Why is this?

Is it a matter or pride?

We all want to be right.

We all dislike admitting we were wrong about something.
We would oftentimes rather blame someone else than accept responsibility. It can be embarrassing to be called out on something we did wrong.

Think about the last time you hurt or offended someone. Were you quick to ask them for Forgiveness or did you let the resentment build up until it became nearly impossible to swallow your pride and ask for Forgiveness? Sometimes we can hold onto those resentments for years.

I, Janeen, would like to tell you a story.

I know a family of six siblings – three brothers and three sisters. When their parents passed away, the house was left to be divided among the siblings. But there was some disagreement on how that should actually work. There was one sister who did not have a house, and the other five siblings owned homes.

The sisters believed the right thing to do was to give the house to the one sister who actually needed it. The brothers believed the house should be divided among all six. They could not come to an agreement, so the house was divided as per the request of the parents who had passed on.

As a result of this, the sisters were angry with the brothers and didn't speak to them for – well, the rest of their lives. The brothers and sisters all went to their graves without making amends.

What was the point?

Every one of them carried the burden of resentment with them throughout their lives. They ruined the chance for family gatherings and destroyed any chance of their own children having a relationship with their cousins, aunts and uncles. And on down through the generations.

I wish I could say this story had a happy ending. But unfortunately, the best we have here is a learning experience for the rest of us.

If you find it difficult to Forgive, either others or even yourself for things that have happened, pray to your Father in Heaven and ask for His help. He will give you the strength and the ability to Forgive. He will soften your heart so you can repair your relationships with others and let go of the pain and resentment that is holding you back.

Let yourself be free – find it in your heart to Forgive.

We'd like you to take some time and complete the activity below.

Think of someone in your life – a parent, a child, a friend, an ex-spouse, a current spouse – whoever it might be for you whom you need to Forgive.

First: Think about what they did.
Try to put yourself in their shoes.
Look at it from this whole new perspective and take notes.
Ask yourself, "How could I have reacted differently to the situation?"
Take yourself out of the equation and understand that you probably had nothing to do with the choice they made – was it something they needed to do for them and you were the innocent bystander who suffered?
Think of times you may have done something similar that hurt someone you didn't intend to hurt.
Cut this person some slack.
Cut yourself some slack.

Second: Write a letter to the person you need to Forgive.
Be intentional and deliberate in your words.
Explain how you felt when you were hurt and why you felt that way.
Be completely honest.
Tell them you are working on Forgiveness.
If you are ready, tell them you have Forgiven them now.

The purpose of this activity is to get you thinking about and acting on Forgiveness. If you can do it, it will set you free.

As we reflected upon the story of Jesus earlier in this chapter, we know that Jesus suffered through human torture during the many hours leading up to his crucifixion. Although difficult, this event is worthy of deeper contemplation since we can learn so much from it. Yes, it is very hard to visualize and recall what Jesus went through, as He willingly did this for us, as one of His greatest gifts and, therefore, it's painful to recall the events.

I, Elizabeth, remember taking my teenage daughter to a movie theater to see the movie "Son of God," produced by Roma Downey and her husband, Mark Burnett, and so many people in the audience cried out loud watching Jesus be tortured. We cried hard also. After the movie, my daughter could hardly speak in the car, and she just cried out loud and asked, "How could they do that to Jesus? He was so good and so full of love?" Her questions echoed what most of the people watching felt during the movie. Yes, very difficult to watch indeed, but therein lies our great spiritual awakening and understanding of how much Jesus sacrificed for all of us, in the name of love.

We know from reading in Matthew 27:46 and in Mark 15:34, that Jesus pled in prayer as he hung on the cross in about the ninth hour, asking His Father in Heaven,

"My God, My God, why hast thou forsaken me?"

This question clearly shows that Jesus was anticipating and experiencing the pain of the moment, based on the current circumstances and the previous visions He had seen. We also know from Luke 23:34 that shortly before Jesus' body died, he asked in prayer, "Father, forgive them; for they know not what they do."

So, given all of this information and the history of these events, it makes us wonder, "How could Jesus possibly have the strength to muster up the words, let alone the spiritual conviction, to ask His Father in Heaven to Forgive the people who were killing his body?"

Given all of the physical torture and pain that Jesus endured on the cross during his crucifixion, it makes us wonder how Jesus could even have the strength to muster up the energy to push the words through his lungs and vocal cords. It would seem logical, from a physical aspect, emotional level, and mostly, a spiritual level, to believe that there was an additional spiritual source supporting Him and giving Him strength on all levels.

From a practical and medical perspective, the loss of blood, the beatings, and shear pain, would have a disabling affect upon most human bodies. From the Bible, we know that Jesus had spiritual gifts while on earth, but He was also given a human body, just like ours, that would feel and experience the same joys and pains of life that human bodies experienced. So from this account, Jesus clearly felt the pain and torture He had been put through for many hours leading up to his death on the cross. We read in the Bible, about the pain of his loved ones, while watching Him endure the hours of torture. Physically, Jesus and his loved ones were helpless to stop the end result. So they endured and suffered through it.

Therefore, when Jesus was able to say, "Father, forgive them for they know not what they do," it makes logical sense that there must have been some type of divine intervention to help Him as He made those words come through his tortured and beaten body.

We share these reflections and thoughts with you because we know that there will never be an exact science or formula that points to how, when, and why the gift of Forgiveness is embraced or not. Therefore, we should consider all of the other miraculous possibilities that could accompany a person, once the thought of Forgiveness is even considered.

One thing we have noticed as a common factor with the gift of Forgiveness is that is usually begins with a clear decision to embark upon the path. This is a commonly reported experience, and there is much work ahead as we surrender our emotions to the grieving process and move beyond the anger stage. Even after we journey through the roller coaster of emotions in the grieving process, we often need to repeat certain steps in the Forgiveness process.

New life experiences tend to re-trigger old wounds, and they open up again needing a fresh bandaid to heal past memories of pain. The key to this process is to realize that Forgiveness often needs to be renewed and it is worth doing. It's not easy, but for all of the same reasons described throughout this chapter, it is so worth it.

Without Forgiveness, climbing to the top of the Christmas tree to experience the full love of Christlike living will be diminished.

What are your thoughts and impressions now about the gift of FORGIVENESS?

Has anything changed or come into your awareness that wasn't there before?

Jot down your thoughts now after 30 days of reflection:

_____

_____

_____

_____

_____

_____

_____

_____

_____

_____

_____

_____

_____

_____

"That seeing they may see, and not perceive; and hearing they may hear, and not understand; lest at any time they should be converted, and their sins should be forgiven them."
~ Mark 4:12 ~

CONCLUSION:

After reading through the stories and thoughts shared about Forgiveness, it feels fitting that we should try and wrap it all together, in an orderly manner. As we discussed it for many hours and prayed throughout the process, we can honestly conclude that Forgiveness is probably one of those life mysteries that none of us fully understand, on a universal level. There are so many variables, circumstances, questions and true mysteries about why and how some people can Forgive life events, and why so many people cannot even consider the possibility of Forgiveness.

We all know that there are many life experiences with valuable lessons learned that would not fit into the category of, "one size fits all." The topic of Forgiveness seems to be one of those elusive, but strongly sought after gifts, that keeps even the best of the theologians debating and studying. Forgiveness will most likely be one of those mysterious life wonders, for which we will seek greater understanding when we are given the chance to gain spiritual wisdom as we cross over to heaven (It will certainly be at the top of our questions and curiosity)! Forgiveness is a powerful life changing experience for those who seek it, choose it and embrace the power of it. It is perceived as a way of "taking the high road in life" and moving beyond the infractions and injustices that have occurred in our individual lives and in the lives of others.

If we can engage ourselves in a life that will allow us to be kind, thoughtful, considerate, respectful and loving toward others, maybe we won't hurt people so much, and maybe we won't need to be Forgiven as often. And maybe those positive attributes will help us as we sincerely Forgive others. People are going to make mistakes – it's part of living and becoming who we will ultimately become. But learn to live your own life in such a way that when you look back you can honestly say, "I harbor no ill will toward anyone."

DAILY REFLECTION

(Repetition is what creates new habits.
Read this page daily as a reminder.)

Each chapter is meant to be read slowly,
Absorbing the deeper essence behind the words and stories.

This allows for continual reflection,
Prayer and listening for answers,
Which opens the door to
Greater insight and awareness of
The Gift of Compassion.

If we devote one month of the year,
To learning and living the Gift of Compassion,
Our awareness of the precious Gift of Compassion,
Will be spiritually heightened,
And our daily existence will emulate this awareness.

As we make this shift to mindful attentiveness to the Gift of Compassion,
We will be less likely to take for granted,
The beauty, the power, and the mystique of Compassion.
We will have developed a habit,
Which becomes part of who we are.

As we develop a new habit each month,
Based on a different Gift each month,
A Gift that Jesus came to earth to give each one of us,
We will become more like Jesus in the way we live.
As this happens,
We will be living a more Christlike life, every day.
As we do this,
We are expressing our deepest gratitude to Jesus
And our Heavenly Father.

As we share the 12 Gifts with others,
We cannot help but bring the same love and peace
To our own hearts and spirits.

5

The *Gift* of

COMPASSION

What does it mean to have Compassion? As we began writing this chapter, we had to think about that question. Truly having Compassion isn't just about seeing people suffering and saying, "Oh that's too bad." To us, Compassion is more of an act. It's a way of treating people. And that's why we wanted to include it as one of the gifts.

Having Compassion for those living on the earth with us is something we want to strive for. Imagine a world filled with Compassionate people. What a beautiful world it would be. There are many, many people in the world doing good. Let's work to expand that so that ALL of us are doing good.

Being Compassionate isn't just about helping those who are sick or afflicted in some way. It's also about truly accepting and loving people who are not like us. And that, in today's world, seems to be the real challenge. We want to help that cause in some small way.

Why did we choose COMPASSION as the fifth gift?

*"Then the lord of that servant was moved with
compassion, and loosed him, and forgave him the debt."*
~ Matthew 18:27 ~

*"And when the Lord saw her, he had compassion
on her, and said unto her, Weep not."*
~ Luke 7:13 ~

Compassion seems to come easy for some, but the rest of us have to work at developing it throughout our lives. My friend, Elizabeth, who co-authored this book with me, has an amazing capacity for Compassion. She has the ability to truly care about pretty much anyone who is in a tight spot or having a difficult day – or life – for that matter. I have learned so much from her example and am very grateful for a new perspective on caring for and about people. A kind word or even just a smile can have such an impact on someone who is struggling.

Is it possible to develop Compassion when it doesn't come so easy for some of us?

I think so.

It starts with being aware and taking a look around to see what's going on in the world around us. Actually taking notice to see if someone is sad or disturbed, or having a bad day, is a huge part of developing Compassion. Trying to see things from the other person's perspective is another important step toward becoming a more Compassionate person. And how about asking yourself what you think YOU would need in this particular situation –

what would make you feel better? It might just be a listening ear, or an encouraging word. And sharing some of your own experiences can help in a really big way.

Compassion is the awareness of the suffering of others, and the compelling desire to help them overcome it. It isn't enough just to notice someone's heartbreak or difficulty. We should want to help them and do all we can to take some of their pain away.

I have seen Elizabeth spend time listening to people on several occasions – even when it is not easy. I have seen her offer to pay a small parking fee or forgive the last $5 when someone didn't bring enough money to attend a mandatory class. It makes all the difference in the world to these people who are already in a difficult circumstance. She works hard to help them laugh and make their negative experience as enjoyable as possible. This is an example of true Compassion and concern for others.

"So Jesus had compassion on them, and
touched their eyes: and immediately their
eyes received sight, and they followed him."
~ Matthew 20:34 ~

"Instead of putting others in their
place Put yourself in their place."
~ Amish Proverb ~

When we think about Compassion, we might also contemplate closely-related words that help us to embrace a deeper meaning. These words could include: EMPATHY, HUMANITY, KINDNESS, SYMPATHY, GRACE, MERCY, TENDERNESS, BENEVOLENCE

I am sharing the following story because it shows the ability of someone to show true Compassion at a time when it was not easy. My friend could have easily been hurtful toward the other person, because she too was hurting, but she chose to take the high road and try to help someone feel better.

"I UNDERSTAND YOU ARE IN PAIN"
by Janeen

A close friend of mine, Janet, had an experience recently where someone had been hurt by a third party and lashed out at her. It involved a man whom they both cared for, and he told this other woman that he had meet someone he was very serious about pursuing – my friend, Janet. The woman was hurt, and she was angry. In desperation, she displaced her anger and worked very hard to cause pain to my friend.

Janet was completely controlled and extremely professional, but also very Compassionate in a situation that could have turned ugly very quickly. She said things like, "I am very sorry that you have been hurt and disappointed. It's never easy to lose someone you care about, but I hope you will be okay." The mean spirited messages continued, and still my friend persisted. "I understand you are in pain." "I hope you have a solid support system to help you through this."

After a few exchanges, Janet had to finally say, "Again, I am very sorry, but please do not contact me again." After asking her to stop a second time, the messages finally stopped coming, and the last message showed a tiny bit of Compassion back to my friend.

It never pays to be hurtful back to someone who has hurt you. People who lash out do so because THEY are hurting. They don't know what to do with their anger. I know this because I have done it myself. I have been in that position of not knowing what to do with my hurt or my anger. So, what do we do? We push it onto the people we love most or who do not deserve it.

I am not always great at doing so, but I truly believe if we can stop for a moment, put ourselves in the other person's shoes, try to understand their point of view, have Compassion for what they are going through, and be kind, we will be a lot farther ahead. We might even help that person heal faster.

"Shouldest not thou also have had compassion on thy fellow servant, even as I had pity on thee?"
~ Matthew 18:33 ~

And Jesus, when he came out, saw much people, and was moved with compassion toward them, because they were as sheep not having a shepherd: and he began to teach them many things."
~ Mark 6:34 ~

In order to begin thinking about Compassion and what it truly means to you in your life, we'd like you to contemplate and then answer the following questions just to get the ideas flowing. Really put some thought into these questions and see how deep you can dig to come up with your best answers. Take your time. There is no rush to complete these.

What breaks your heart?

_____

_____

_____

_____

_____

When you realize you've hurt someone, what do you do next?

_____

_____

_____

_____

What emotions do you experience when you see someone begging for money?

_____

_____

_____

_____

_____

How do you treat people who are not like you?

_____

_____

_____

_____

_____

Think about the last time you had to forgive someone – were you able to put yourself in their shoes – do you still hold a grudge against that person?

_____

_____

_____

_____

_____

How do you feel toward people who are weak or struggling?

_____

_____

_____

_____

_____

Think back on your life and the times you received Compassion from someone.

Maybe your mother was really good at making you feel better after your feelings were hurt, or after you did something naughty and felt bad about it.

Maybe you had a teacher in school who was particularly great at showing kindness to all of her students, and knew how to make you feel loved no matter what.

Did you know a healthcare provider who had a particularly kind bedside manner, or a neighbor who always brought soup when you were sick?

Were you blessed with a child who loves animals and other children, and can make them feel included no matter what?

Compassion is a blessing that comes in many forms. When we stop to realize how good it has felt over our lifetime to have others show Compassion to us, it makes us want to do the same for others. It truly is a gift, and it comes more easily to some than to others.

How wonderful it is to know that Jesus Christ has Compassion

- for those who have been hurt,
- for those who have lost a loved one,
- for those who have lost a job,
- for those who are alone,
- for those who have divorced,
- for those who have had a child go astray,
- for those who feel lost,
- for those who sin – that would be ALL of us!

Knowing that Jesus Christ has Compassion for each one of us is so comforting to us. Does it make you feel like you owe it to people to have Compassion for them? We wouldn't want any less from others, right?

Keep this in mind as you make if your GOAL this month to make it a point to go out of your way to show someone COMPASSION – someone you might otherwise have overlooked.

Put your arm around someone who has recently experienced a difficult situation.

What are your thoughts and impressions about the gift of COMPASSION? We'd like you to write about it.

As you begin reading this chapter, write down a few thoughts you have as you contemplate the gift of Compassion. We will ask this question again at the end of the chapter after you have completed your study of the gift of Compassion.

_____

_____

_____

_____

_____

_____

_____

_____

_____

_____

_____

_____

_____

_____

What did Jesus say about COMPASSION?

"And Jesus went forth, and saw a great multitude, and was moved with compassion toward them, and he healed their sick."
~ Matthew 14:14 ~

When Jesus spoke to His disciples, he commanded them to "Be ye. .merciful, as your Father also is merciful." (Luke 6:36) We can all follow our Heavenly Father's example of mercy in our own relationships, if we so choose. If we work hard to set aside our pride, it will become easier for us to be Compassionate, patient, forgiving and respectful of others.

We all have our shortcomings. Because of the Savior's suffering on the cross, God is able to be merciful AND be just. He is able to show Compassion to us human beings who don't necessarily DESERVE Compassion. It is our willingness to repent and accept the atonement that allows Him to do so.

Don't each of us want those in our lives to show us Compassion when we don't deserve it? Of course we do. So, in turn, we should also show Compassion to them.

"But when he saw the multitudes, he was moved with compassion on them, because they fainted, and were scattered abroad, as sheep having no shepherd."
~ Matthew 9:36 ~

Stories to help us reflect on the Gift of COMPASSION:

Stories of Compassion are some of our favorites. It's uplifting to read about people who change a person's life or really make a difference. We want to share some of our own stories here to help you learn some of the things we have learned as we've watched others.

As you read our stories, contemplate your own stories and experiences and jot them down to help you in your quest to develop more Compassion in your life.

_____

_____

_____

_____

_____

_____

_____

_____

_____

_____

_____

_____

_____

_____

_____

_____

_____

_____

TAKE A DEEP BREATH
by Janeen

Compassion is one of the most difficult of the gifts to practice because it requires getting outside of ourselves and seeing through the eyes of another. I witnessed a most beautiful example of Compassion just last night as I watched a good friend of mine handle a very rattled and upset young man.

He had come to a class he was required by law to take because his wife had left him and filed for divorce. He was angry about having to be there, upset about the fee he was having to pay for the class, and mad that he didn't have enough money for parking. It was obvious there were many underlying causes for his anger, but I will admit I didn't have Compassion for him right at first. I felt annoyed that he was pushing his negative emotions on to the people in the room who were just trying to do their jobs. I felt he ought to buck it up and get ahold of his emotions and his life, and just stop being angry.

While I was having my own set of negative emotions towards this young man, I saw my friend begin to ask him questions – a lot of unrelated questions in order to gain his trust and validate his pain. She was working to give a little something to this young man to show kindness – to show she cared no matter what his attitude was.

There is a skill set involved in showing someone Compassion. It involves looking for the source of someone's pain and then paying attention to it. By asking a lot of unrelated questions, the person feels validated and will open up to you. My friend knows how to do this very well and can get anyone, no matter how difficult, to talk to her.

Once she was able to get his attitude to soften, she offered to pay for his parking, and invited him to sit down for a few minutes and take a deep breath. Before long, he was telling her about his 5-year-old son who was caught up in this divorce and the fact that he is between jobs because he is having a hard time coping. Pretty soon, he began to soften. My friend was so kind and compassionate toward him that she changed his whole demeanor. By the end of the class, he didn't want to leave. He wanted to stay near my friend and partake of her positive energy and kind words.

Honestly, it was fascinating to watch all of this take place.

I learned yesterday that Compassion is truly a gift, and my friend is definitely blessed with that gift. As I watched her take care of him, I wanted to be like her. I made a commitment that very moment to work harder to try and understand people and the trials they face. We don't all handle things the same way, and some are not as strong as others.

I don't believe our Father in Heaven put us on this earth to only have our own trials and become stronger because of them. That is part of it, yes. But he also put us here to help each other and lift each other up. That is exactly what my friend was doing. She truly understands the meaning and sincere practice of Compassion.

So let's go more in depth about the skill set we talked about earlier:

How To Show Compassion To A Person Who Is Obviously Struggling

1. In a kind tone of voice, say something that **validate**s the truth of what they might be feeling. For example, if you spot a person who is obviously upset about something. You could say, "It looks like you might be having a hard time right now. Is there anything I can do to help you?" Or, "I'm sorry you seem upset. Can I help in some way?"

2. **Listen** to what they say, and use the skill of Reflective Listening – which basically **re-states what they said** in a slightly different way. For example, if he said, "I'm just really mad that I have to take this class and that I have to pay for parking in addition to the class fee." You could say, "It sounds like you're angry that you are required to attend this class because it's inconvenient. And, on top of that, now you have to pay for parking." This validates to the person that you understand why they are upset and/or frustrated.

3. Usually when another person validates a person's comments, it feels good to know that another person "gets it" and it often invites the person to continue venting.

FIRST RESPONDERS INCLUDE FIREFIGHTERS, POLICE, AND EMERGENCY MEDICAL PROFESSIONALS

by Elizabeth

We now live in a society where many scenes and situations are filmed and recorded, especially when there is some type of confrontation occurring. A quick reaction for many is to pull out the cell phone and begin recording. Capturing things on film is necessary because film footage reveals the truth. The availability of so much footage has caused our society to re-think and study the manner in which police officers and citizens interact. Clearly there is work to be done in order to find an acceptable way to approach dangerous situations, while making quick decisions and seeking peaceful resolutions.

The issue of racial profiling is under scrutiny and is being fully examined. Changes are in progress as I write this. I am a single white mother, and my youngest child is 17 years old, 6'4", and African American. His mother had a severe drug addiction, and I brought him into our family when he was five months old. If you didn't know him, it might be easy to feel intimidated by his large presence. My son played football for about four years, and he eventually quit. When he finally admitted why he wanted to quit, tears welled up in my eyes as I listened. He said, "I don't like hurting other kids. One kid that I tackled, had his wrist broken from it." My son has a gentle and kind spirit and clearly, football was not the right sport for him. He still does not like hurting others, and he is sensitive to the feelings of others. But simply based on his size and appearance, others might be fearful or quick to judge. They just don't know. This is why stereotypes need to be broken down and looked at.

Now at seventeen, he is a gentle giant. But to simply look at him, his large presence could intimidate others, including a police officer, if there was ever a confrontation. I understand it. Quick judgements are typically made in a very fast moving, dangerous situation, and the appearance of a strong, tall African American might worry some people. This is exactly why new approaches to handling dangerous situations are being examined and new policies are being implemented.

More police departments are re-training their officers on topics related to perceived racial bias, dealing with a person who is mentally ill, understanding more about individuals who are homeless, drug addictions with paranoia, and much more. We are an intelligent society, and we will find methods for solving the relationships between law enforcement and private citizens. Professionals are busy working on this as I write these words. We need to trust that our society is capable of advancing policies and protocol for responding to fast moving, dangerous situations. Just the fact that most police departments are having their officers wear cameras on them demonstrates that their agencies also want the truth to be known. Change takes time. Oversight and patience are needed while changes take place.

Hope, Faith, Prayer and Compassion are Needed, as Policies and Protocol Improve

Having said all of the above, we all need to take a deep breath and remember our society depends on the dedication and service from the men and women in police uniforms. We need them. We need their service, and we need them to come to our aid when we are having a crisis. They help maintain law and order in our society. There are millions of highly professional officers who have dedicated their lives to keeping the public safe. There is probably footage of many appropriate arrests, which show professional integrity from many officers. But it is the footage of the controversial situations that get media attention. We need to remember that media coverage is not balanced with what is actually happening in our society. We must refrain from making generalized judgements about police officers who have chosen their profession to make a difference in maintaining law and order.

I am sharing these stories, thoughts and reflections in the chapter about Compassion because I know there are millions of individuals who have dedicated their lives, each and every day, to protecting innocent people. These officers put their lives on the line, and they take a risk each day as they leave for work early in the morning or late at night, and they kiss their loved ones goodbye. They do not know what that day's shift will be like or what might happen to them. They take this risk to protect us, the people who depend on them, if and when there is a crisis. We all know we can call 911 in an emergency, and the police will respond. What a secure feeling to know that these services are available. We all depend on the police, whether we admit it or not. If our loved ones were in danger, we would call 911.

So let's come together and remember, in every organization, there are always a few individuals who will break the rules, bend the rules, or react in a way that is not fair or appropriate. Yes, these individuals need to be accountable for what occurred, but each situation needs to be thoroughly investigated. Justice and accountability will happen as we are all enlightened by truth, evidence and listening to many stories. WE can solve this.

Pray for solutions. Have Compassion for those officers who do their job with integrity and dedication. For all of the officers, both men and women, who serve their profession in a noble manner, we thank you. We appreciate you. Our society depends on you. You take the risks for us, which we are not willing to take. You come to the rescue during a crisis. Sadly, during the course of doing your job, some of you will be faced with tragedy and possibly death. If this happens, your families will grieve and there will be many losses. Yet, you continue to do your job knowing all of the risks. So thank you!! You are appreciated, and our society relies on your integrity, service and Compassion.

**To lighten the mood and learn why
I have such Compassion for first responders,
I will share a few memorable stories aboutmy family's
encounters. Some of our stories are probably
still circulating amongst them, whenever
they need a good laugh.**

My youngest son was about ten, and it was the 3rd of July. It was permissible to light fireworks the day before the 4th. One of our neighbors sold their home to a rental group, and a house full of loud and late night college guys moved in. From our backyard we could hear every word they were saying, and don't even get me started on the language. We dealt with it. But about 4 pm on July 3rd, they began shooting off big fireworks, and many of them landed in our backyard where my kids and their friends had been playing. So I did what any parent would do. I called the non-emergency police number and reported it.

I had ushered my son and his friends into our house while we waited for the police to arrive. Obviously, on July 3rd, the police were busy, and our situation was not an emergency. A couple of hours later they arrived. But the boys had gone out to the backyard again, and they had been filling up water balloons to have a water balloon fight. One boy decided it would be funny to throw some water balloons over our fence when he heard a car coming. So he did. Several boys, including my son, told him not to do this.

As fate would have it, the police officer responding to my complaint about the neighbors,(who lived around the corner) had just pulled up in front of our home. Just as the officer was about to investigate, a water balloon hit his windshield and made a loud bang and then burst. Not okay at all. I did not know any of this when the officer approached my front door. I thanked him for coming, but he was clearly upset. He asked me, "Is anyone here throwing water balloons over the fence at cars?" and of course, I said "No."

The officer quickly went to our backyard. There were four boys, looking scared, with water balloons filled up. The officer said, "There's the evidence!" and I quickly began apologizing. The officer asked who threw the balloon, and three of the boys looked at one boy. This boy admitted it, and he became upset. The officer was very upset about it, understandably so. But instead of getting angry, he brought all four boys, and me, of course, to his patrol car. He explained to us how he was sitting in his car finishing up a report and was about to come out and help us with the neighbor's fireworks problem, when he heard a loud boom on his windshield. He said it was so loud he thought someone was shooting at him. He explained how his heart was racing because he didn't know what was going on. He told the five of us that he worries about getting shot at, and the water balloon sounded like a gunshot when it exploded on his windshield.

He was kind, and he used this situation as a teaching moment for the boys, and yes, me too. He did ask for the boy who threw the water balloon to call his parents, and then the officer took the phone from this boy and invited the father to come over. The officer had a firm discussion with the boy and his father, and he told the rest of us to stand there and listen (clearly so he could teach all of us a lesson), and then he prepared to leave. He asked, "Is there anything else?" and I quickly thanked him and let him be on his way. He had more important things to do on the eve of July 4th. I decided not to worry about the fireworks coming into our yard. We went to a neighbor's house where they were lighting fireworks safely. I fully appreciated how kind this officer was, and he taught all of us a great lesson. Under the stress of feeling fear, he was able to turn things around, and he used the situation to teach all of us about how intense the job of any police officer can be. I know that I felt much more gratitude and respect for all officers after that incident.

What are the odds of calling the police on your neighbors and it turns out the police end up reprimanding the caller? Our family remembers this incident with a bit of humor, but mostly with Compassion for how the officer taught us about the fears and worries he faces every day on the job. Being a police officer is not a stress-free job, and as officers respond to situations, they never know what they might encounter. This officer enlightened all of us, and he did it in a very firm but polite manner. Thank you officer, if you ever read this story and recognize yourself, we admire you. We care about you. I have Compassion for you, and I clearly saw Compassion demonstrated by you that evening. You taught us valuable lessons that night. We wish you all the best.

A Firetruck with Four Fireman (two younger ones in training) Arrived at My House Early One Saturday Morning, to Help Rescue a Kitten.

My daughter, Amanda was about eleven years old, and she had been begging for a kitten for years. Finally, I agreed and we rescued an older kitten from an agency where we thought it had the necessary shots and neutering. We would later find out this sweet cat was able to get pregnant, which she did. She had five adorable kittens, and we loved and nurtured them. We had to keep them until they were at the right age to be weaned from their mother. But, if you are a cat lover, you can imagine how hard it is to think about parting with any of them. Yet we knew we had to. They had all been trained to use the kitty-litter box, and they were almost ready to be given to loving homes.

Several weeks before, the front door to our home had cracked and I had purchased another one. I bought the package where the sub-contractor comes out to your house and installs it. We made the appointment, and then he changed it several times. I had the door laying on its side in my front entry way, with the two empty holes for locks and knobs near the floor. I was thinking the installer would be handling this in a few days. But this lasted for about two weeks. Finally, one Saturday morning about 6 am, the one day we could all sleep in, my seven-year-old son woke me up and said, "The kitten's head is stuck in the door." I asked him if he could get the kitten out, and he said he tried and it was definitely stuck.

So, I got up and assessed the situation. I decided we needed some butter to smooth the kitten down and make it easier to slide its head out. The front door was lying on its side so it wouldn't tip over, and the two empty holes waiting for locks and handles were at the right height for a kitten to slip its cute little head through. The kitten slid its head through the lower hole and couldn't slide back out. The kitten's body was too big for the rest of the kitten to get through. With the way the kitten's ears are attached to its head, it's not possible to bend them back enough to slide the kitten backwards. It would have injured the kitten. I called a few neighbors. It was early Saturday morning, and they all came in their pajamas, just like the rest of us. Each one suggested butter again. The poor little kitten was so slicked down, but it still didn't work.

After an hour of at least three adults and quite a few kids trying to solve the dilemma, we had no choice but to call the local fire department. Again, I had the non-emergency phone numbers on hand. (When the kids were younger, 3 and 5, they called 911 a few times when I was in the shower. They later said they wanted to see fire trucks. I soon learned when an adult does not pick up the call back from 911 after a hang up, they send a firetruck or police car to check on things. After several times of greeting firemen or police officers in a wet towel, with shampoo dripping into my eyes, I learned how to take a 3-minute shower, with the kids in the bathroom, and the phones hidden.) This is just one more reason I appreciate firefighters and police officers. I ultimately memorized the non-emergency phone numbers to prevent another 911 incident after a few stern conversations.

The firetruck parked right in front of my house and four firefighters came in. (I later learned that many neighbors who were just waking up, still in their pajamas I'm sure, were calling each other asking, "What's going on at Elizabeth's house, again?") At first, the four firefighters joked around, partly because two of them were younger and still in training, and the situation looked a little comical. At first sight, we all thought we could slide the kittens back, and it would be an easy fix. After we each tried the butter, olive oil, and then peanut butter method, we all knew we couldn't get the kitten through the hole.

I asked if anyone had a saw or chainsaw so we could cut the door up and release the kitten. I was willing to ruin the $450 plus door to save the kitten because I could see it was starting to struggle from the stress. It wasn't choking, but it was getting anxious. The door didn't matter, but the kitten did. However, I had bought a very strong door this time, in an effort to prevent future cracks. It was solid. So cutting it up took time.

Here is the part where a funny story turns into a lesson for many others. No one had a saw! The firemen thought they had a few, but when they looked, there were no saws at all. The firefighter in charge told me to go find a saw from a neighbor. So I ran from house to house, in my pajamas, and brought back a saw. The saw was not sharp, so it took at least forty minutes to cut through the door. By the time these two young firefighters were done cutting through the door, taking turns, they were both dripping with sweat. They all exhibited Compassion for this sweet kitten.

This kitten was a living creature, and they clearly saw the kitten needed to be rescued. There was no way I, or any of my neighbors, could have saved this sweet kitten without the firefighters' help. The door was cut open, the kitten was rescued and nurtured. One of the young firefighters wanted to adopt the kitten. We were all very grateful. I had been praying for help throughout the ordeal, and I knew the firefighters were an answer to my prayers. Their efforts saved the kitten. My gratitude was huge!

During the course of the rescue, the head firefighter asked me to take pictures. I could not find a camera. He was a little annoyed. This was during the time when cameras were new to cell phones, so one of the young firefighters took a photo. I never saw it. I'm sure his photo circulated through fire houses everywhere. Here's why I know this to be true.

After the Door was Cut Up and the Kitten was Saved...

I took time to love the kitten back to peace and express my gratitude, and then I regrouped from this very stressful situation. I called this popular home box store where many of us shop, and I told the supervisor about my ordeal. I explained that if the sub-contractor had not changed the schedule so many times, this situation would not have happened. They agreed, and they

asked me to bring the door back to their store. This was about
11 am Saturday morning, and I pulled into the big store with a
sawed up door on top of my SUV heavily tied down, of course.
(I try to be extra cautious about items flying off of a car roof or
truck. This is another one of those life events where a few extra
minutes helps. I was driving on the freeway once when a plastic
garbage bag flew off of a truck and landed on my windshield. It
worked out, but this is just another example of taking extra time
to do the right thing.)

My young son and I were trying to get the door off the roof of my
car when these firefighters in the parking lot approached me and
asked if I needed help. They were different guys, not the ones
who sawed up the door. My emotions got the best of me, and I
started telling the story about the kitten and the door, and they
reassured me they knew all about it because fire stations talk to
each other, and it was all going to be fine. They carried the door
to customer service for me, where a new door was waiting. Word
spread quickly. The store employees even carried it out and tied
it up on my SUV. They promised the sub-contractor would be
there within an hour, and he was. The new door was installed
that day, and all of the kittens were fine!

I have learned there are so many ripple effects in life that happen
from the positive things we do and say, and also from the negative
acts and thought patterns we might have. When we pay attention
to these patterns, we realize there is a flow of energy associated
with them. I have focused my energy on being a positive person,
and I imagine the positive energy, kindness and love I share is
rippling towards others. It is a comforting feeling. We may never
realize the ripple effect of our events or behaviors, but we can
know that everything does ripple forward. We can choose the
positive ripple, and if we don't choose the positive, the negative
ripple might find us, simply by default. Choose for good. It
brings you peace, and you can feel the love from Jesus.

To bring this story full circle, I often pray to be used as a source for good to help others. When we say this type of prayer, we never know how we will be used, but we have faith that it will be fine because the Holy Spirit is leading us. I believe the kitten ordeal was one of those times where I was used to help.

The firefighters who helped me bring the sawed-up door into the store for return told me their story. After hearing my story, they checked their trucks for saws. They noticed they did not have enough, and that is why I ran into them at this big box store. They even said, "It was a funny story, and we're glad it all worked out for the kitten, but it made us check our trucks for saws, and that's why we're here." When we walked into the store, I saw their captain paying for quite a few saws at the check-out counter. Firetrucks need to have many types of saws simply because, in a crisis, you need the right equipment to save lives. The firefighter who carried the door in for me said the story went to all the fire stations in the state, which was good, because they all went out and checked their trucks for saws.

When you pray to be used for good in the world in your morning prayers, you never know what events will happen. But it all worked out for the kitten and every fire station who heard about this story. Each fire station checked out their saw supply and made the necessary purchases. You just never know when you might need a saw – and a sharp one too!

From the guys who spent an hour or two at my house to the firefighters who helped me carry the chopped up door into the store, I give you all a very big "Thank You!" You were all very Compassionate as you helped me throughout the day. I know you don't choose to go into firefighting for the thrill of it. You do it because you care about people, and you want to save lives. This is Compassion in action, and we thank you for what you do every day, and for risking your lives. Our prayers are with you.

Never hesitate to ask for prayers.

We hope you feel the love and peace from working hard as you save the lives of people and animals.

As you've read some of our stories, we hope you have been able to reflect on some of the people in your own life who have shown you or your family Compassion at times when you really needed it.

Think about a person who made a huge difference in your life at a time when you really needed someone to acknowledge your pain.

Now, make a phone call to that person, if you are able, and tell them you were thinking about them and how much they helped you at a difficult time in your life. If you can't call them, write them a letter or an email. The Lord works in mysterious ways, and just maybe your communication will give that person the boost THEY need today.

As we've been working on this book, we have noticed so many opportunities around us to show true Compassion. There is great power in acknowledging someone else's pain – not only can we make another person's day a little bit better, we can make our own life more meaningful.

If we are not showing Compassion, we are most likely making judgements about people, and that is not a comforting feeling when we're engaged in it. We like to think that those we show true Compassion for will turn around and show true Compassion to someone else. Because when we feel cared for, we tend to want others to feel the same way. Try to think of ways and look for opportunities to show Compassion throughout your day:

- Look for the beggar on the street;
- Watch for the frazzled mother with the crying baby;
- Look for the elderly person trying to get out of a car;
- Be aware of those who seem sad and need a friend;
- Listen for the person who is having a stressful day;
- Pay attention to your teenager when he is angry;
- Watch for those who are different from you.

Be that person who makes others feel important, loved and safe. Always make an effort to make others feel like they matter.

We attended a fundraising meeting recently where we were greeted by the two women who owned the company. They threw their arms around us like we were long lost friends. We immediately loved them. They made us feel like we mattered. They made us feel safe in an unfamiliar environment. They talked with us and asked a lot of questions. They made a huge effort to help us feel important, and their efforts did not go unnoticed. We left there wanting to work with them. We felt like they were our family by the time the meeting ended.

People like this are gems. They are genuine in their love of people. And when we can truly love ALL people, that is when we are in a position to show sincere Compassion no matter what the circumstances.

We came across the following quote by Thigh Nhat Hanh and it hit home for us. We have all been around people like this, and it helps to realize why they are the way they are. This is one more reason why Compassion is such an important gift:

"When another person makes you suffer,

It is because he suffers deeply within himself,

And his suffering is spilling over.

He does not need punishment; he needs help.

That's the message he is sending."

Here is a sample affirmation to say each day so you can reinforce the commitment of living each day mindfully, while appreciating the gift of Compassion:

AFFIRMATION: I will remember every single day that people all over the world are struggling. My own struggles will take a back seat at least for a time – so I can focus on helping others and acknowledging their pain. I will be proactive, not just sympathetic.

"And Jesus, moved with compassion, put forth his hand, and touched him, and saith unto him, I will; be thou clean."
~ Mark 1:41 ~

Applying the gift of COMPASSION:

We have compiled a list of 75 ideas to help each of us begin appreciating and practicing the gift of Compassion – ways we can all begin thinking about, feeling and acting on it. Remember, this is what forms the habit, and we all know by now how powerful habits are. We all want to develop GOOD habits that will change our behavior in a positive way.

I, Janeen, have been influenced by my very own daughter as she has taught me to have more Compassion for people. Because of her, I have worked on changing my attitude towards people who are less fortunate. One day when we were out and about, someone approached us asking for money. Typically, I may have made a judgment and told the person no, but because my daughter was with me, I reached into my wallet and gave the man a little bit of cash. I will admit, I wasn't able yet to completely withhold my judgments, but it is not for me to decide whether or not that person was truly in need. It's all about baby steps, and I felt happy that I was at least able to part with a few dollars.

My daughter said to me, "Wow mom. You're making progress!" Her comment made me want to work harder to change my attitudes and do what I can to help people who may or may not be in need.

So start by browsing through this list, and then begin to add your own ideas to it. Come up with a few ideas that mean something to YOU:

- Take soup to your sick neighbor
- Hold a dog in a shelter
- Visit your friend in the hospital
- Take your parents or grandparents on errands
- Call and talk with someone you know is having a difficult time
- Listen to someone
- Offer to buy a homeless person a meal
- Visit a care center and play music for the patients
- Speak kindly to an elderly person
- Tell you children you love them when they have done something wrong
- Read stories of compassion
- Be kind to yourself
- Offer to tend the baby of a tired mom
- Hug someone who is sad
- Sit with a friend who is hurting
- Let the slow moving older person ahead of you in line
- Give a few dollars to the person who's shortchanged in the grocery line
- Let the car in ahead of you, even if the driver seems rude
- Remember, your compassion will make a difference in someone's life
- Let someone vent to you without judgment
- Stop and help someone whose car is pulled off to the side of the road
- Teach your children to be tolerant and have understanding
- Be who you are and accept others for who they are
- Have compassion for someone who hurt you – they are most likely hurting too

- Turn your pain into compassion for others
- Be aware of those around you
- When someone snaps at you, return with kindness
- Remember, everyone is going through something difficult
- Make someone feel special today
- Assist someone in a wheelchair
- Be patient with elderly people and children
- Help a mom who has her hands full with kids
- Hold the door open for people behind you
- Tell a woman when she has lipstick on her teeth
- Tip your waiter nicely
- Ask the cashier how her day is going
- Avoid judging people based on the way they're dressed
- Strike up a conversation with someone who is very different than you
- Rub your husband's shoulders after a long day of work
- Smile at someone who looks stressed
- Refrain from criticizing
- Place yourself in the other person's shoes and try to understand
- When someone hurts you, be polite to them rather than aggressive
- Sit with a grieving friend
- Help a disabled person across the street
- Speak kindly to someone who seems angry or upset
- Volunteer at a hospital
- Spend some time with hospice patients
- Adopt an animal from a shelter
- Take your dad to his doctor's appointment
- Help out your single-mom neighbor with her yard work
- Cry with someone who has a broken heart
- Tell your spouse how much you appreciate what they do for you
- When people do bad things, remember it's because they are in a bad place

- When people do hurtful things, remember it's because they are hurting
- Let people go through their own process of getting to a better place – it's different for each of us
- Take care of a stray cat
- Apologize to someone you don't think deserves it
- Put your arms around your kids when they are sad
- Take a cupcake to someone who has been disappointed
- Make dinner for someone who just had a baby
- Do kind acts of service often
- Tell your parents you love them every time you see them
- Tell your kids you love them every chance you get
- Read to cancer patients
- Be kind to people you may misunderstand
- Refrain from saying mean things to the person who has hurt you
- Volunteer to prepare dinner at a homeless shelter
- Give your hand-me-downs to someone who really needs them
- Learn to control your own hurt and anger and focus on making someone else feel better
- If there is someone in your life you have not spoken to for awhile – make amends
- When someone has a burst of anger, put your hand on their shoulder and ask them if   everything is alright
- Whenever you speak of someone, make sure you speak kindly
- Give a blanket and some hot soup to a homeless person
- Remember that Jesus showed compassion to everyone

Choose a few items from our list that you'd like to tackle right away. And DO THEM.

Take some time to complete a fun activity. You can take a week to complete this task and then do it again later on as you think about it. Remember, the more you do something, the more it becomes ingrained in who you are.

We want you to think of three 'random acts of kindness' that you can perform and complete them all within one week.

Need some inspiration?

How about a few ideas. .
> *Help someone put their groceries in their car.*
> *Give someone a few dollars if they find they are short in the grocery line.*
> *Offer someone a bottle of water who is working hard.*
> *Mow your neighbor's lawn without them knowing.*
> *Leave some anonymous treats at someone's doorstep.*

The point of this activity is to help you begin to ENJOY being Compassionate and putting others first. There is great satisfaction in helping others and showing them that you care. Get out there and make a difference in someone's life. In turn, you will be making a difference in your OWN life.

"Howbeit Jesus suffered him not, but saith unto him, Go home to thy friends, and tell them how great things the Lord hath done for thee, and hath had compassion on thee."
~ Mark 5:19 ~

"A person who practices compassion and forgiveness has great inner strength, whereas aggression is usually a sign of weakness."
~ Dalai Lama ~

When we have Compassion, we have concern for another human being. We have a desire to help someone in need and relieve their suffering if at all possible. There are so many people in the world who need to feel of that Compassion from others – and we don't need to go very far to find them.

What about the members of our own family?

Our Savior has asked us to bear one another's burdens, comfort those who need comfort, mourn with those who mourn, and visit the sick, among other things. So think about it:

- Does your spouse ever need you to carry the load for them? Absolutely!

- Do your teenagers ever need you to help them feel better after they had a bad day? You bet!

- Do your family members ever need you to cry with them when something devastating affects their life? Certainly!

- Do your aging parents ever need you to visit them when they aren't feeling well? Yes!

We have opportunities right beside us everyday to practice Compassion. If we can start by helping our very own families feel more loved, it will spread throughout the world.

If we can become more Compassionate people, we will be more able to step outside our own issues. Learning to become less absorbed in ourselves and with our own problems, lessens the amount of pain we experience. Compassion is truly a gift we can use to become happier, more content individuals.

*"Our days are happier when we give people a
bit of our heart rather than a piece of our mind."*
~ Anonymous ~

Think back on a time in your life when someone showed you genuine Compassion.

- What were the circumstances?
- Were you experiencing hardship or heartache in your life at the time?
- What did that person do that made such a difference to you?
- How did you react?
- Did the experience change your life in some way?

Write about this experience in your journal.

The purpose of the activity above is to help you realize you have been the object of someone else's Compassion at times in your own life. We want you to think about how you felt in your heart, and hopefully it will inspire you to want to be more Compassionate toward others who are struggling either for just a short time, or long-term.

It's important to remember that the way we treat others is a direct reflection of the way we feel about ourselves. But we as co-authors believe that as we practice Compassion toward others, our own self- worth will be directly affected. The more we show Compassion, the more we will love and respect ourselves, and the more we will want to continually show Compassion towards people from all walks of life – the more we will want to do something to help someone through a difficult time or a challenging event.

As we practice Compassion on a daily basis, we are showing a commitment to love more and help more. Compassion is something we choose. When we see someone in need of support or comfort or love, we are being handed a chance to change a life. We came across the following quote and it reminded us that when someone in need crosses our path, we ought to DO something, not just FEEL something.

"When God puts love and compassion in your heart toward someone, He is offering you an opportunity to make a difference in that person's life. You must learn to follow that love. Don't ignore it. Act on it. Somebody needs what you have."
~ Spiritual Inspiration ~

What are your thoughts and impressions now about the gift of COMPASSION?

Has anything changed for you or come into your consciousness that you didn't recognize before?
Jot down your thoughts now after 30 days of reflection:

_____

_____

_____

_____

_____

_____

_____

_____

_____

_____

_____

_____

_____

_____

*"But a certain Samaritan, as he journeyed, came where
he was: and when he saw him, he had compassion
on him, And went to him, and bound up his wounds,
pouring in oil and wine, and set him on his own beast,
and brought him to an inn, and took care of him."*
~ Luke 10:33-34 ~

CONCLUSION:

Compassion is one of the greatest gifts of all. As we learn to have Compassion for each other – for those who are ill, for those who are less fortunate, for those who are struggling, for those who are different than we are – we will feel love come back into our own lives, and our capacity to have more Compassion will grow.

Compassion is not just about caring – it's about DOING. If we truly have Compassion for another human being, we will do something to help them. It isn't enough just to have sympathy, we must act on those feelings and actually DO.

So as we practice the gift of Compassion on a daily basis, may we be filled with the Spirit to help us know who we can help and how we can help. Make it your goal to make a difference and to even change the life of another. Let us all look to Jesus Christ as the ultimate teacher of Compassion, and strive to become more like Him as we find it in our hearts to be more Compassionate toward ALL of Christ's children.

DAILY REFLECTION

Each chapter is meant to be read slowly,
Absorbing the deeper essence behind the words and stories.

This allows for continual reflection,
Prayer and listening for answers,
Which opens the door to
Greater insight and awareness of
The Gift of Connection.

If we devote one month of the year,
To learning and living the Gift of Connection,
Our awareness of the precious Gift of Connection,
Will be spiritually heightened,
And our daily existence will emulate this awareness.

As we make this shift to mindful attentiveness to the Gift of Connection,
We will be less likely to take for granted,
The beauty, the power, and the mystique of Connection.
We will have developed a habit,
Which becomes part of who we are.

As we develop a new habit each month,
Based on a different Gift each month,
A Gift that Jesus came to earth to give each one of us,
We will become more like Jesus in the way we live.
As this happens,
We will be living a more Christlike life, every day.
As we do this,
We are expressing our deepest gratitude to Jesus
And our Heavenly Father.

As we share the 12 Gifts with others,
We cannot help but bring the same love and peace
To our own hearts and spirits.

— 6 —

The *Gift* of

CONNECTION

We believe experiencing a Connection to the Holy Spirit is one of the most special gifts we can ever hope to be blessed within this life. That Connection can guide us and prompt us throughout our lives and help us to live the most fulfilling life possible, if we will listen. Just as with each of the other gifts in this book, we desire that each of us practice strengthening our Connection to the Holy Spirit throughout our lives.

Practice is so important, because even though we may feel very connected at times, that Connection can be interrupted because of difficulties we are experiencing, attitudes we embrace, or behaviors we engage in, and it isn't unusual to be on that roller coaster throughout our lives. None of us is spiritually connected at all times. And so, our constant attention and effort is required if we want to have the Holy Spirit with us, and if we want to become more like Jesus Christ.

Why did we choose CONNECTION TO THE HOLY SPIRIT as the sixth gift?

*"Now the Lord is that Spirit and where
the Spirit of the Lord is, there is liberty."*
~ 2 Corinthians 3:17 ~

*"And the spirit of the Lord shall rest upon him, the spirit
of wisdom and understanding, the spirit of counsel and
might, the spirit of knowledge and of the fear of the Lord."*
~ Isaiah 11:2 ~

As we contemplated which gifts to include in 12 GIFTS, we quickly decided on Connection to the Holy Spirit. We are all born with the gift of the Holy Spirit which gives us the ability to discern right from wrong. And it makes sense that, if we use this gift throughout our lives, that connection will lead us and give us guidance.

We are certain if each of you think back on the many times you have been directed by the Holy Spirit, you will feel much gratitude. We have all been blessed in one way or another by this gift. Think about the times you may have been influenced in one way or another to do something you didn't plan on or to do something differently than you had anticipated.

We chose Connection as the sixth gift, because we agreed there is almost nothing more precious to either of us than our Connection to the Holy Spirit.

I, Janeen, have had many experiences where I knew I was being warned – sometimes I have listened – other times I have not.

Let me tell you about a time when I DID NOT listen:

Have you ever had an experience where you were dating someone or thinking of getting married to someone, and you felt that, well, that 'feeling?' You had a gut feeling that you should not be with this person – for whatever reason. Did you listen?

Many, many years ago, I had this feeling.

I remember driving home one night and the thought came to me. "Heavenly Father is not going to let me marry this man. He will not allow it to happen." I knew it in my heart, even though I thought I was in love with this person, that something was going to stand in the way. It made me sad, and I had a difficult time dealing with the thought. But lo and behold, I found out he had been seeing a couple of other women at the same time. Even though he denied it, he broke things off with me in a letter that he coldly placed in the mail.

Now, all you ladies out there are thinking, 'Wow, she dodged a bullet!' Right?

Well, let's fast forward 15 years.

I had never fallen out of "love" with this man, and when I found myself in the dating world, once again, I decided to look up my old flame and see if I could get some closure. A letter in the mail left me feeling helpless to fight for what I thought I wanted. And I wanted to find out what exactly happened. So, I wound up meeting this guy for lunch. When I first saw him, I thought, "Wow, he hasn't taken very good care of himself." And yet, those feelings were still there, so I thought I could help him get back to a good place.

I told my Heavenly Father at that point, "I don't care if I'm not supposed to marry him. I am going to do what I want this time!"

Eighteen months later, we were married. Eight years after that, I received a phone call. My husband had been carrying on a relationship with the woman on the other end of the phone for the past eleven years!!!

Wow!

And THAT was just the beginning.

Why must we ignore the Holy Spirit when we KNOW it is speaking to us – when we KNOW it is warning us? Probably because since we have our free agency, most of us human beings enjoy being able to make our own decisions, our own mistakes and our own messes!

After all, what fun would life be if we did everything by the rules all of the time?

Well, it might not be as much fun in the moment, but it would bring a lot more joy and peace into our lives over the long haul. And isn't that really what we are all searching for in this life?

Now, let me tell you about a time when I DID listen:

When I was about to marry the man in the last story, we bought a house. We had been looking around for a plot of ground so we could build our own home, but as we were driving through a neighborhood one day, we saw a couple of homes for sale.

We stopped to look at the first house. It was about the right size, in our price range, and an okay house in a really great neighborhood.

Across the street was another house. It looked too big, and even though we couldn't get in to see it that day, we knew it would be way out of our price range, so we didn't even call.

We went back the next day to possibly place an offer on the first house, but there was already an offer in place. We lost that house.

"Oh well, we'll keep looking," we thought. We drove away, but I kept thinking about the second house for the next three days. "Let's at least call and find out how big it is and what the asking price is," I said. So we did.

The house WAS a little big, but absolutely gorgeous inside with upgrades and special touches all throughout. The yard was amazing. And guess what? It was going into foreclosure! The house, as it stood, was a steal!

We bought it!

My daughter and I have lived in this house for nearly 11 years now. I live in a beautiful neighborhood surrounded by wonderful, caring, friendly people. I have formed life-long friendships here. I was called as the leader over the youth in my church, and it changed my life in many ways. My daughter has formed meaningful friendships and loves it here. Since my divorce, I have been surrounded by people who watch out for me and help me with things that I might not be able to get done.

I firmly believe I was prompted by the Holy Spirit to call about the house that day. This is where I am supposed to be. This was no mistake. I was guided here. I know it.

I choose to look at life in this way:

I would not live in this beautiful home and have all these wonderful people in my life if I had not married my husband. Even though my marriage to him caused great pain to me and my family, my life, in the long run, is better for it. Even though I chose not to listen to the Holy Spirit about that very big decision in my life, I WAS willing to be directed to move into this neighborhood. I will forever be grateful for that.

Suggestions for getting in tune to the Holy Spirit:

Take a road trip by yourself and drive in silence – no music playing.
It's difficult to listen to music AND listen to the Spirit at the same time because they both require the use of the senses. Spiritual music can help us FEEL the Spirit, but silence makes our Connection and ability to HEAR much greater.

Ask someone to share a personal spiritual experience they might have had.
The testimonies of others can support our own faith, just as sharing our own testimonies
can increase our faith.

Pray and then listen.
Getting up right away and plopping into bed or hopping in the shower doesn't give us the time needed to listen for answers. When you speak to Heavenly Father, let him speak back to you.

Get outside of yourself.
Serving others gives us the chance to answer someone else's prayer, and by so doing, we may find the answer to our own prayer.

*"The Holy Spirit is a living gift of energy from
the Divine to comfort, strengthen and heal!
~ wingedpoetry ~*

When we think about Connection to the Holy Spirit, we
might also contemplate closely-related words that help us
embrace a deeper meaning of Connection. These words could
include: ASSOCIATION, FRIEND, KINSHIP, MENTOR,
MESSENGER, COMFORTER, SPIRIT OF TRUTH

I chose to share this next story because it was such a powerful
experience for me that it changed me in many ways. When it
happened I realized just how possible it is to Connect to the
Holy Spirit.

"ARE YOU ALRIGHT?"
by Janeen

Several years ago, I was living in a neighborhood where I
bought my first house. I had lived there about four years when
my husband and I experienced an unfortunate divorce. I had
two small children, and I was working a full-time job and going
to school part-time working to finish my degree. I was more
than busy and sometimes I would cry myself to sleep from the
exhaustion I felt and the stress I was under.

No one suspected. Not even my own family. I was working so
hard to be strong – an example to my children.

None of my friends or neighbors knew that I was struggling
because I always had a cheerful attitude and a positive outlook
when in their presence, but sometimes I would simply become
overwhelmed.

One day in particular, I had experienced a heartbreak that left me lying on my bed sobbing until I had literally cried out all the tears I could find. I felt lifeless as I lay there wondering what I could do to make myself feel better. I began to pray, and as I did so my phone rang. Thank goodness! A reason to get up off that bed! I answered the phone and my neighbor asked, "Are you alright?"

I was stunned. I was speechless. And I was grateful. I said to her, "How did you know something was wrong?" And she replied, "I just had an overwhelming feeling that I should call you."

That was my first experience of its kind. Before that incident, I had never had anyone be that in tune with the Holy Spirit on my behalf. It changed me.

I have been mindful of my own Connection to the Holy Spirit since then. I have grown to realize what a significant impact that Connection can have on my life each and every day if I am listening and paying attention.

"If ye then, being evil, know how to give good gifts unto your children: how much more shall your Heavenly Father give the Holy Spirit to them that ask him?"
~ Luke 11:13 ~

"There was a man sent from God, whose name was John. The same came for a witness, to bear witness of the Light, that all men through him might believe. He was not that Light, but was sent to bear witness of that Light. That was the true Light, which lighteth every man that cometh into the world."
~ John 1:6-9 ~

We all want to know more about our Connection to the Holy Spirit, so we have provided you with some questions to help you learn to understand how to listen for it and understand it. Put some significant thought into each question before answering:

Think about a time when you had an impression to do something and acted on it. How did it turn out?

_____

_____

_____

_____

_____

When you have a thought to do something insignificant like change lanes on the freeway, do you ever consider that the Spirit is prompting you for a reason? Explain.

_____

_____

_____

_____

Think of an experience you had where you believed the Holy Spirit was prompting you. Write in your journal about how you felt.

_____

_____

_____

_____

The Holy Spirit will help guide us. But we must realize that the path is not always direct. Sometimes we make a choice that feels right, only to realize later it was wrong. Why does this happen?

There was a time when I, Janeen, had moved a new city and had set my sights on a particular place where I wanted to work. I had always landed the jobs I wanted in the past, and I was confident things would work out in my favor now.

I applied for the first job I was qualified for and made the initial cut. Three of us were interviewed for the position and, lo and behold, I was not hired. What? How can that be? I was disappointed, but decided to apply for the next one. This went on for the next four positions I applied for. Each time, I would make the initial cut to the top three, and each time, I would not be selected for the position.

Looking back now, I realize the Spirit was trying to guide me away from this place of employment, but I persisted. I did finally land job number six. And my seven years there were wonderful, but I had some experiences that I believe I could have avoided had I listened and moved on. Is that to say my choice was wrong? Not necessarily. The choice gave me experience, and I believe sometimes our decision to ignore the prompting and use our free agency to do what we choose is what we are in need of learning. Maybe my path would have been easier had I paid attention in the first place. But I have no regrets because I know it is our experiences in life that make us who we ultimately become.

I do realize that some of us are more stubborn than others and need to learn lessons over and over before we finally get it knocked into our brains. I am one such person! Maybe you are too.

But sometimes a choice that turns out to be wrong can lead to an inspired opportunity.

Not long ago, I was looking at starting a business – something I had never done, but it sounded like a great idea so I started looking for a building or a spot to build one. I called on one piece of land, in particular, that led me to a gentleman who showed me the property. As we started talking, he realized I would be a great fit for a project he had just funded, so he gave me the contact information.

The short story is – I never started the original business I had in mind. Instead I became involved with his project and am still involved today in a major way. These people have become lifelong friends and business partners, and I never would have met them had I not ventured out to see the property that day.

I have a testimony of living righteously. As long as we do all we can to stay true, we can have access to the Spirit in our lives to help us make correct choices. But we have to keep our hearts open to divine inspiration and have hope for the future, especially at times when it seems like nothing is going right.

With this in mind, make it your GOAL this month as you think about the Gift of the Connection to the Holy Spirit to listen to the still small voice when you have a big decision to make and let it guide you.

Come up with your own GOAL that you personally want to set as a way to improve your ability to hear the Holy Spirit as it tries to direct you.

We would like you to begin your journey by thinking about what your thoughts and impressions about the gift of Connection.

As you begin reading this chapter, write down a few thoughts you have as you contemplate the gift of Connection. We will ask this question again at the end of the chapter after you have completed your study of the gift of Connection.

_____

_____

_____

_____

_____

_____

_____

_____

_____

_____

_____

_____

_____

_____

_____

_____

_____

_____

_____

_____

_____

What did Jesus say about
CONNECTION TO THE HOLY SPIRIT?

"Then Jesus said unto them, Yet a little while is the light with you. Walk while ye have the light, lest darkness come upon you: for he that walketh in darkness knoweth not whither he goeth."
~ John 12:35 ~

"While ye have light, believe in the light, that ye may be the children of light. These things spake Jesus, and departed, and did hide himself from them."
~ John 23:36 ~

Our Savior wants to help us in this life. He want to guide and direct us, and help us see the light. He doesn't want us to flounder. He wants our path to be clear, and it is possible for us to have that direction if we truly want it and seek it out.

If we pay attention to the way we feel, the things that are being whispered quietly to us, and the thoughts we are having, we can use that Connection throughout our lives to be safe, help others, and make decisions.

Have you ever had that experience where you felt prompted to leave a few minutes early or you were inadvertently running a few minutes late? Do you ever wonder as you come upon an accident on the freeway, if you were prompted with a change in your schedule that allowed you to miss being a part of that accident?

Have you ever been thinking about someone out of the blue only to be called by that person the very same day?

Have you ever been prompted to do something that turned out to be the greatest thing you could have done?

We often talk about 'women's intuition.' Is that intuition actually the Holy Spirit prompting us as wives, as mothers and grandmothers to guide and protect ourselves and our children?

Our own mothers save us from harm, from pain or from illness many times throughout our lives because they feel we should or shouldn't do something. As we became mothers ourselves, we realized just how real and true those feelings or promptings are. We are so confident in them – and would bet all of you mothers can relate – that we tell our kids, "When I tell you I have a feeling about something - you'd better listen."

Think back about some of those times in your own life when you had a prompting, or your mother had a prompting and asked you to listen. Write about them.

_____

_____

_____

_____

_____

_____

_____

_____

"Cast me not away from thy presence;
and take not thy holy spirit from me."
~ Psalms 51:11 ~

**Stories to help us reflect on the Gift of
CONNECTION TO THE HOLY SPIRIT:**

**Keep in mind that when we listen to the stories of others, we
can learn so much by example. Just as when we share our
own stories, we are teaching our own truths to others so they
can learn from us.**

LIFE'S TRADEOFFS
by Elizabeth

Throughout my life, depending on many different circumstances,
I have had various degrees of awareness about the need for
prayer, and about the power of prayer. I think it is safe to say that
most of us say a prayer in desperate moments where something
very challenging is coming our way. I know that I have sent
many compelling prayers in a moment of crisis and, amazingly,
many of the most bizarre situations were answered with safety
and the ability to be able to live on earth.

There were other prayers sent up in moments when things
weren't going in my direction, and most of those prayers were
not answered in the way that I hoped and pleaded for. Sometimes
I had the benefit of realizing why later. Other times, I had to just
believe that God knew better than I did and, therefore, He said
"No" and my plans were rearranged. I must admit that it takes
maturity and life experience to fully appreciate why God would
not go along with my very desperate plans. (They sounded so
important when I was "prayer begging", but I can't even recall
most of those prayers years later, except for maybe one prayer
about getting asked to a prom by a certain boy which did not
happen.) So, if you are a teenager or perhaps in your twenties,
maybe even thirties, (Okay, let's stop there… I'm 56 as I write
this, but I appreciate the life wisdom I've gained with each year.

I'm not so appreciative of the gray hairs that accompany each year, but that's between me and my many boxes of hair dye.)

Life is about trade-offs too! It's great to keep life in balance and to maintain a healthy sense of humor. Laughter is good for the soul. Jesus had a sense of humor too. Jesus is able to know everything about each of us. He knows our quirks, our goofiness, our kind deeds, our prayers, our mistakes, and what's happening with us. Since He already knows everything about us, why not be honest and laugh a little about the funny side of our thoughts and life experiences?

Regarding humor, there are ways to laugh when it is not offensive to other people, and there are also many jokes and times in life where it might be very easy to laugh, but it could offend another person. It's wise to think about humor so that we can find ways to laugh and lift others up in the process. I know that I was so sensitive when I was teenager, and I was nervous about other's criticizing me. It would have been hard to laugh at myself during those years. But now in my fifties, I'm usually the first one to laugh at my ridiculous antics, and since others know this, we can all enjoy a good belly laugh at my expense. I think this is because the more we reflect on ourselves as spiritual beings and we gain a sense of who we are on earth and our purpose, we become more secure with our spiritual identity. We learn that the world does not get to define who we are. We learn that by seeking our connection and identity to Jesus, we develop a faith in this identity, and we can laugh at the silly aspects of our life choices. Here is one example about this from my own life.

"Do Not Take Yourself Too Seriously - Laugh and Love"

A few years ago, my family was preparing for our annual trip to the beach where we have created some of our best family memories together. It was the day of our trip and I was just beginning to pack. I brought out a suitcase and my daughter announced that the zipper on this particular suitcase had broken on our last trip. There wasn't much time to look for another suitcase so I told everyone that I could fix anything with super glue, since I had just recently repaired a lamp with super glue. Yes, I was bragging and feeling happy about our beach trip, so I was being silly. I carefully applied the super glue where the zipper had come apart from the suitcase, and it appeared to be working. With two fingers still covered in super glue, I sneezed, and then I accidentally wiped my eye. You can imagine what happened next. Yikes. Within seconds I realized that I couldn't open my eye. Since I had just been bragging about how I could fix anything, I quietly slipped into the bathroom and tried to undo the super glue on my eye. Unfortunately, I had super glued my "good eye" shut with my long eyelashes completely stuck to my lower eye area. It was hard to see what to do using only my "weak eye", so I fumbled around for reading glasses and, I think the longer I delayed, the more time the super glue had to adhere to my skin. (DO NOT try this at home!!! I am serious! The glue could have gotten into my eye, and I could have lost my sight in my "good eye", so please, DO NOT do this!)

Finally, I went back to the kitchen and showed three of my children what happened. They laughed so hard, and I laughed along with them because I deserved it due to my goofy bragging. In between all the laughs we did the typical things to get my eyelashes unstuck, such as smearing my eye with peanut butter, regular butter, olive oil, Neosporin (Why? Because it was handy.) When my son started getting out the cleaning supplies, I said, "Whoa! We need to think about this more." Now I started to worry a little. My teenage daughter suggested one of her make-up removers. She was playing around with it and then without any notice, she put her fingernails on my upper eye lid, holding my eyelash, and just ripped across!!! I can still feel it! She said, "Problem fixed, open your eye." I did. I was so grateful to have the sight back in my good eye (still blurry though) that I hugged her. She looked at me a little weird and said, "You need to pack or we'll miss our flight!" So I ran off and I heard some laughter in the kitchen. I went to the bathroom and looked. Not one eyelash remained on my "good eye!" But problem solved!

So I packed. The suitcase zipper was also frozen in super glue and would not budge, (but at least I tried) so I found another one, and we made the flight. We had a great trip with lots of laughs about my eye and the glue. My family still laughs about this. Laughter is so good for the soul. Endorphins release and happy hormones come out. There are studies that show that opening up a serious talk with a few jokes relaxes the group and helps the audience to be more receptive to the topics presented.

It only took two months for the "good eye" to grow back its lashes! Just for the fun of it, I did not wear fake lashes as the lashes grew back. None of us are perfect, and I was comfortable telling the funny story and using it as a way to make others laugh.

However, losing your hair to cancer treatments is never a joke or a reason to laugh. That situation is completely different, and my heart and prayers have gone out to many people who have endured the side effects of chemotherapy, including my own beloved mother. My mother lost her battle with melanoma years ago. But she would have been the first to laugh at my super glue eyelash story! So while I share my silly and funny story about not having an eyelash for two months, I am fully aware of the difficult sacrifices that many cancer patients go through, including myself.

So my family embraced this story for the fun and laughter we had, and they now hide the super glue. As a family, we try to find the silver lining after a problem and, in this case, we concluded that the "weak eye" finally had a chance to shine, and the "good eye" worked on growing back it's lashes for nearly two months. Both eyes eventually returned to their naturally wrinkled look, with lashes of equal lengths. Both eyes still smiled with love and laughter, and they were wide open looking for more lessons to be learned and humor along the way. One very wise person who gave me advice once said, "Don't take yourself too seriously. Try and find the funny side in things and laugh at yourself. You will be much happier as you go through life if you do this." Thank you Sue! She was so right!

"Pray About All Of Your Dreams"

So, if you are a person reading this book in your teen years, twenties, thirties, or more, it really doesn't matter. Each of us will develop and grow on our own individual courses, and, in accordance with our awareness about our soul journey. I fully understand how important your dreams and desires are at the time you are having them. If the ideas, concepts, and solutions were born within your brain and heart, there is a reason. That is valid enough. Explore them. Be open minded and flexible with them. But more importantly, it is completely worthwhile to pray about all of your dreams and aspirations. No one in the world should squash another person's dreams if they are based in positivity and strong conviction and there is a realistic chance of success. (The reality of a fully grown young man pursuing a career in the NBA when he is 5'2" probably should not be encouraged or pursued, simply because the odds are against it, in practical terms.)

Believe in you and your connection to Jesus, and He will give you guidance about the path that is right for you. Stay alert, because sometimes the messages are like whispers from heaven. But also believe in the wisdom of your Father in Heaven and your Savior, Jesus Christ. They love you more than any words in any book can possibly convey. They want you to pursue your highest good and to develop your spiritual awareness. Heaven has a perspective that those of us on earth cannot possibly understand or even begin to fully conceptualize. Therefore, once we develop a strong spiritual relationship with Jesus, who is our conduit to God, we will have many moments of confirmation when we are on the right path. Although Jesus will not drop a "Life Map" down to us from heaven so that we can spread it out on a table and follow the course, He will give us so many other signs and direction if we listen and stay close. Our job is to stay close through prayer and making choices that support a lifestyle that is in accordance with His plan for us.

Prayers, listening for answers, and staying close to our Savior, Jesus, will always light a path for us that leads us down a meaningful and purposeful life. Jesus wants us to feel joy and peace, and He will be there to help us find this. Prayer is the way to learning and finding our direction. We can't go wrong with prayer if it is true, sincere, and open to God's will.

All Prayers Are Heard

There are various ways to pray and different churches suggest different formats on how to approach our Heavenly Father in prayer. There are some religions that promote praying with a rosary. Other religions suggest praying in various tongues. Some religions show a style of showing lots of emotion and praising while praying. Other religions are more reverent in their way of praying.

The point is, there are many different ways to pray and seek a closeness with Jesus. But we believe that Jesus and God will listen to a sincere heartfelt prayer, prayed in a childlike, innocent voice, perhaps more than an intellectually calculated prayer, which is stated in a proper format. Heaven wants to hear the sincerity in our hearts. Honesty and openness allow the communication and closeness to flow back and forth.

In my own life, I've had many different styles of prayer, as I'm sure many others have had also. Most of us would agree that we have all said the "desperate prayer" at one time or another right before a crisis, or when we thought our lives had to have an exact outcome or experience. Of course, there are the prayers for loved ones who are suffering and we want Jesus to comfort them. There are actually double blind studies that show that the patients who are being prayed for in a hospital setting, compared to those who are not listed on an active prayer roll, actually do better in their recovery process. There are also many prayers for guidance, direction, and answers about what to do in a particular life situation. There are prayers when we have time to be patient and reflect while waiting for an answer. And then there are desperate prayers, needing help immediately. Most of us in adult years of life can recall a time or two in our lives when we had a desperate pleading prayer. I have had my share of them. Now, in my 50's, I must remember to thank the Lord for not answering many of the requests when I had many impulsive ideas and dreams.

Some of those pleading prayers were imbedded in my own personal desires for how I thought certain situations should turn out (I thought I knew for sure how things should turn out). But often, years later, I thanked God for not listening to me when I begged. We are lucky that God has a great deal of patience with us. Perhaps He and Jesus even have a keen sense of humor as they watch the antics we might go through just to have our "must have prayers" at the moment be answered according to us. I even laugh hard as I recall some of the important things that I pleaded about, only to see the silliness of it all later. It's good to chuckle at ourselves at times! It lightens up the seriousness of other pressing matters.

But there have been life and death prayers that were truly desperate, and after these prayers were answered, I was so grateful for a very long time, and my faith grew deeper, and kept me close to Jesus. But we are human, and even after such profound memories and experiences, many of us get comfortable again and go out into the world with a sense of confidence and forget the depth and importance of staying close to our spiritual connections. I know I did. More about that later, but just realize that learning life lessons is a process, not a one-time event. This is why I will share many different stories that might seem repetitive throughout the book, so that we can all recognize that patience with ourselves along our journey is a necessary thing if we truly desire to grow spiritually.

Desperate Prayers

Here are some examples of desperate prayers that we all have all heard about and most likely uttered, if not screamed, during critical moments in our lives:

Imagine the seconds before we realize that we are about to be in a car accident and we see the oncoming car or truck about to hit us head on; or the hours, minutes, and finally seconds, where we have heard the warnings about a natural disaster, such as an earthquake, tornado, hurricane, wildfires, etc, and we plead desperately that "If you just save us all God and Jesus, we promise that we will do so much more to live a better life, so please spare our family, home and our community..."; or possibly the moments right before we recognize that we have been confronted by an evil or dark energy (being robbed, raped, or hurt by another person), and we instinctively know that we should pray, and we are able to live and tell about it and hopefully learn from the ordeal.

For me, these types of moments and life-altering experiences pushed me to the very core of what I know is true in life. It was an automatic response to pray. In those frightening moments, the core of my soul knew without a doubt that I didn't have time or ability to call 911, even if they could have responded in a timely manner, which was not even possible, and my soul went straight to Jesus. I begged Him. I knew He was my answer, and the only way. He was my one and only Savior, my truth and my light.

I'm alive and well to share these stories, so clearly my desperate prayers in extreme moments of chaos and confusion were answered. As a result, my faith was cemented and I knew the true power of prayer. But we're all human and, at times, we stray and test the waters again. Some lessons I reluctantly had to repeat over and over until I really knew for sure in my soul. This is how we all evolve and grow. But once we learn a lesson, it is very hard to go backwards and pretend that we "didn't know". We can't fool God or Jesus. They know if we know better or not.

Pray To Be Used For Good

During times when I was most in tune with my spiritual existence and identity on earth, I often asked to be used every morning as an instrument for good, peace, hope and healing. And this prayer works and doors will open for you. So be ready. It happens. I assure you, if you say this prayer with a sincere heart, all kinds of opportunities await you. This prayer seems to remove a veil or two so that we can see more closely into the heart and soul of another person, or even an animal. It feels like a sixth sense is more in tune, and you get a sense that the lady checking you out at the grocery store is grieving the loss of a loved one.

Here's a true story about this. I was at my local grocery store and I did the usual chit chat of being friendly, and then I had a feeling to ask the clerk about her husband. She started crying. She said, "Today would have been our anniversary and no one remembered. My husband died four years ago and now, no one ever mentions our wedding anniversary. But I still think about our wedding day every year on our anniversary. Just because he has passed on, doesn't mean that I don't want to celebrate our wedding day." I hugged her. Then the other clerks and customers who overheard her story, joined in and hugged her too. Some even shared similar stories, identifying with her sadness. (Luckily, it was a slow time of day, mid-morning, and most people were not in a hurry. Many customers seemed to be of the retired age. I actually found this morning pace at the grocery store very relaxing because most people did not have another pressing appointment to get to, and they took time to say hello and chat.) The entire experience was very tender and warmed my heart. If I had not trusted the prompting in my heart to ask about her husband, none of the subsequent joy and connecting would have happened. I knew it was an answer to my prayer of asking to be used for good today. It was easy to do and it didn't cost a penny. It just involved a prayer and paying attention for an answer. Most of us can afford to do that.

However, it would have been easy for my logical mind to talk me out of asking about her husband, but I had a strong sense that I was supposed to ask (and I recalled that I had prayed to be used just a few hours earlier...). So, after you offer the prayer to be used for good throughout the day, it's important to pay attention and listen for the prompts. Logic will often try to persuade you from speaking up, but the angels are counting on you to do the opposite. Speak up. Notice others. Sense their emotions. Allow yourself to be empathetic. Kindly ask sincere, non-invasive questions. With a kind tone of voice, most people will sense that you are just interested in them. Tone of voice is almost more powerful that the choice of words. (Just to prove this point to my questioning young kids years ago, I did an experiment for them. I said some rude words to our dogs in the nicest tone of voice and, of course, the dogs wagged their tails and licked me with joy. Animals don't understand our vocabulary but they know exactly when we are loving or when we are upset.)

So a kind, sincere, interested tone of voice can put others at ease, and they listen. As humans with the ability to speak, angels rely on us to share the words or questions that they prompt us with. We need to trust that angels would not put us in an awkward situation unless some good could come from it.

So on the days where I shared a morning prayer of this nature, it would go something like this, "Lord, use me today to reach out to others and share your love and compassion with another person, or with others. I want to be an instrument of your love today. Thank you for all of my blessings and for always loving me." (There is no formula for how to say a prayer such as the above. I have never written it down before because I rely upon the sincere desires in my heart to find the right words. I doubt that I have ever said the exact same prayer twice. I wait for my heart to be still and then a beautiful flow of words would rise to the surface and they are spoken, often out loud, even though I am humanly alone. Try it. Experience it for yourself. Just being still enough and waiting for your heart to feel the words or message is a spiritual experience in itself. But much more happens after the prayer!)

There might be days when you skip that specific prayer to be used, because maybe you are still catching up from things you need to follow through with from past prayers. This is completely understandable. I took many breaks because of the "To Do Lists" that are generated when heaven shows you the full menu of what's waiting to be done. We all need a break and a vacation here and there. It refreshes us and renews us. But in pure honesty, the days that I took a "vacation from praying to be used for good," I was able to "catch up" with personal responsibilities, but I didn't feel that peace in my soul and heart when you know for sure that you made a difference in the life of another.

I missed the good vibes of the karma peace you get from helping others. It's a day off, but then you might feel sad and miss the good vibes that you get from doing good. So there is a natural payoff that occurs from sharing love and light in the world. These good vibes of kind karma will be missed when they are not showing up in your heart.

When I've taken a break from my prayer of helping, I notice the difference in my soul satisfaction. The more love I share in the world, the more love I feel and the greater the joy is in my heart. I envision angels in heaven looking for willing partners to align with to do some good, and make some miracles happen. Therefore, if you are asking and willing and paying attention, these angels will notice your pure intentions and race to you. A willing vessel and person on earth can truly be a vehicle for heaven to work through.

When You Give With Love, It Re-Gifts Right Back To You

Be ready if you ask, because it's worth it. The peace and joy in your soul after making a difference in other people's lives cannot be measured in earthly terms. It is the peace from heaven and from Jesus. I've learned that when you live your days trying to be kind to others, and you ask for help from heaven, you just know that you are guided. I never know exactly who is directing and guiding me, but I trust it, because I know it's an answer to my prayers. It could be angels. It could be Jesus. It could be the Holy Spirit, or it could be our Heavenly Father. The main point here is – it really doesn't matter. When I ask to be used as a vessel, as an earthly instrument for good in the world, I believe that heaven hears those prayers and will send us guidance and direction for the good of others.

My responsibility is to listen with my soul and heart, and pay attention. We should all be reminded that heaven and guidance will never tell us to harm another person or hurt society in any way. Heaven and all of the gifts that we have access to, through prayer, would not answer a prayer in a way that could harm others. God and Jesus ask for love, kindness, compassion, and thoughtful understanding. If anyone feels confused about their direction after praying, please remind yourself that God is all about love and He would not ask you to hurt innocent people to make a point. However, this might be a confusing and difficult topic for some people who are not sure about the answers they hear after praying.

If you are uncertain about any answers after praying, please seek the guidance of a trusted spiritual advisor who can assist you with seeking more understanding about your worries or concerns. There are times when a negative influence can get mixed up with the answers to our prayers, if we are not paying close attention to the truth and light. It is very important to stay close to Jesus and pray often for these very reasons. Jesus is the way, the truth and the light.

*"The Spirit of the Lord is upon me, because he hath
anointed me to preach the gospel to the poor; he
hath sent me to heal the broken-hearted, to preach
deliverance to the captives, and recovering of sight
to the blind, to set at liberty them that are bruised."*
~ Luke 4:18 ~

"I HEAR MOM'S VOICE"
by Janeen

Being Connected to the Holy Spirit is a wonderful way to live. Everyone is born with the ability to connect with the Holy Spirit if they so choose. We are all given this gift, but each of us must decide to live our lives in a way that will keep us connected.

This is truly one of the reasons we are writing this book.

When we choose to live our lives in a mindful way, focused on principles of Christ-like living, we become more sensitive to the promptings of the Holy Spirit.

We should not take it for granted that the Spirit will guide us at all times. The Spirit's ability to help us depends upon our willingness to listen. We have to do our part by being in tune so we can receive the promptings. And we then need to have the faith to act upon those promptings.

My son, Dirk, was serving a Christian mission for our church in Iowa a few years ago. His first six months were particularly difficult, and he was feeling pretty homesick. He wanted to come home and just be back among his family and friends.

I did what I could to encourage him to stick it out and fulfill his mission to the end.

One afternoon, he and his companion were out knocking on doors, and not having much luck with people wanting to talk with them – the lonely life of a missionary – when they came upon a house that looked inviting. They knocked on the door and, to their surprise, they were asked to come inside. The woman who answered the door was friendly and kind to the boys, and was asking them about themselves when my son suddenly stopped her. "I hear my mom's voice," he said. She laughed and he said, "No, I really hear my mom's voice!" He asked if he could walk into the next room where the television set was on. Well, I had done a national commercial a few months prior, and my commercial was on the air at that very moment in Iowa. My son became emotional as he was able to watch me for a few moments and hear my voice.

He was overcome by the connection he felt to the Holy Spirit at that moment. He was missing me so much, and Heavenly Father knew what he needed. He believes he was directed to that house at that very moment – to the house where a kind woman would let him in so he would be able to catch a glimpse of his mom. It settled him down and helped him get over the hump so he could complete his mission and return home 18 months later.

The Holy Spirit is there to direct each of us if we will only listen and keep ourselves in tune to the promptings. I was so grateful that my son had put himself in a position to receive divine inspiration that day. It changed his life at a time when he was truly struggling.

MIRACLES HAPPEN - WATCH FOR THEM
by Elizabeth

Life presents each of us so many opportunities to make choices in many different scenarios, and we simply don't know what the outcome of our choices might be. Sure, we can make a calculated guess based on knowledge, statistics, and other research. But then again, there is often a feeling or gut instinct about what we should do. There are times when we can turn a situation like this into a mental vs. spiritual debate. Our logical mind gets in the way of talking us out of the whispers or guidance, and it may be that the practical and logical side wins the debate on occasion.

If, instead, we follow the hunch, prompting, or inspiration, we often move forward and may even forget the valuable guidance we were given because it might have prevented a bad situation from happening, but we didn't get to see what the result was, simply because we listened.

So after trusting and listening and following the course, we typically don't get to learn what the outcome of the other choice would have been. Therefore, we cannot prove or disprove whether or not, listening to that inner feeling was the right thing to do or not. Even though we can't prove it to ourselves, or to others, there is often a feeling of peace about the decision, even if there is still a lingering curiosity about the other outcome.

Quite often, it might be that others in our life might try to persuade us to take the logical path, simply because they did not experience the same type of spiritual prompting that we felt. Without this awareness, it is understandable that our friends and loved ones would coach us towards a pragmatic direction.

A good debate team could effectively argue both sides of this, and usually, it would be hard to declare a winner, due to the "faith" issue of believing in the wisdom sent from heaven. Based on so many moments where we have been guided to take one path versus another, and then we DID realize why it was necessary, those experiences should increase our faith in "hunches" or promptings.

I know that I would not like to see what the outcome might have been if I had not changed course and listened to what I believe the Holy Spirit was telling me to do.

So many experiences have shown me that I was very fortunate to be guided and told what to do and what not to do. As I share these stories, ponder your own past stories, and pray about any lessons learned from them. Even if we have a regret or two about choices made, we can always grow and learn from this. That is so important because we were also given the gift to be able to repent, learn and grow. Jesus and God are so much more powerful than we can imagine, so always say a heartfelt prayer in the midst of a crisis. These prayers will surely be heard in heaven. Don't ever doubt saying a prayer. Just do it, especially in the midst of a great challenge. (You can sort out previous lessons learned later.)

A strong prayer can summon angels even before the crisis happens. We often forget here on earth, that timing is completely different in heaven than it is on earth. So there are always adjustments that can be made by Jesus and God, because they are all powerful and capable of miracles. Our rational earthly minds cannot even begin to comprehend the infinite possibilities and awareness that they hold. This is where trust and faith come into play. We won't be able to understand it, but that doesn't mean we shouldn't believe in the power of miracles. Doctors say this quite often when they see a patient who has made a miraculous recovery, against all logic and odds. They say something like, "It can only be explained as a miracle."

I have several powerful stories that I will share about miracles that I know happened in my life. I am not sharing to act as if I were more deserving than another person, because I was truly humbled during and after these times. I am choosing to share these stories because I have learned much from listening to other people's stories, and my faith and prayers increased as a result of listening to others. It is my hope that through sharing my stories, you might experience a similar pattern of growth. I have learned great lessons through other's stories.

The first lesson I learned was to simply pay attention. Notice when you are having a feeling, or prompting, or something inside of you that is not at peace. Usually, there will be greater guidance about what to do, once we are tuned in to the warnings.

Prayer Helped Me Avoid A Head-On Collision

Here is a recent story regarding a warning about an upcoming situation that could have been tragic and deadly. I was about to get on a busy freeway to drive to a class that I was scheduled to teach, and the drive usually takes about an hour. As I was driving, I had an anxious feeling about my car and the road conditions, so I turned the music off and prayed. I did not know why or how, but I sensed an urgent feeling to pray. I prayed for "extra guardian angels surrounding me" that night as I was driving. After I said those continual prayers, I felt a sense of peace.

I arrived at the class, interacted with participants, felt warm feelings regarding the class, and I knew in my heart that it was a great class. As I entered the freeway again to return to my city, I had no worries about the previous anxious feelings from the drive to the class. I was feeling the peace of knowing that I made a good connection and shared a valuable message at class. When I was about ten minutes away from my home, I took the exit closest to my home, as I had done hundreds of times in the past. It was almost habit to exit and follow the streets toward home.

As I drove through this winding, one way exit to get off the freeway and into a residential area, I saw a car heading straight towards my car on a one way winding exit. As I screamed out loud, something like, "Ahhhhh... yikes, etc.," I realized that the car heading straight for my car was heading into a head-on collision and was not turning at all. It was almost as if the driver in the car did not even see me, and was planning to drive straight through my car. As I screamed and prayed quickly, my car moved up towards a winding uphill bank on this exit ramp. This pivotal action prevented a head on collision at about 50 mph.

I know it was a miracle because I don't recall turning the steering wheel, simply because I was trying to figure out which way the other driver was going to turn. The steering wheel, I believe, was taken over by the extra angels that I had prayed for about six hours earlier. Moments after this, I pulled over and said thank you prayers. Then I called 911 and explained what happened, trying to prevent that car from heading into another car. They listened and sent a patrol car into that area. When I followed up the next day, there were no accidents in this zone.

However, I now believe, that the prayers I sent up, six hours earlier, asking for extra angels to protect and guide me, were for this very situation. I had been warned about some upcoming danger, and I was very uneasy about it, so I prayed with full attention. I recall, deliberately asking for extra angels, as I was driving to the class. Once I arrived safely, I sort of forgot about the warnings and prayers, and I focused on the class and the participants.

During after-thoughts and reflection, I finally realized that the anxious feelings I had experienced as I began the hour drive to class, were actually meant to warn me about the drive home, not the drive to the class. However, one of the best lessons that I learned from this ordeal, is to never second guess a prompting, a feeling, a warning, a spiritual message, or anything similar. There is always a reason that we feel and have these experiences. Trust and faith in how divine order works is something that we learn without a doubt, after enough earthly experiences.

I wish I could sit here and write that I was one of those individuals who heard the truth the first time, and from there on out, I just lived by that truth and wisdom. But I am not that type of person. Speaking of truth, most of us are here on earth to learn these lessons in a very real way and in a way that affirms in our heart and soul, that Jesus is the way, the truth, and the light. The more we experience profound life lessons, that reveal and show us the spiritual truths which will lead us home to heaven, the more we will grow in our soul and share this love and wisdom amongst our brothers and sisters. So there really is a reason that we stumble at times, until the lessons resonate in our hearts in a secure and knowing way. Peace follows.

Life Is Full Of Lessons

But don't worry. Learning great lessons does not release any of us from learning many other significant lessons. There are so many life classes that we can take until it is our time to rejoin our Father in Heaven and greet our Savior and brother, Jesus Christ. Usually, it is not part of our earthly plan to know the exact time and way that we will depart earth. Having said that, it is way beyond any of us here on earth to speculate about how our loving Father in Heaven decides upon how to share wisdom with each of His children on earth. It is always within His realm to make the rules, bend the rules, change the rules, and do so, according to His will. Heavenly angels will always be there to accompany any God's decisions. "Thy will be done." It is not our will or plan, but His, that will allow for the greatest peace and love in our souls. We turn these decisions over to our Father in Heaven and pray, through our Savior, Jesus Christ, for guidance as we live to learn the highest lessons according to our soul's plan.

In faith, we accept the guidance and wisdom that are bestowed upon us, in various discerning ways. It is not for us to have full knowledge while upon earth, but we can accept the glimpses that are revealed to us. These glimpses are pure comfort, and motivation that we are on the right path.

Again, peace follows. This peace is not of the world, but it is a peace and gift from our Savior, Jesus. Seek it, live the gifts, and the love and peace you will experience from doing this will fill your heart and soul in ways that cannot be communicated with words on paper. You will know that Jesus and angels are smiling upon you and the beautiful efforts that you have made to live a life, reflecting Christ-like habits and gifts. It's very real. But it is also not tangible enough to put inside a box and gift wrap. It is a gift from the heart, and it multiplies while it is in your heart, if you tend to it often. There is no way to "contain" a gift from the heart, because real love in the heart, only multiplies over and over. We really don't want to even try and contain the love or the emotion or any of the gifts that we share with another. It would be better if we allowed the gift to find its own course and continue to ripple along and touch other hearts. It's a good thing that we can"t stop the flow of love and all the goodness it brings to others.

"In whom ye also trusted, after that ye heard the word of truth, the gospel of your salvation: in whom also after that ye believed, ye were sealed with that holy Spirit of promise."
~ Ephesians 1:13 ~

We know as you've read our stories, you have thought of many times in your own life where you were inspired or directed by the Holy Spirit.

Spend 15 minutes one morning this week meditating. Once you have completed your session, sit quietly and think about a powerful example, either in your own life or the life of a friend or family member, of a Connection to the Holy Spirit. Write about it in your journal.

Here is a sample affirmation to say each day, to reinforce the commitment of living each day mindfully, while appreciating the gift of Connection to the Holy Spirit:

AFFIRMATION: I will sit quietly at least once each day and contemplate the way the Holy Spirit has had influence and guidance over my life. I will seek for ways to bring the Holy Spirit into my life on a daily basis, and I will learn to listen to the promptings. I will be aware through my feelings and my thoughts, and will not close the Spirit out.

Applying the gift of
CONNECTION to the HOLY SPIRIT:

With much thought, we have placed 75 ideas below to help each of us to begin appreciating the gift of Connection to the Holy Spirit – ways we can each begin thinking about, feeling and acting on it.

Once you have gone through our list, add ideas of your own and create your own personal list, if you prefer. We noticed as we worked on these lists of ideas, things came to us that we, ourselves, realized we need to work on. It has been an inspiring experience and, hopefully, one that will be thought provoking for you as well.

So here is our list to get you started:

- Get on your knees and pray at least morning and night
- Meditate
- LISTEN
- Read from the scriptures daily
- Listen to spiritual music
- Talk to others about their experiences with the Holy Spirit
- Write in your journal when you feel promptings and how you handled them
- Share your experiences with your children
- Spend time in nature appreciating all God's creations
- Sit outside in a beautiful place and be still
- Do your best to love everyone
- Talk to Heavenly Father throughout your day
- When you feel you are being guided, go with it
- If you have an impression to do something – do it
- Keep in mind that we are all connected on this planet
- Pray for your enemies

- Trust your connection with Heavenly Father
- Watch for people who have connected to the Spirit on a deep level
- Read stories of spiritual experiences had by others
- Play music that lifts your soul
- Teach your children about God and Jesus Christ
- Search for peace – that's when everything tends to come together
- Work on your relationship with your Savior
- Remember, faith is what will connect you to the Holy Spirit
- Believe that God is in control of your life – there is no need to worry
- Make peace with your past so you can fully enjoy the present
- Make your home a place of peace where the Holy Spirit can dwell
- Trust that God has put you where you are for a reason
- Breathe deeply
- Live your life in a way that will allow you to have access to the Holy Spirit
- Be grateful always
- Talk about your blessings
- Live for the approval of God – don't worry about what others think of you
- Show concern for others
- Be humble
- Be kind to all you come in contact with
- Love and respect yourself
- Share your thoughts and impressions with those you love
- Work on getting a deep connection with God
- Have integrity
- Have a heart to heart with God whenever you feel the need

- Contemplate the purpose of your life
- Show compassion for those in need
- Pray for opportunities to help someone or influence someone
- Take the time to understand who you are
- Adopt an attitude of service toward others
- Put the names of those who need help on a prayer roll
- Sit outside and close your eyes when there's a breeze blowing
- Don't forget to LISTEN for the Holy Spirit
- And LISTEN after you pray
- Surround yourself with wonderful, spiritual people
- Do what it takes to learn to love yourself
- Live a life of truth
- Work to have a meaningful life
- Learn to listen on a deeper level to the spirit
- Be authentic
- Be silent and listen with your heart
- Look for quotes about connection
- Be watchful and you will find those who need your help
- Be mindful of the things going on around you
- Lay on the grass and watch the clouds
- Sit by a fire and let your mind think deep thoughts
- Think of the times in your life when the Holy Spirit guided you
- Do your best to have a positive influence on the lives of others
- Keep a gratitude journal
- Create connections with people who are important to you
- Decide what you need to change in your life – and then change it
- Be forgiving
- Become a more thoughtful person
- Take long walks

- Ponder the meaning of life
- Be hopeful
- Change one thing today that you've been wanting to change
- Encourage others and help them succeed
- Remember the Holy Spirit is given to everyone if they will just LISTEN

Now, choose a few items from this list that you would like to do right away. And DO THEM.

Be DELIBERATE about trying something new that will help you understand your own personal Connection to the Holy Spirit. Work to make it stronger, and work on mindfully listening.

Now take a break from reading for a day and sit somewhere quietly – preferably in nature – maybe in your own backyard. Complete the activity below by filling a couple of pages in your journal.

Think about a time when you felt inspired to do something.
- Maybe you wanted to write a book
- Maybe you felt you should change jobs
- Maybe you got excited about a new project
- Maybe you felt a need to do some service for someone

Write about what prompted you – how you went about it – how it turned out – how you were blessed.
- What positive things came from it?
- Describe the path you started out on and where you ended up.
- What did that inspiration ultimately lead you to?
- What changes resulted in your life?

The point of this exercise is to get you thinking about how to recognize that Connection to the Holy Spirit and act on it. The more you become familiar with it, the more it will bless your life.

When we begin to truly rely on our Connection to the Holy Spirit – when we start to see how safe we feel, and how lost we may have felt without it, there is no greater gift.

The stronger our Connection, the easier it is to become stronger in our practice of all the other eleven gifts in this book. The Spirit can truly guide and direct our lives. We have the great opportunity to chose what we will do in this life, but how comforting to know that we can rely on divine intervention when we seek it.

As Elizabeth and I have been writing this chapter, my thoughts have traveled back to my grandmother who passed away several years ago. She had been staying with my parents temporarily because she had not been feeling very well. She had a bronchitis-like cough, and was ill. I stopped by to say good-bye on my way out of town for a 2-day trip, and told Grandma to "get better and I'll see you in a couple of days." She said she would get better, and told me to have a nice trip. I left the house and went to get into my car and had the thought, "I didn't tell her I loved her." I thought about going back in, but I was in a hurry to leave, so I decided I would tell her the next time I saw her. I returned home to my grandma in the hospital. She was incoherent and didn't even know who I was. She passed away the following day.

I ignored the prompting, and I have not forgotten. I know my grandma knew I loved her, but I let an opportunity to tell her pass me by, and it turned out to be my LAST opportunity. I learned to never ignore a prompting – even one as simple as "tell someone you love them."

What are your thoughts and impressions now about the gift of the Connection to the Holy Spirit now that you have spent time contemplating and learning?

Has anything changed or come into your awareness that wasn't there before?
Jot down your thoughts now after 30 days of reflection:

_____

_____

_____

_____

_____

_____

_____

_____

_____

_____

_____

_____

_____

"He therefore that despiseth, despiseth not man, but
God, who hath also given unto us his holy Spirit. But as
touching brotherly love ye need not that I write unto you:
for ye yourselves are taught of God to love one another."
1 Thessalonians 4:8-9

CONCLUSION:

Our Connection to the Holy Spirit is a very special gift that can make all the difference in our lives. Practicing this gift will help us become closer to the Spirit, and help us learn to listen to the promptings that will guide and protect us throughout our lives. We hope this chapter has inspired you to want to have a daily Connection. And we would like you to get yourself prepared to experience the whisperings on a more intense level whenever you seek guidance.

If we stay close to the Spirit throughout our lives, we will have the privilege of feeling and hearing promptings even when we are not directly asking for them.

Our attitudes and our willingness to be in tune with our Savior play a big role in setting us up to form a deep Connection with the Holy Spirit. As we near the end of our lives, we hope we will all be able to look back and see how Divine intervention played a big role in helping us accomplish the things we were sent to this earth to do.

DAILY REFLECTION

(Repetition is what creates new habit. Read this page daily as a reminder.)

Each chapter is meant to be read slowly,
Absorbing the deeper essence behind the words and stories.

This allows for continual reflection,
Prayer and listening for answers,
Which opens the door to
Greater insight and awareness of
The Gift of Teacher.

If we devote one month of the year,
To learning and living the Gift of Teacher,
Our awareness of the precious Gift of Teacher,
Will be spiritually heightened,
And our daily existence will emulate this awareness.

As we make this shift to mindful attentiveness to the Gift of Teacher,
We will be less likely to take for granted,
The beauty, the power, and the mystique of Teacher.
We will have developed a habit,
Which becomes part of who we are.

As we develop a new habit each month,
Based on a different Gift each month,
A Gift that Jesus came to earth to give each one of us,
We will become more like Jesus in the way we live.
As this happens,
We will be living a more Christlike life, every day.
As we do this,
We are expressing our deepest gratitude to Jesus
And our Heavenly Father.

As we share the 12 Gifts with others,
We cannot help but bring the same love and peace
To our own hearts and spirits.

7

The *Gift* of
TEACHER

Jesus Christ was the ultimate Teacher. He spent His years on earth Teaching people how they ought to treat others. As we pondered the gifts we wanted to choose for this book, we decided on Teacher because of Jesus' Example, and also because learning to follow Christ's Example and be an inspiration to others is a big part of what we'd all like to be doing in this life.

Practicing the gift of Teacher is important because we have to constantly be on our toes in order to live so we can be an Example to those around us. And even though we may be that Example at certain times throughout our lives, we may, at times, fall short because of the trials we are having or the circumstances we find ourselves in.

The gift of being a Teacher or an Example is no different than any of the other gifts we have shared – it takes our constant attention if we want to become like our Savior, Jesus Christ.

Why did we choose TEACHER as the seventh gift?

"With men this is impossible, but
with God all things are possible."
~ Matthew 19:26 ~

"By him therefore let us offer the sacrifice
of praise to God continually, that is, the
fruit of our lips giving thanks to his name."
~ Hebrews 13:15 ~

Let's face it. Each and every one of is an Example of some kind. We don't have a choice. Just by living and being, we are influencing those around us. We can adopt an attitude of not caring what we do and how we affect others, OR we can make a decision that we want to enhance the lives of others.

We have a choice in the KIND of Example we will be.

As we think about the people who have had the most influence in our lives, for good or bad, we can say we have chosen to follow not so much what they say, but the way they live – the things they do.

Think about it for a minute. We tend to watch what others do. Words are meaningless unless a person is practicing what they preach. It is their Example we choose to follow.

This is why we tell our children to choose good friends. As parents, we all know how friends can lead our kids away from the things they know to be right. But friends can also keep our kids on track – doing the things that will help them grow up to be responsible adults and contributing members of society.

We personally know the heartbreak that comes from watching a child walk away from the things they have been taught to be true, simply because they decided, from watching others, that a different lifestyle would be more fun. And, as a result, others will be influenced by our children to do the same thing.

As we have researched this chapter, we have come to the conclusion that the only way we can hope for a child to come back to Jesus Christ, is to:

- Continue to be an influence for good,
- Never stop trying to be a good Teacher,
- Be a consistent Example,
- Love and respect their right to make choices,
- Pray.

I, Janeen, have a couple of friends in my life who are as solid as they come. Liz and Karen never waiver. They never consider backing away from their values. They are Examples of Jesus Christ, and I always turn to them in times of heartache, confusion, or just for advice.

They would never lead me astray, and they always have my best interest at heart. I trust them completely. And the reason for this is because they have chosen to live their lives in order to influence others for good.

They live close to the Savior, so I know the things they say to me are thoughtful and influenced by the Spirit.

Each of them have had a major impact on my life, and have helped me to become a better person. Just a side note – I met both of these friends when I was married to my second husband. I like to look at them as the silver lining that came out of a difficult marriage. It has taught me that regrets are a waste of time. Had

I not been married to my husband, I would not have met these two women. And they have become my closest, dearest friends.

"And saith unto him, All these things will I give
thee, if thou wilt fall down and worship me."
~ Matthew 4:9 ~

There have been times when all of us have been influenced to step away from our values and do things that were against the person we wanted to become. We all face this dilemma at certain points in our lives because we are here to learn and to grow. Making tough decisions is part of that learning process.

- Of course we are going to make mistakes;
- Of course we are going to choose the wrong path sometimes;
- Of course we are going to feel regret;
- Of course we are going to have to make things right;
- Of course we are going to have to get right back up and try again;
- And of course we are going to need to ask for forgiveness at times.

This is all part of learning to follow those who are good Examples for the kind of life we want to live. And following Jesus Christ and those who worship Him is, we believe, the very best thing we can do to become EXAMPLES ourselves.

"Then saith Jesus unto him, Get thee hence,
Satan: for it is written, Thou shalt worship the
Lord thy God, and him only shalt thou serve."
~ Matthew 4:10 ~

As we think about the gift of Teacher and Example, we might also contemplate closely-related words that help us embrace a deeper meaning of the gift of Teacher – of being an Example. These words could include: COACH, EDUCATOR, ADVISOR, MENTOR, DEVOTION, EXALTATION, ADORATION

I am sharing the following story because I believe examples of Teachers are all around us – those who do extraordinary things or simply lead lives of kindness, integrity, faith and inspiration. I was inspired by a dear friend of mine just last night. She was a true Example of great faith, hope and love.

"HEAVENLY FATHER HAS A PLAN"
By Janeen

It was Sunday, and I decided early in the evening that I would drive to my daughter's house about 30 minutes away to deliver a gift to my son-in-law who had a birthday the day before.

As I was driving, I received a phone call from my dad who informed me that Katie's daughter had been in a horrible car accident the day before and was fighting for her life in the hospital near where my daughter lives. My dad had been a close friend of the family for several years, and he was devastated at the thought that this precious girl had been so severely hurt. I told him I was on my way, and that I would pick him up so we could stop by the hospital and offer our love and support.

I picked my dad up and learned on the way to the hospital that Katie's beautiful daughter had been a passenger in a small car that was involved in a crash when they turned in front of an SUV going about 50 mph. Her daughter's side of the car was broadsided, and she was unconscious at the scene. She was facing several internal injuries.

As I entered the hospital room, Katie welcomed me with open arms. She was amazingly strong as she told me her daughter had suffered major brain trauma and was in a coma. She lay there in her hospital bed with her head now shaved, hooked up to life support. I couldn't help but notice that her eyelashes were amazingly long and beautiful, so I commented on them. Katie laughed as she told me she had just had them done the day before. She looked so peaceful and so beautiful lying there, helpless, in her hospital bed.

I was caught off guard by how stable Katie appeared, and I asked her how she was really doing. She replied, "I am good. I have always had faith, but I have decided to put my money where my mouth is and leave this in the Lord's hands. I feel like I have a blanket around me. I feel the Savior's love and comfort. I know Heavenly Father has a plan, and I am going to trust in that plan."

Katie then proceeded to say how grateful she was that my dad and I had taken the time to come by. She asked me about some of our mutual friends, and talked to me about some of the things I was doing. She shifted her concern from her precious daughter to her welcomed visitors. I was so amazed at her composure, and her ability to get outside of herself at a moment of intense trauma to make her friends feel at ease. I remember thinking to myself, "Wow, she is so calm. She has trust in her Savior." She was so pulled together and so full of faith.

Katie's Example of faith and trust was one of the most amazing things I have ever witnessed. She is a true Example of living what she believes in.

"The same came to Jesus by night, and said unto him, Rabbi, we know that thou art a teacher come from God: for no man can do these miracles that thou doest, except God be with him."
~ John 3:2 ~

"My doctrine is not mine, but his that sent me."
~ John 7:16 ~

Take a good look at the following questions and think about them before answering. We want you to start thinking about the concept of Teacher or Examples of people in your life who have influenced you to be a better person. See what you can come up with:

Think of a person you recently noticed who made you want to be like them because of the way they treated someone. Write about it.

_____

_____

_____

_____

_____

Think about a time you reacted to something and then regretted things you said. What would you do different next time?

_____

_____

_____

_____

How would you like to be treated be others?

_____

_____

_____

_____

Think of a person who has been your greatest influence. Why?

_____

_____

_____

_____

_____

Have you ever had someone tell you that you are a great Example? Ask yourself why or why not.

_____

_____

_____

_____

_____

What one thing could you change in your life to make yourself a greater Example to those around you?

_____

_____

_____

_____

_____

_____

_____

_____

_____

_____

We bundled a few descriptions together in this chapter as we chose Teacher - Praise and Worship as one of the 12 GIFTS. Jesus was the ultimate Teacher. As we read the Bible, we see that He used parables and symbolism so those who really wanted to learn could understand and relate His stories to their own lives.

But as Elizabeth and I discussed what this chapter is actually about, we agreed that Example is where we are really focused.

The greatest tool we have for teaching others is our Example. The way our children learn from us is by watching our Example.

Jesus didn't walk around telling people how to live and then go do what He wanted. He practiced what He preached. He followed His own teachings and was an Example to all who knew and followed Him.

Because he is our Teacher and our Example, we express love, thanks and respect to our Savior, Jesus Christ. We Praise Him. We Worship Him through prayer because He has taught us how we must live in order to return to our Father in Heaven.

Jesus Christ is our Teacher.

If we want to be more like our Savior, we need to live what we believe. We can't expect others – especially our own children – to do what we tell them to do if we aren't willing to do it ourselves.

"What we are speaks so loudly that our
children may not hear what we say"
~ Quentin L. Cook ~

Make it your GOAL this month as you ponder the gift of Teacher - Praise and Worship to find one area in your life where you can be a better Example to those who look up to you.

What are your thoughts and impressions about the gift of Teacher (Example) - Praise and Worship?

As you begin reading this chapter, write down a few thoughts you have as you contemplate the gift of Teacher (Example) - Praise and Worship. We will ask this question again at the end of the chapter after you have completed your study of the gift of Teacher.

_____

_____

_____

_____

_____

_____

_____

_____

_____

_____

_____

_____

_____

_____

_____

What did Jesus say about Teacher (Example) - Praise and Worship?

*"Ye call me Master and Lord: and ye say well; for so I am.
If I then, your Lord and Master, have washed your feet;
ye also ought to wash one another's feet. For I have given
you an example, that ye should do as I have done to you.
Verily, verily, I say unto you, the servant is not greater than
his lord; neither he that is sent greater than he that sent
him. If ye know these things, happy are ye if ye do them.*
~ John 13:13-17 ~

All of us learn to do things – good and bad – by watching others. We watch the Examples of our parents, siblings, friends, schoolmates, teachers and others who come into and out of our life.

Friends are almost more important in a teenager's life than family members. That's why we as parents are involved with and want to know who our children are hanging around with. The influences are far reaching, and it puts a lot of pressure on each of us to live a Christ-like life so that others, including our own children, will benefit from watching our Example.

Jesus wants us to choose the right path, and do the right thing. He doesn't want us to follow the crowd. He expects us to stand up for what we believe to be right and true. It isn't always easy.

We are impressed by young people who stick together in defending what is right. When groups of teens stand together and honor their Savior, make good choices and live clean, honorable lives, they are sending the message that it's cool to love Jesus Christ. They focus on helping others, respecting their peers and setting an Example for others to follow.

There are many kids in our world today who are defending what is right. We sincerely want to thank them and openly support their efforts.

**Sometimes we have to
take a stand simply because
it's the right thing to do.**

**Children need to know that
regardless of what everyone
else is doing, if God is not
honored, we won't be
participating. Period.**

Stories to help us reflect on the Gift of Teacher - Praise and Worship:

The stories we have chosen for this chapter will, we hope, help you be inspired to think of people in your own life who have brought you to a higher level and helped influence you to do good in your life.

Write stories of the people who mean the most to you in your journal so you can always remember what they did that had a significant impact on you. Strive to be like them.

Hearing and relating the stories of others is one way to learn great lessons and, as we learned in the chapter about life, find truth for ourselves.

SHOWING UP ON TIME
by Janeen

A close friend of mine pointed out to me the other day that she appreciates so much that I am always on time (translation = early) and so responsible.

She is not the first person to point this out to me. Others have been appreciative and commented that it shows my respect for others. It feels good to have others notice such a quality, but it feels even better when someone tells me they were inspired to follow my Example and began arriving to their obligations, not only in a timely manner, but early.

My friend has started arriving 30 minutes early to classes in order to get set up, decompress, relax and be ready for the rush when it begins. She told me it has changed her life, and she feels so much more organized, less stressed, and respectful of others. She has worked hard to change her behavior in this regard, and I truly have respect for any person who can make a change like that. It isn't easy.

In contrast, I know a person who is late to everything. It doesn't matter if it is a casual lunch or an important meeting – she is late. I can always count on it. I have had several people comment to me that they have no respect for a person who doesn't care enough about other people's busy schedules that they cannot and will not show up on time. I was sitting in a restaurant recently with a client, waiting for this person to arrive. She showed up 15 minutes late, and by the time she ordered her salad and walked over to our table, it was 30. It's frustrating and difficult to work around someone who is always late.

Being late is something that spills over into all areas of a person's life. And it is something that affects the way people look at the person who is always running late. They can begin to stop trusting, respecting and believing a person who only cares about her own world and her own self.

That might sound like a drastic reaction, but I know we have all experienced this in some form or another and, you have to admit, it is hard to take.

This is just one very small area where I feel I have had a positive impact and been an Example to others. Inspiring others to change their habits makes me want to work harder in other areas of my life in order to be a better person.

We have talked about habits in this book and how important they are. It isn't easy to change our habits, but it is possible. A true desire to change is required first. And then, if we can work hard at something good, it can replace the bad habit we are wanting to set aside.

TEACHING FOR A PURPOSE When We Notice an Unmet Need in Society, And We Happen to Have the Expertise, Along With Some Solutions to Improve the Situation, and the Lives of Others, We Could Wait Around and Ask for Permission, Or, We Can Go Forward with Prayer, Faith and Hope, And Expect that Solutions Will Find a Way.
~ By Elizabeth ~

Over twenty five years ago, I was working for a state agency in a position where I conducted child custody evaluations for the courts. These were cases where parents who were going through a divorce, were both seeking custody of their children. The court would appoint a professional person with special training in this area to do a thorough assessment of the family situation, and make a recommendation to the court regarding which parent should have custody. Clearly, these were sad situations, and there was plenty of pain to go around.

After a few years of interacting with these parents and children, I began to see patterns of common behaviors and emotions. I recognized that many family members had not healed from the emotional pain and disruption of divorce. As a result of the lack of healing, there were many emotions filled with anger, resentment, feelings of revenge, and other unhealthy emotions. It was evident that these negative emotions were creating an environment of stress and conflict. Children of divorce absorb the stress of this.

Since I saw these patterns of emotions over and over, I could just keep going along doing my job, which paid very well as custody disputes are not cheap, or I could put my energy into trying to solve this problem. My conscience and creative mind would not allow me to sit idle, but neither would the Holy Spirit. I kept feeling a prompting to start a class for parents who were going through a divorce. I realized that I should teach about how parental conflict affects children. I noticed that many parents, involved in a child custody dispute, did not fully understand how their disputes were affecting their children. So along with a colleague, we put together a wonderful two-hour class about divorce and children. We advertised all over the city, and even in the court house, with court approval. But attendance was low, and most of the parents who attended the class were already trying to do the best things for their kids. The parents who were still angry and bitter did not realize that they could benefit from the class. The class was free and offered at night and on Saturdays.

Finally, one of the miracles happened. A state senator attended one of our classes and, after class, she invited us to come up to the state capitol the next week and share information about our class to a new committee which she co-chaired. It was the Legislative Task Force on Child Custody and Visitation.
We attended the meeting and there was overwhelming support for our class. One committee member suggested they make our class mandatory for parents who are going through a divorce, and another committee member slowed things down a bit. He

suggested that they make it a pilot program for eighteen months, and then decide about making it a mandatory law. They all agreed.

It was a huge success as a pilot program, and some of the courts across the state asked if they could implement the class prior to the end of the pilot program. The class became a state law. Our state was the first in the country to enact the law and many other states followed. Listening to promptings can help solve problems for many others. We just have to pay attention. I am grateful for the miracles which helped to put thousands of similar classes in place across our country. It all began from listening and following through. Promptings are our way of following through with what heaven wants us to do.

And the law was nationally recognized as the "Significant Legislation of the Year" when it was passed. We knew the classes were helping because 96% of the parents reported this on the evaluations. But the icing on the cake was to get a little validation with the national award. The classes have continued, and they have been helping many thousands of parents.

"Listen When You are Being Prompted"

Here's a tip that I've learned in life: When the Holy Spirit, through Jesus, gives you a prompting to do something, don't try and ignore it with logic. The prompting will just continue. And if you decide not to listen, for whatever reason, the Holy Spirit will take the amazing idea to someone else, and you might feel a sad ache in your heart for not following through. On the other hand, if the Holy Spirit is counting on you to follow through with an idea or project, forget the logic about why it's not possible. We know Jesus has the power to make miracles happen, and all the doors that you previously thought would be shut in order to make your idea happen will start to swing open. This doesn't mean you don't have to follow through with the day to day meetings and many steps, but Jesus will make it easier. You will feel it and you will know it, and it will make you smile and feel such great peace in your soul.

I am sharing this story and the insights I've learned as a professional person working with couples, individuals, and family members, when a divorce has taken place in a family. As a master's level social worker, mediator, educator, former child custody evaluator for the courts, and a co-author of a successful healing book on divorce, I have learned a great deal about families and divorce over the decades.

Just for the record, and before I get into the topic of relationships, marriage and families, I want to acknowledge that I am not encouraging divorce in any way. As a professional who educates parents who are going through a divorce, I see and feel the pain frequently. No professional person would casually encourage divorce after they have felt and witnessed the pain of family members who are going through it. But once a decision to divorce is made, many efforts should go in the direction of healing so that all family members can proceed, with time, and they can find peace, acceptance and hope again.
Whenever a marriage can be strengthened, during or after difficult times, I applaud the efforts of individuals who work hard to make this happen. Working through hard times is not easy, but it is worth it, especially when it can restore and improve relationships. Divorce should never be taken lightly.

Having said this, when divorce happens, it is not a situation where on-lookers should peek into a few situations and make judgements. It is always complicated, and most people do not reveal the details so it's hard to truly understand. Some situations have more obvious reasons to divorce, especially when there are issues of domestic violence, child abuse, substance abuse and other problems that create risk factors. These situations need professional help. Safety is the most important concern when there are high risk factors. Changing the status of a family deserves and requires considerable thought and contemplation. It is a major life decision and, many times, there are regrets. Seeking professional help when a serious life change is about to be made is always wise.

I must acknowledge and make a statement that as I work in the professional arena of divorce, and work with the court system, I keep my personal views and beliefs very private. As I teach classes to parents, I stick to the research, statistics and practical methods for helping all family members to heal and adjust to a divorce between parents. However, since this book is about the gifts of Jesus, it allows me to go beyond the professional boundaries and share some personal beliefs and promote spiritual concepts that could assist in the very necessary healing process.

When healing does not happen for family members, both children and parents, it can cause individuals to retreat emotionally and become depressed. Other times, the repressed pain can turn to anger, resentment, conflict and jealousy. Unresolved pain and sadness will usually play out in how we behave and conduct ourselves. It is very important for all family members to have an environment which allows for the healing and grieving process to occur.

There are many healing methods available to heal from the disruption of divorce and the many emotions it brings forth. It is not an easy task, but a very important thing to do. Without healing, emotions fester and will interfere with decisions about life, hope, future relationships and more. Healing the heart is one of the most important things each family member can do as they navigate through the course of divorce. Healing holds the power to open doors for hope, peace, joy, forgiveness, lessons learned, compassion, and love. Without healing, it is difficult to achieve the above gifts on a deeper level.

Support, Education, Reassurance and Hope are Needed, During a Life Changing Event

I am a mother, a former spouse, and a professional who has worked in the area of divorce for many years. I can state all of this, but when it comes right down to it, when you are the person going through the pain and sorrow of divorce, there are no credentials in the world that can help make it easier. It is very hard. This is one of those situations where a person might read this and think, "Oh, that is so sad that she went through divorce, with a child and a large extended family. How upsetting!"

I can fully appreciate these thoughts, and there have been many times when I had the very same feelings. No one enters into a marriage expecting that they will later get divorced, especially after starting a family, so there is always disappointment, regardless of the reasons why. Divorce is NOT expected or hoped for, and it is one of the greatest life challenges that a parent can experience.

However, when the national divorce rate continues to hover around fifty percent for all marriages, this is a topic that needs to be addressed and talked about. If a couple you know is considering divorce, listen and offer support. If it appears that it might be an impulsive decision, it would be helpful to encourage a time out, professional counseling and other resources.

Once a decision is made, one person has filed, and it appears like all options have been tried, showing love for a loved one and sharing comfort, reassurance and hope are always helpful strategies. Steering a person away from anger and revenge towards the other person is sometimes necessary.

However, there are stories of hope where individuals decide to work hard to heal, and they restore trust and hope again. There is no formula for how to go about this. And yes, miracles can happen, and love can be restored. None of us truly know what is best for a person until that individual person makes an honest and sincere connection with what is going on, and then prays frequently for insight and guidance. Jesus will answer. The Holy Spirit will reveal direction and truth for each person. And Heavenly Father will always be loving you unconditionally from above. What beautiful gifts to be able to receive and embrace when a person is going through one of their most painful adult life experiences.

"How Can I Get Through This Dark Time in my Life?"

When a parent who is struggling, during a painful stretch of time, would ask me, "What should I do?" I would provide a series of options, choices, and considerations. I knew that ultimately each person needed to choose how they would cope and move through their decision making process. I remained professional in my response to those types of questions.

However, if I was not working as a professional, when I was talking to a friend, or relative about the same type of things, I would always end by saying that prayer will help you tremendously. When I went through my divorce, it was prayer and love that ultimately helped me to heal. I felt the love from friends and family, and I strongly felt the love of Jesus. The power of that love can and will heal hearts from all types of life disappointments. It doesn't happen overnight, and it is a process, but it is a powerful process. And it comes from Jesus. Therapy is always helpful. But the love of Jesus is something difficult to put into words. If you seek His love, Jesus will show it to you.

I share this story because I went through it. As I felt the love from Jesus, it opened the doors of my heart so that I could heal the pain. It can be the bridge from your pain, as you cross over to hope, love and forgiveness. If I had discovered a short cut through the healing process, I would have shared it by now. But the way to heal the pain is to allow yourself to feel it, so you can heal it. And then to ask Jesus to be with you as you go through it. This is the best short cut that I know of. If you know anyone, adult or child, who is struggling with the painful emotions of a divorce, please consider sharing some of these insights with them.

Supporting Loved Ones Going Through a Family Change, Such as Divorce

Offering reflections and thoughts for healing, listening with love and brainstorming solutions are ways that a loving person can support loved ones through a difficult time.

Parents who are able to heal from the sadness of divorce are much healthier parents, and they are more emotionally available to meet the needs of their children. Healing is truly such an important part of getting through a significant family change. Parents, please focus your efforts on healing, and you cannot go wrong.

Jesus will always be there to assist to you as you pray with your full heart for peace, guidance and hope. Our personal job is to be patient and trust. It's not easy to listen for answers to our prayers in our hurry up society. We have become accustomed to having things answered for us quickly. Jesus wants us to exercise our faith, patience and hope, and listen for guidance. The Holy Spirit will reveal the path and direction. Most of tend to want things to happen quickly.

With more life experience, I realize there are gray areas in life (besides the roots in my hair line) that do not fit neatly into the box of "black and white." Some people think that "one size fits all," and if we could just provide a list of things to do for a successful marriage, then marital problems could be solved. Yes, education is always beneficial, and there should be much more emphasis upon educating couples prior to the wedding.

Yet, over generalized scenarios and simplifications about statistical data do not explain the sensitive aspects of an intimate relationship. It is a process of evolving together as a couple, understanding how complicated it can be, and being willing to seek help when needed. Relationships are wonderful, fulfilling, beautiful, and challenging. Having lived this story, in addition to twenty five years of professional time in this field, I know that marriage is not easy. Neither is divorce. Much more attention in our society should be focused on educating our youth, teens, young adults and adults about the reality of the delicate balance of relationships. However, RELATIONSHIP AWARENESS is a huge and worthy topic that we plan to fully explore and write about in the future.

My Personal Story of Marriage, Love and Family

I married my former husband in my early twenties, and we were both full of hope for the future. We felt so blessed to receive the beautiful gift of our daughter, who is now a happily married mother of two young children. We stayed married for about ten years, and then divorced. There have been so many lessons learned from our relationship, and our beautiful daughter was a gift from our union. So it is not possible to ever say that a marriage was a mistake. It was not. The children who are born into a family, or adopted in, are NEVER a mistake. They need to hear this message loud and clear. They are a precious and amazing gift to their parents.

They are children from our Heavenly Father, entrusted to their earthly parents to be cherished. Each child has their own life and destiny on earth in accordance with their divine plan. As parents, whether married or divorced, we are responsible to honor the gift of raising a life with love and hope for the future. This is a gift and a privilege. The following is a poem I wrote many years ago after praying about the sadness of my divorce. I know the words were inspired, and I was moved and changed by the message.

Separate But Connected, Forever

My private spaces blended with yours
We shared beds
Tables, Destinations
In one spirit, on one path,
Till words created distance
Now we walk on different paths
Yet we share the same legacy
A Child, a Life, a Soul, a Breath
Depending on our support
A Life hoping for,
A family, parents, unlimited Love, unlimited acceptance
A Life that knows
There are no sides,
That Love is not finite, and the world is kind
How will we open our arms
Our hearts, our spirits,
To our children?
We are the Teachers...
What will we Teach?

The above poem was included in a previous book published in
1994, titled, **Healing Hearts: Helping Adults and Children
Recover From Divorce,** which was written from my professional
perspective, but mostly as a parent going though divorce. I
recognized how many conflicts between parents had an impact upon
the children. I dedicated many years of my professional career to
advancing discussions about how to approach divorce from a multi-
disciplinary viewpoint. I knew that healing efforts were critical for
parents and children. I was successful in getting laws implemented
which focused on assisting parents, in the divorce process, with
healing strategies for themselves and also for their children. As a
national leader in this field, I was very humbled and appreciative to
be on the front lines of advocating for changes.

Here is one of the points for sharing the above story. In my profession as a child custody evaluator for the courts, I was obligated to find a sensitive way to interview the children who were in the middle of their parent's custody dispute. I could feel their pain and conflict, and I searched my heart for creative ways to ask questions that would not cause the children to feel like they were in the middle. The children in these cases were my greatest Teachers, and I thank them for sharing their truths with me. These children provided insight about the common experiences that many kids of divorce deal with. Their stories taught me lessons that I have been able to use to educate other professionals and parents for decades. Honesty is a gift. It provides insight into common human challenges that many of us face. Honesty connects us because we then realize we are not the only ones struggling with the same pain. We realize we are not alone. This is another gift, feeling connected to others.

With connection and honesty, we also realize that even if we feel alone on earth, we are not. Jesus is always there for each and every one of us. When I teach public classes, I focus on topics that are clearly accepted and recognized by therapists. I do not infuse any spiritual content simply because there is a clear line between separation of church and state. It is truly a personal choice for how an individual decides to heal from the pain of a loss in their life. There are many methods for healing. But the most important thing is that a person who has felt the pain of loss, through divorce or some other major life situation, will decide upon a healing plan. It will be life changing. I know it. I have seen it. I've experienced it.

You are never alone. There are always ways to connect through prayer and listen for guidance. Jesus will be there for you when you seek Him. Be still and listen for answers. Remember, the relationships classrooms on earth are some of the most advanced classes because they teach us some of the hardest lessons in life.

Loving and forgiving those who have hurt is a very big challenge. But it is part of our healing process. Take time, contemplate and seek peace. Healing your heart will lead you back to peace. Of course, peace leads to hope again. And joy will follow. But you can't get to true peace and joy until you heal the pain.

As you read the stories of others, it is impossible not to think about Examples in your own life – the people who have really made a difference and influenced you to do better or to strive for something greater.

Take a moment to think of one such person. Write a note or a letter to them, thanking them for making a difference in your life. Get personal with it, and be specific about the way they have touched your life. Then mail it or hand deliver it. Challenge them to do the same – to think of a person they could show gratitude for and send them a note of appreciation as well.

---

*The world is changed by your **example** not by your opinion*
~ Paulo Coelho ~

Here is a sample affirmation to say each day, to reinforce the commitment to living each day mindfully, while appreciating the gift of Teacher (Example).

AFFIRMATION: I will be the Example that others look up to. I will do what is right at all times, not what is popular. I will remember that others will do as I do, not as I say and that standing up for what I believe to be right and true is always the best choice.

"But the hour cometh, and now is, when the true worshippers shall worship the Father in spirit and in truth: for the Father seeketh such to worship him."
~ John 4:23 ~

**Applying the gift of TEACHER (Example)
PRAISE AND WORSHIP:**

It's so enlightening to sit down and think through ideas to put on these lists. We've started our list for you with 75 ideas to help jumpstart your progress toward appreciating the gift of Teacher (Example) - Praise and Worship so you can begin thinking about, feeling and acting on it.

- Think of one person who inspires you and why
- Share your testimony of Jesus Christ
- Speak to people in a way that makes them feel worthwhile
- Teach your children about Jesus Christ
- Get in the habit of serving others
- Learn something new each day that you can share
- Study the scriptures
- Show compassion to those less fortunate
- Watch your actions at all times
- Ask yourself, "what would the Savior do in this situation?"
- Be honest in everything you do

- Be the kind of person others respect
- Express your thanks to Heavenly Father on a daily basis
- Live your life as an example to those who come in contact with you
- Show respect to every person you come across
- Attend church services
- Pray with others for a cause
- Help people who are in need
- Write down positive things about others in your journal
- Always speak the truth
- Be an inspiration to others
- Boost the confidence of young people around you
- Involve your kids in acts of service
- Let your husband or wife teach you something
- Strive to be more like Jesus every single day
- Be forgiving
- Help others feel better when they are hurting
- Get outside yourself and always try to make others comfortable
- Watch the things you say – speak with a kind voice
- Smile often
- Show others that you are happy
- Work hard
- Always give others the benefit of the doubt
- Help someone who is overwhelmed – do some small thing for them
- Always show up on time
- Let others know how important they are to you
- Tell your spouse you appreciate them every day
- Think about teachers in your life who had a huge impact – and why
- Be the kind of person others want to emulate
- Be helpful
- Be understanding
- Be conscious of the needs of your family
- Sing or dance while you clean your house

- Stay positive
- Laugh with someone at least once a day
- Ask your neighbor how you can help them
- Watch your language
- Adopt a healthy lifestyle
- Be the first to volunteer
- Start a service project and get the neighborhood involved
- Help others find purpose in their life
- Be a leader
- Be productive each and every day
- Learn to persuade people in a positive way
- Read about great things people in the world are doing
- Watch movies about inspiring people
- Take a trip with family or friends to the Holy Land
- Meditate and listen to the Spirit every morning
- Start a nonprofit
- Share your experiences in order to help others who are trying to cope
- Write a blog of inspirational stories
- Listen to others when they are talking
- Don't be judgmental
- Make your kids feel important
- Decide on something about yourself you want to improve – and work on it
- Let the people you love be who they are – inspire them with your actions
- Be a motivator
- Try to put yourself in someone else's shoes
- Don't raise your voice
- Always be excited to meet someone new
- Ask people about themselves and what's important to them
- Stay up on current events
- Be the first to congratulate someone on a good job
- Let others have the spotlight
- Say thank you and be polite to everyone

Choose a couple of things from the list above that you can do right away. And DO THEM. We want you to work on getting outside of your comfort zone and doing things you've never done before. This is a powerful way to grow in areas where we may be weak.

Take a break from your reading now for a day or so and complete the following activity. Fill a couple of pages in your journal.

Think for awhile about the people in your life that you could call Examples.

- Come up with family members,
- Think about friends who have stuck with you through thick and thin,
- Consider teachers, neighbors, co-workers,
- Look back on leaders in your church, your community.

Take the time to write a paragraph about each person you come up with.

- What did each person do that had an impact on you?
- In what ways did you change the way you were doing things because of them?
- How were you inspired to be a greater Example?
- What long-lasting affects did each person have on your life?
- Consider a way that you can show gratitude and appreciation at this time to each.

The purpose of this activity is to get you thinking about more ways to be an Example in your own life. Get yourself in tune with what it takes to change people's lives or, at least, have a significant impact on them.

Imagine being the person who could have some influence in changing the life of another human being. We never know who is watching us. That is great motivation for always doing our best to live as Jesus Christ did. People may be looking to us to see how we act, how we treat others, how we speak, what we do when we're under stress, what we do when we others are unkind to us. Be the person who takes the high road. Be the strong one under all circumstances, no matter what. You will have greater respect for yourself, and others will look up to you.

I love the following poem. My co-author, Elizabeth wrote it and published it in her book, "Healing Hearts." It blends so many of the gifts we speak of in this book, but ultimately, we decided to put it in this chapter about Teacher and Example. You will see why when you have finished reading it.

My private spaces blended with yours
    We shared beds
        Tables
        Destinations
    In one spirit, on one path
    'Till words created distance

Now we walk on different paths
Yet we share the same legacy
    A child
    A life
    A soul
    A breath
Depending on our support
A life hoping for
    A family
    A father
    A mother
    Unlimited love
    Unlimited acceptance

A life that knows
    There are no sides
    And love is not finite
    And the world can be kind

How will we open our arms
    Our hearts
    Our spirits
    To our children?

We are the teachers...
    What will we teach?

Some things to think about doing that could create change in someone's life:

- Love them unconditionally;
- Listen with your heart when they confide in you;
- Don't judge them – you don't know what they've been through;
- Have compassion;
- Try to put yourself in their shoes;
- Open your mind and get outside your own opinions.

We are all teachers in this life – even when we are completely unaware of it.

- We teach our children,
- We teach our family members,
- We teach our friends and neighbors,
- We teach our colleagues,
- We teach people who don't even know us,
  just simply by the things we do and say each day.

Now that you have studied the gift of Teacher for the past month, try and make it a point to be more conscious of your actions and your words. Remember, you are an Example to people who are watching you for good or for bad.

But don't be too hard on yourself. Sometimes, we all let our guard down and do things that we didn't mean to do. Like when we're stressed out in the grocery store line or irritated at the driver behind us, or upset with our child.

With that in mind, we know we need to make a point to cut people some slack. We all have a bad day now and then, and we need to remember to be kind to those who may appear to be a bad Example at the moment. In reality, most of us try to be the GOOD EXAMPLE most of the time.

What are your thoughts and impressions now about the gift of TEACHER (Example) - PRAISE AND WORSHIP?

Has anything resonated with you or come into your awareness that wasn't there before?

Jot down your thoughts now after 30 days of reflection:

_____

_____

_____

_____

_____

_____

_____

_____

_____

_____

_____

_____

_____

_____

"And when he was come nigh, even now at the descent
of the mount of Olives, the whole multitude of the
disciples began to rejoice and praise God with a loud
voice for all the mighty works that they had seen."
~ Luke 19:37 ~

"By him therefore let us offer the sacrifice
of praise to God continually, that is, the
fruit of our lips giving thanks to his name."
~ Hebrews 13:15 ~

As we emulate His perfect example Our hands can
become His hands Our eyes His eyes, Our heart his heart
~ Deiter Uchtdorf ~

CONCLUSION:

Being an Example that others will ultimately follow is really what we ought to strive for in this life. When we look back on our lives, the things we did that influenced others for good will bring us joy. If we can have one tiny bit of satisfaction in knowing we made a difference, our lives will be well lived.

At the same time, look to others who live the Example that YOU want to follow. Look for those individuals who you want to emulate, and ask yourself what it is they do that you admire, respect and know to be right.

If we can engage ourselves in a life that serves an important purpose – showing others how to live a Christ-like life through our Example – we will make life better for ourselves AND for others. When we reach the end of our lives and can say, "I truly made a difference – even if it was just in one person's life," we will be content.

DAILY REFLECTION

Each chapter is meant to be read slowly,
Absorbing the deeper essence behind the words and stories.

This allows for continual reflection,
Prayer and listening for answers,
Which opens the door to
Greater insight and awareness of
The Gift of Humility.

If we devote one month of the year,
To learning and living the Gift of Humility,
Our awareness of the precious Gift of Humility,
Will be spiritually heightened,
And our daily existence will emulate this awareness.

As we make this shift to mindful attentiveness to the Gift of Humility,
We will be less likely to take for granted,
The beauty, the power, and the mystique of Humility.
We will have developed a habit,
Which becomes part of who we are.

As we develop a new habit each month,
Based on a different Gift each month,
A Gift that Jesus came to earth to give each one of us,
We will become more like Jesus in the way we live.
As this happens,
We will be living a more Christlike life, every day.
As we do this,
We are expressing our deepest gratitude to Jesus
And our Heavenly Father.

As we share the 12 Gifts with others,
We cannot help but bring the same love and peace
To our own hearts and spirits.

8

The *Gift* of
HUMILITY

One of the most precious of all the gifts we've been blessed with is Humility. When we are born, we are innocent and Humble – precious children who recently left home where we dwelled with our Father in Heaven. We see things differently, we love everyone, and we are happy.

As life happens, some of our innocence and Humility might become less noticeable. We may have to work a little harder to let our Humility come to the forefront. Our Heavenly Father wants us to be as little children – that means setting aside our arrogance, our anger, our attitude, our bitterness, our judgements, and anything else that drags us down. He wants us to love everyone, and He wants us to get outside of ourselves and help those around us who are in need.

Humility is a gift that we must practice on a regular basis. And part of practicing is being aware of our attitudes so we can change them. Keep in mind as you read this chapter that our constant effort is required throughout our lives if we want to become more like Jesus Christ.

Why did we choose HUMILITY as the eighth gift?

"Take my yoke upon you, and learn of me; for I am meek and lowly in heart: and ye shall find rest unto your souls."
~ Matthew 11:29 ~

"But with righteousness shall he judge the poor, and reprove with equity for the meek of the earth: and he shall smite the earth with the rod of his mouth, and with the breath of his lips shall he slay the wicked."
~ Isaiah 11:4 ~

We chose Humility because there is so much we can accomplish when we work at all the necessary changes we need to make within ourselves in order to be Humble.

Jesus Christ was the ultimate example of Humility as he hung on the cross, waiting for His body to die, in order to fulfill the atonement. His purpose was about to be fulfilled, and He never wavered in His responsibility to accomplish it – no matter how much He suffered. He loved us all that much. His words speak volumes of His control, His faith, His ability to forgive, and His Humility.

Jesus spoke the following seven statements
as he hung on the cross:

"Father, forgive them; for they know not what they do."
Luke 23:34

To the repentant thief:
"Verily I say unto thee, Today shalt thou be with me in paradise."
Luke 23:43

To his mother, Mary:
"Woman, behold thy son!"

To John:
"Behold thy mother!"
John 19:26-27

"My God, my God, why hast thou forsaken me?"
Matthew 27:46; Mark 15:34

"I thirst."
John 19:28

"It is finished."
John 19:30

"Father, into thy hands I commend my spirit."
Luke 23:46

What a pure and wonderful example for each and every one of us. Jesus could have called in legions of angels to rescue Him from His pain and suffering. But He did not. He stayed the course and died that we might live – that we might be resurrected and have everlasting life – that we would have the possibility of eternal life with God and Jesus Christ if we are willing to repent of our sins and have faith in our Savior.

*"He hath shewed thee, O man, what is good; and what
doth the Lord require of thee, but to do justly, and
to love mercy, and to walk humbly with they God?"*
~ Micah 6:8 ~

*"Serving the Lord with all humility of mind,
and with many tears, and temptations, which
befell me by the lying in wait of the Jews:"*
~ Acts 20:19 ~

Think of all the things we could influence if we accept Humility as something we want in our own life:

- Our relationships would be stronger and more special;
- We would be able to communicate with others on a more respectful level;
- We could be loved more deeply by those who mean the world to us;
- Others would look up to us and value our opinions;
- We would have an easier time fulfilling our responsibilities;
- We could truly make a difference in the lives of others.

When we think about Humility, we might also contemplate closely-related words that help us embrace a deeper meaning of Humility. Some of these words could include:

MEEKNESS, OBEDIENCE, LACK OF PRIDE, LOWLINESS

I am sharing the following story because I am deeply moved by people who experience a lot of heartache and can bounce back with healed hearts to move forward and look constantly for a better life. It takes being truly repentant and letting the Lord know we understand we cannot do it alone.

"CHOOSE HUMILITY OVER BITTERNESS"
by Janeen

I have a close friend who has lived a life filled with tragedy and disappointment. When she was very young, she lost one of her siblings to a devastating disease. As a teenager, she lost her mom to cancer. Other deaths within the family added to the toll and caused my friend much grief.

Tina also suffered two divorces – one because of infidelity on her husband's part, and the other because of a very difficult set of circumstances that led her to stray during her marriage many times. She is not proud of that fact, but she has worked hard to make things right.

Tina has accepted her life and continues now to look for a better way. She owns the part she played in the breakdown of her marriages, and takes full responsibility. She is sorry. Her spirit is contrite and her attitude is Humble. She has done all she can to keep her relationships positive and make amends where possible.

We all do the best we can with what we are given. It is easy to make mistakes when we are hurting or suffering emotionally. It is important that we cut each other some slack in this life, because none of us is perfect.

The losses we suffer in this life can lead us to either bitterness or Humility. Many of us are so stubborn, we will endure years of heartache before we finally get on our knees and Humble ourselves before the Lord. He will come our way one hundred percent if we will just go to Him and ask for His forgiveness and promise to do better. An amazing burst of energy and a desire to live a better life will come to us through His love. Heavenly Father doesn't expect any of us to live a perfect life. He only expects us to do our very best. He will meet us the rest of the way if we are truly Humble.

Humility is not something that comes easy. It is something we must learn through experience. The trials we have in life serve the purpose of making us Humble, and I believe if we can keep that constantly on our mind and in our hearts, we will come to be grateful for the things that happen to us in this life. It is through these trials and hardships that we become stronger, more faithful, more compassionate, loving human beings.

Work for a cause, NOT for applause.
Live life to express, NOT to impress.
Don't strive to make your presence noticed,
Just make your absence felt.
~ Unknown ~

"Whosoever therefore shall humble himself as this little
child, the same is greatest in the kingdom of heaven."
~ Matthew 18:4 ~

"And whosoever shall exalt himself shall be abased;
and he that shall humble himself shall be exalted."
~ Matthew 23:12 ~

Let's begin thinking about Humility and what it means to truly be Humble. Review the questions below, and start to really think about the word, Humility.

Write your thoughts in your journal:

Think about the last incident you had that required you to show Humility. Were you able to do it, or did your ego get in the way? Write about it.

_____

_____

_____

_____

_____

Who is the most Humble person you know? What are the qualities that stand out and make you respect them?

_____

_____

_____

_____

_____

What would it require of you to increase your own Humility?

_____

_____

_____

_____

_____

When you are around a Humble person, how does it make you feel?

_____

_____

_____

_____

_____

What does it mean to you to be truly Humble? Think about Jesus Christ's example.

_____

_____

_____

_____

_____

If we are truly Humble, we begin to recognize that we are dependent on our Savior, Jesus Christ. We are able to acknowledge that we need Him and that all of our talents and abilities are a gift from God.

We don't think being Humble is not a sign of weakness or fear, as some would have us believe. We believe it is possible to be both humble and courageous. When we are Humble, we trust in our Lord, and He gives us what we need to succeed.

When Jesus Christ served his mortal ministry, He constantly acknowledged that His strength came because of His dependence on His Father.

"I can of mine own self do nothing. ...I seek not mine own will, but the will of the Father which hath sent me."
~ John 5:30. ~

He taught us by example to do the same.

Our Savior will actually strengthen us as we Humble ourselves before Him. We are submitting ourselves to the will of the Lord when we do this, and saying to Him, "Thy will be done." How empowering it is to have the Savior on our side, leading and guiding us to do good and to succeed in all our endeavors.

According to some in the world, Humility is not a highly sought-after character trait. Think about the business world – we are taught to be assertive, we are taught the art of negotiating by intimidation. What would happen if we all decided to practice a little bit of Humility instead? What would happen if we all invited the Savior into our lives to help us in our business dealings? Thought provoking question isn't it?

The opposite of Humility is pride. Just as Humility leads to other virtues like unpretentiousness and teachableness, pride leads to many other vices like selfishness.

The following quote from C.S. Lewis says it like it is:

"Pride gets no pleasure out of having something, only out of having more of it than the next man. We say that people are proud of being rich, or clever, or good-looking, but they are not. They are proud of being richer, cleverer, or better-looking than others. If every one else became equally rich, or clever, or good-looking there would be nothing to be proud about. It is the comparison that makes you proud: the pleasure of being above the rest. Once the element of competition has gone, pride has gone."

With the gift of Humility heavy on your mind, make it your GOAL this month as you ponder this most special gift to think of a person much different than yourself and make the effort to get to know that person so you can begin to see them as a child of God. Try to Humble yourself to the point of being able to apologize to someone you have been needing to make amends with.

Ask yourself probing questions to determine where you are at on the Humility scale

The following comparison of Pride versus Humility may help each of us determine where we need help:

PRIDE	HUMILITY
Focuses on others failures	Realizes how far they fall short and have overwhelming sense of their need to grow
Self righteous, overly critical, and fault finding	
	Compassionate and forgiving
Looks at their life through a telescope but others with a microscope	Looks for the best in others
	Seeks to win people, not arguments
Looks down on those who aren't as 'spiritual' or 'committed' as they are	Realizes only God knows a persons true motives
Thinks they know who is truly proud and truly humble	Leaves the judgement of the heart in God's hands
Thinks everyone is privileged to have them involved	Thinks they don't deserve the opportunities that God gives them

What are your thoughts and impressions about the gift of HUMILITY as you begin your journey?

As you begin reading this chapter, write down a few thoughts you have as you contemplate the gift of Humility. We will ask this question again at the end of the chapter after you have completed your study of the gift of Humility.

_____

_____

_____

_____

_____

_____

_____

_____

_____

_____

_____

_____

_____

_____

_____

_____

_____

_____

_____

What did Jesus say about HUMILITY?

"For thus saith the high and lofty One that inhabiteth eternity, whose name is Holy; I dwell in the high and holy place, with him also that is of a contrite and humble spirit, to revive the spirit of the humble, and to revive the heart of the contrite ones."
~ Isaiah 57:15 ~

"A man's pride shall bring him low: but honour shall uphold the humble in spirit."
~ Proverbs 29:23 ~

We chose the gift of Humility as one of the 12 GIFTS because of the importance Jesus puts on it. In Psalms 37:11 we read,

"But the meek shall inherit the earth; and shall delight themselves in the abundance of peace."

In our opinion, the ability to be Humble is a true gift. It is not always easy, and it requires effort to put others before ourselves, but the promises and blessings we can receive make the effort seem very well worth it.

The idea of Humility goes along with "loving our neighbors as ourselves." We have had many discussions with friends about this very thing. We have talked about how learning to love others, get along with those who are not so easy to get along with, treating our families with love and respect, and, in general, being able to love everyone – including those who are different from us – is really the main purpose of our lives here on the earth.

304

One of our good friends has often said, "I think when each of us meets God after death, His main concern isn't going to be, 'Did you hold family home evening every week? Did you read from your scriptures on a regular basis?' He will ask each and every one of us, 'How did you treat your wife? Did you show love and respect to your family? Your friends? Your neighbors?' Those are the questions I believe He will ask us."

There are many issues in the world today that are dividing people and creating rifts that run deep. We all have difficulty sometimes accepting the beliefs and actions of others, but we think we would all agree – the answer lies in following Jesus Christ's teachings to love one another.

One of our favorite hymns is 'Love One Another."

As I have loved you, love one another.
This new commandment, love one another.
By this shall men know, ye are my disciples,
if ye have love one to another.

We believe the hymn is saying that if we can honestly and sincerely love each other, we are true followers of Christ. We are bearing witness of Him by showing love and respect to all men, just as Jesus did.

Humility is a very important gift. Imagine a world where everyone was able to practice and show Humility. What a difference it would make!

Stories to help us reflect on the Gift of HUMILITY:

As we reflected on stories from our lives that would illustrate the Gift of Humility, we began to realize that lessons in Humility can take many forms. Sometimes we are being guided to Humility without even realizing it. Sometimes a "wake up call" comes to us as a way of helping us increase our Humility.

Many of us have had experiences that brought us down from the pedestal and back into reality. Sometimes, when things are going our way, we can begin to think we're pretty great. That's why we want to impress on all of us – Elizabeth and Janeen included – just how important it is to continue practicing the gift of Humility throughout our lives. Because walking around acting like we're awesome doesn't set well with anyone. After awhile, we might find we have no real friends any more because we have pushed everyone away with our arrogant attitude. We may all have had experience with this – no matter how small.

I was immediately reminded of an experience I had several years ago that I will relate to you in the following story:

"WHAT IF SHE DIES AND I LIVE"
by Janeen

When I was in my late twenties, there was an amount of time that I was lacking in the Humility department. I thought I knew everything, and I was not about to take advice from anyone – especially my parents.

Looking back, I'm not entirely certain why I was like this at such a late age. I had been a good teenager – straight A student, student-body officer, sterling scholar, and all the things that go with those "perfect child" titles. I was respectful of my parents, had a lot of friends and loved high school. Honestly, I think I may have become a little cocky because of all my good fortune.

But the ten years post high-school had brought me some experiences that brought me to my knees. I was divorced with two children and was working full-time and going to school at night. My parents took care of my children a lot because of my schedule. And I will admit, I was feeling a little resentful, rather than appreciative that my mom was able to spend so much time with my kids.

So, one day, when I decided to drive to Las Vegas with my daughter, who was five at the time, to see our friends, I was going to do things my way.

I stopped by my parents' to pick up a couple of things before we headed down the road, and I had my daughter in the front seat. She was very tall for her age, and I was not at all concerned that she should be in the back seat locked in a secure seat belt. I drove a Jetta at the time, and there were no lap belts in the front seat – only a shoulder belt.

When my mom saw the situation, she begged me to put her in the back seat, but I said, "No, she will be fine." I could see the panic in my mom's eyes, but she worried about EVERYTHING so I thought nothing of it.

We had a fun drive and talked a lot along the way. We were excited to spend some time together on a trip. We had gone just about half way when I decided to look in the door pocket for the address I would be needing when we arrived. I looked down just long enough that my car began heading toward the median. When I looked up, I panicked and overcorrected my car. It went berserk! The next few moments were pure torture. Time passed extremely slowly. It felt as though we were moving in slow motion. The only thought that kept passing through my mind was, "what if I live and she dies." I could not accept that fate. I was terrified. But at the same time, I was calm. I felt our car was being gently guided by angels. I remember thinking as we were going through the crash that it felt as though our car was being lifted and carried.

I simply couldn't overlook the feeling that our guardian angels were watching over us and seeing us through that accident. We finally rolled and landed down an embankment where the car came to a rest. I told my emotional daughter we needed to get out of the car, so I tried to open the door but couldn't. I was so disoriented. I finally unlocked her seatbelt and she fell on top of me, and that's when I realized the car was on its side. We crawled out the sunroof to safety – not a scratch on either one of us.

The car was completely totaled – windshield shattered, tires flat, frame twisted. I remember sitting on the side of the road wishing the police would hurry up so we could get going again. I was in shock! It was a couple of hours later when we reached a phone and I called my parents that I began to cry.

My mom had been waiting for that call. She had a prompting and she knew it, but I had been unwilling to listen.

That accident changed my life.

The deep Humility that overcame me that day was undeniable. I knew my mom was living her life in such a way that she had a connection to the Holy Spirit. I was not doing the same. But since that time, I realized I could have it too. I have been blessed by having many experiences where I have been prompted and I have learned to listen. What a difference it has made in my life.

"If you are humble, Nothing can touch you. Neither praise or discouragement. Because you know who you are."
~ Mother Teresa ~

CREATE YOUR OWN UNIQUE RELATIONSHIPS
BASED ON LOVE, HOPE AND FAITH
by Elizabeth

As I shared the story of my divorce in the Teacher chapter, I explained how emotionally intense divorce was for my family and all of our extended family members, including my former in-laws. This story is about how relationships can be defined according to your own creative thinking, especially when you let love guide your choices. For over ten years, I formed close relationships with my former husband's side of the family. When a divorce occurs, it doesn't mean that a person suddenly loses their love and appreciation for their in-laws and other relatives.

If a divorcing couple can navigate through their own emotional healing process and allow the grieving stages to be worked through, each person can reach the final stage of acceptance, and I might add FORGIVENESS also. This allows each individual to release any resentment and pain. Without the bitterness, each person in the divorce can see the logic of maintaining established relationships with the other person's family, because they don't feel threatened. Each partner gets it; a divorce does not erase the love that has been built up with extended family relationships.

The stories that I am about to share relate to the special type of relationship I formed with my former mother and father-in-law. They have both made their transition to heaven, and I was able to continue a loving relationship with each of them after our divorce. I will always be grateful for the memories and love we all shared. It was an unusual type of relationship following a divorce, but they were astute and wise enough to pursue a path where they could love all of us. They clearly wanted to keep a close relationship with their much-loved granddaughter. They had enough love in their hearts to love beyond their biological family connections. Their awareness about love extended in many directions. I recognized this from the many unconditional acts of love and service they provided to others, and their generous acts of giving back to those in need.

Here are a few of my favorite stories about them and some of the lessons they taught me.

Hugh Was Brilliant, Humble, Generous, and a Person Who Learned and Embraced Lessons

Hugh was a very accomplished orthopedic surgeon, and I specifically chose the word "accomplished" instead of "successful" because he was humble about his work, and he never bragged about any of the many contributions he made in the field of medicine. I noticed he would share a story about his work if there was a reason to tell it, or a lesson to be learned, or to inspire others towards achieving their goals. He never bragged about anything for the sake of boasting. He knew his talents, and he was always so grateful to God for giving him hands that could heal others' pain. One of his daughters made a beautiful sculpture of Hugh's hands, symbolizing how his hands had helped so many people. Hugh would recognize when there could be a better way to do an orthopedic surgery, and he would carefully go about creating a new procedure. He didn't do this for fame; he did this quietly because he wanted to help improve lives and decrease pain.

For example, Hugh noticed that children who were born with spina bifida – a condition where an opening in the back exposes their spine, often leading to paralysis – needed additional services, along with more advanced types of surgeries to improve outcomes. He put his efforts into both areas. He took it upon himself to establish one of the first spina bifida clinics in the country, and then he created new methods for how to improve the current surgeries. This was about thirty years ago, and I'm sure more advancements have been made since then. However, Hugh had this sense of pioneering new methods, and he hoped that others would continue to make advancements in the field. Hugh would be very pleased to see progress and how these newer practices could improve lives. His intention as a doctor was to improve the quality of life for a patient. Hugh had this type of pioneering spirit, to see beyond the current situation and always look for better ways. It was never about him or getting recognition. It was even difficult for the family to learn about his accomplishments, simply because he kept them quiet. It seemed like it was a spiritual thing, between Hugh and God.

Hugh also made many significant teaching contributions to developing countries, and he went to areas where local doctors wanted to learn more about updated surgeries. Hugh and his wife Sue shared their gifts as quietly as they could while, of course, informing their loved ones about their trips and the purpose. The people on these islands grew to love them for their desire to improve lives. The locals could feel their love, Humility and compassion. Hugh and Sue were devoted Christians. They had a strong faith, and they lived by example. Preaching was not necessary. It was the love and their demonstration of it which was felt by others.

Of course, there are many stressors while raising a large family, and Hugh and Sue were no exception. They would be the first to admit they were not perfect. We're all human, and part of our experience on earth is to make mistakes, grow from the past, adjust course (Hugh loved sailing), improve always and learn lessons in life. As we all grow older, we tend to look back and wonder how we could have done a few things differently. Many times, we are doing the best we can during the moments in time. It is in hindsight where we can put the larger picture into perspective, and we eventually realize life is a series of many classrooms where we learn different and valuable lessons. Hugh and Sue grew and learned, just like the rest of us, by sharing their love for others.

It is a true gift that I was able to know them and be inspired by their compassion and Humility.

Sue Shared Her Own Gifts

Let me assure you, Sue was not a woman who just followed her husband around cheering him on. Sue had many strengths, and she was as beautiful on the inside as she was on the outside. Sue was stunningly beautiful, with one of the warmest smiles I've ever known. She smiled with her beautiful blue eyes before the world ever heard about "smizing" (which is now a popular phrase for smiling with your eyes). As Hugh once told me, he felt Sue had the highest Emotional Quotient, EQ, (Google it later if you want to learn more about EQ), of any person he knew. Hugh was absolutely right about this.

Sue could walk into a room, with her calm and joyful personality, and instantly figure out how to make others feel comfortable, welcomed, and at ease around her. She had a beautiful gift, and she knew how to be in the moment and make each person she was conversing with feel like they were the only one in the room. She listened, she connected, and she knew how to lighten up the moment with a joke (her humor never offended anyone). Many of her children have a great sense of humor also. It's a great feeling to be around a person who can make others laugh, without hurting anyone else's feelings.

There was a time when I found myself alone with Sue, during a thunderstorm at night, driving a small stick shift pickup truck on a winding state highway as we were trying to meet up with a family member who had accidentally forgotten their airline ticket. So, instead of worrying about the storm, I decided to find out more about Sue. I could tell she was worried about the storm and worried about getting the airline tickets to the relative on time, so I tried distracting her. I asked questions so I could learn from her. She had a charm that fascinated me, and I wanted to know more about her as a person. I was curious.

As she relaxed during the drive, she opened up and shared wisdom that came from living and learning. We enjoyed an honest and open conversation about many things. I asked her about her presence and how she was always able to connect with others, especially at big public events. She told me very clearly, "Before an event, you think about your outfit and how you want to look for the occasion. You do everything you can to make yourself look your best. Once you have done the best you can on your appearance, you forget about it. When you show up, you notice the people around you. Many of them are nervous, and you can help them relax just by being kind. When you let people know you care about them, they relax. None of us want to impress others with our outfits, but we all want to look good. After that, it's about listening, sharing and being kind to each other."

I have remembered Sue's wisdom for decades, and it has served me well. I think many of us go through an awkward phase where we are so self-conscious that we worry about how others are perceiving us. This can make us anxious, and then we get too focused on ourselves. We can often miss the opportunities to make a connection with someone when we get self-absorbed with our own anxieties and worries. Simply by doing the best we can with our physical appearance and then forgetting about it and focusing on the person we are interacting with, can and will promote true human connections. We never know what gifts we can share and learn when we reach out to another with our heart, instead of being concerned with what they think about us.

"Love and Truth Lies in the Tender Connections of the Heart, During the Unexpected Moments of Life."

In short, this is what Sue taught me while I was driving their classic older truck through a major thunderstorm to meet another family member, who was anxiously awaiting their airline ticket. Back in the day you had to have a paper ticket and, without it, you could not board the plane. Through it all, I still recall the precious lessons I learned from Sue that night. It was a special night, and I am so grateful that an airline ticket was left behind, because it gave me the chance to talk one on one with Sue. She was always in demand because she was organizing holidays, busy family schedules, and volunteer work.

On the drive back home, after the airline ticket was delivered, we were able to relax a bit, and we talked about other things. The lightening stopped, along with the loud thunder. I did not dare mention I had never driven an older stick shift truck. I was grateful I was able to figure it out. I did say a prayer before I began. The pressure was off, and we were now on our way back to their home on the lake. We chatted about many things.

Sue shared the value of setting a beautiful table, especially for the holidays, which I had never thought about before. She shared a few of her favorite recipes. She helped me think about things I had not considered when you are fortunate enough to set a pretty table. She understood this detail, and that is where her Humility came in. She said, "Even when people in other places might not have the pretty plates and things we have, they know they have each other, and that's what matters most. They make their time together lovely and inviting."

Hugh and Sue had Humble hearts, and they always wanted everyone to feel welcome in their home. They were grateful to God for all they earned and all that they were able to share.

They knew the value of caring and sharing. They shared their hearts and their love with thousands of people, maybe millions of people, when you add up the ripple effect of their good deeds. They were too Humble to tell how many lives and groups they helped. Their examples made me feel grateful, and they taught me many gifts. But this story is about their combined Humility.

I must say, Sue served the most beautiful Thanksgiving dinners. She paid attention to every detail, and not just with her amazing dishes. She noticed every person and seized the moments to make everyone feel welcome. Her dinners were the best. She cooked with love, and chefs now talk about this. I believe when you cook with love for your guests, they sense it, and it comes through in the wonderful taste of the food too. The guests feel the intention of your LOVING cooking. It matters.

P.S. Sue loved her family, her home, entertaining, making others feel good about themselves and more. But she loved her husband Hugh with her full heart, and when he wanted to teach doctors who needed his expertise, she fully supported him. But she went beyond this. She had graduated from college with a degree in elementary education, but after she married, her husband went to serve in the Korean War as a doctor (in the unit where the hit television show "Mash" was inspired and from). Hugh did not speak much about his time in the war, similar to other war veterans. While Hugh served his country, Sue was busy raising their children. It was hard to be away from her husband with two young children. However, Sue always kept education close to her heart, and eventually she had the chance to make a difference in this area.

When Hugh was busy gathering medical supplies to bring to the doctors on the islands, Sue was busy gathering old textbooks that were going to be discarded because new books were arriving. She arranged for the shipping of these older books to be delivered to the islands where they were not only needed, but treasured. Many students were blessed, and they appreciated the textbooks because they were so much better than anything they had before. The operating rooms in the hospitals were thrilled with the gifts they received. Sue and Hugh followed their hearts and their love for Jesus, and they served in places where they were needed.

Yet, there was no bragging or boasting about it. They knew what Humility was, and they were great examples. There were times when it was difficult to find out what they were up to, just because of their Humility. Thank you, Hugh and Sue. I Love you.

WAKE UP CALL
by Janeen

I have a friend, Dave, who recently had a life-changing accident involving a deer that crashed through his windshield. When I first saw pictures of the accident, I realized that Dave could have died.

My friend was driving along a rural road at 55 mph, minding his own business. It was a typical day, and he was headed to his cabin a few miles away. There were cars in front of him and behind him, and there were cars coming in the other direction. No one was speeding, and nothing was out of the ordinary. When suddenly, out of the corner of his eye, he saw something airborne. Without warning, a great big buck crashed into his windshield. Its body wrapped around the front windshield and the side window taking both completely out. The impact was so great that it cut the deer in half. But the impact to my friend was lessened because of the fact that it hit the panel that goes between the two windows. The deer had been airborne because it had jumped over the car that was coming toward Dave's car. Wrong place at the wrong time? Or was he at the right place at the right time?

The accident most certainly shook Dave up, but as he began to ponder why that accident happened, he started to realize there were some things in his life he needed to change. It was a wake up call for my friend. After all, why had the deer hit HIM? All the other cars on the road, and why was he right at that spot at that very moment? It's hard to deny when something like that happens that it was meant to happen. I believe we are sometimes given things like that to get us to stop and re-evaluate.

My friend since begun to make some changes in his life. He made some decisions that have propelled him forward to the possibility of a happier life, and he is getting to a place of peace.

He was Humbled by that experience.

GARTH BROOKS – A GREAT EXAMPLE OF HUMILITY
by Elizabeth

We mentioned in another chapter how Garth Brooks and his amazing band came to our city recently (November 2015), and how Garth shared a few stories about how grateful he was to be able to do what he does during his concerts. During the same stop on this tour, a different local news station had an interview with him. After this interview, Garth and his team offered their charitable contribution which they do in every city after a series of shows. It was obvious Garth was grateful and Humble.

But just in case a younger reader might not know the history of Garth Brooks, we will share it.

Garth Brooks quit going on tour at the height of his award winning career, sold out concert tours and more, in order to stay home and raise his children. He told the public he had "retired" and it was accepted and understood. Yet, when his children went off to college, he decided to do what he loves again, which is music and performing. After many years of being absent in the music field, the first year Garth went back on tour, he was nominated for "Entertainer of the Year" by the Country Music Awards. He did not win, but he made a very Humble and touching statement the week before while he was in our city. He said:

"The greatest gift from God and the people was to be able to go home and raise my kids and be able to afford to do it. The second greatest gift from God and the people, is the chance to be able to do this again."

Clearly, this man understands the source of his gifts. He is grateful and Humble enough to acknowledge it. His statements, and the way he gives back to others, show his sincere gratitude.

His sense of Humility makes many of us appreciate him even more. We wish you well Garth, along with your family and your band. We hope your sense of gratitude and Humility touches others as they hear your story. We all have much to be grateful for, and thank you for acknowledging your feelings publicly. You are a wonderful example to each of us.

"Now I Paul myself beseech you by the meekness and gentleness of Christ, who in presence am base among you, but being absent am bold toward you:
~ 2 Corinthians 10:1 ~

We know as you have read some of these stories, you have pondered what you could change in your own life to begin practicing greater Humility.

Take some time to write in your journal about a person you know who is a great example of Humility. List their traits and characteristics and the things you admire most about them.

Take this activity to the next level by calling this person or meeting with them to talk about their journey to gaining Humility in their life.

Here is a sample affirmation to say each day, to reinforce the commitment to living each day mindfully, while appreciating the Gift of Humility:

AFFIRMATION: I am striving on a daily basis to be Humble. I will make a difference in as many lives as I possibly can – through kindness, through generosity, through understanding and lack of judgement.

"Being humble means recognizing that we are not on earth to see how important we can become, but to see how much difference we can make in the lives of others."
~ Gordon B. Hinckley ~

Applying the gift of HUMILITY:

Humility is one of the greatest gifts we have been given. We want to do all we can to help you increase your Humility so that loving and accepting others comes easily. We worked on our list of 75 ideas to get you to begin thinking about and appreciating the gift of Humility Start with our list below and see if you can add to it by coming up with some personal ideas of your own that will help you get motivated to begin thinking, feeling and acting on Humility.

Here is our list:

- Speak to someone you have difficulty with in a kind voice
- Pray to Heavenly Father and ask for His help
- Read stories about people who displayed Humility
- Apologize to someone you have yet to forgive
- Notice someone very different from yourself and talk to them
- Accept your trials without complaining
- Work hard to stop needing to be right all the time
- Find scriptures that speak of humility
- Treat others like they are your equal
- When you have done something wrong, make it right as soon as you are able
- Admit that you made a mistake
- Always speak to your spouse in a loving way
- Put forth the effort to get to know people who are different from you
- Talk to your children about what it means to be humble

- Look for service projects to help less fortunate people
- Work at helping others feel important – focus on them
- Be the first to apologize – even if you didn't think you were wrong
- Ask your husband what he needs from you
- Ask your wife what makes her happy
- Show respect to all people
- Think of yourself less often
- Be genuinely interested in other people
- Have a grateful heart and express gratitude each day
- Give credit to others for your successes
- Never forget to say 'thank you'
- Look for the good in others
- Try to laugh when you feel irritated
- Accept insults without firing back
- Always remember we are all children of God
- Bear witness of Jesus Christ
- Get outside yourself and think of others first
- Cook your family's favorite meal from time to time
- Come home early from work and take your kids someplace special
- Always be willing to help others without being asked
- Do away with self-indulgence
- When someone provokes you – be polite
- Notice people who live in humble circumstances – get to know them
- Keep God's commandments
- Honor your elders
- Give people the benefit of the doubt
- Be willing to learn
- Don't allow your feelings to be easily hurt – the one who hurt you is doing the best they know how
- Have a patient heart and be willing to listen
- Never act like you are superior to anyone
- Be selfless rather than selfish
- Be concerned with WHAT is right, not WHO is right

- Go without some wants and save more money
- Don't talk about yourself to people
- Worry about your own affairs – not those of your neighbors
- Be patient with your spouse and your children
- Don't gossip
- Accept everything with joy in your heart
- Smile as much as possible
- Be kind
- Ask questions of others and learn about them
- Understand how much you need others in your life
- Enjoy the people around you
- Get into deep discussions with your husband or wife and connect on a deeper level
- Read from the scriptures as a family
- Talk to your children about the sacrifice Jesus Christ made for all of us
- Realize the people in your family are gifts from God
- Take the focus away from your physical imperfections
- Be courteous in every situation
- Give food or clothes to the homeless
- Hug your family often and tell them you love them everyday
- When you feel distressed – pray to Heavenly Father
- Chose one person and improve your relationship with them
- Meditate each day and surround yourself with thoughts of gratitude
- Realize how blessed you are
- Accept God's will for you
- Search for talks about humility
- Accept Jesus Christ as your personal Savior
- Let go of your ego and do the right thing
- Admit your limitations and shortcomings and work to be better
- Love Heavenly Father and Jesus Christ

Now, take a few items from our list that you can do right away. And DO THEM.

If there are other things you would like to add to your own list, do so.

As we've mentioned before, we want you to get out of your comfort zone and have new experiences as you read through this book and begin to practice the 12 Gifts. Do some things you've never done before. Stretch yourself and reach for your potential. Keep in mind that being deliberate about the things you do will help you form new habits.

"The principles of living greatly include the capacity to face trouble with courage, disappointment with cheerfulness, and trial with humility."
~ *Thomas S. Monson* ~

We all need to have experiences and trials that mold us and shape us into the people that we will ultimately become. We want each of us to appreciate more the gift of Humility because it is the KEY to becoming more Christ-like. So take a few moments and complete the following activity by writing your thoughts in your journal:

Think of a time in your life when you were prideful.
- List the circumstances,
- List the behaviors you were caught up in,
- Think about the interactions you had with others at the time,
- Consider the way you felt,
- What was the outcome – where did you end up?

Think of a time in your life when you displayed Humility.
- List the circumstances,
- List the behaviors you noticed from yourself,
- Think about the interactions you had with people during that time,
- Consider the way you felt,
- What was the outcome – where did your Humility take you?

The purpose of this activity is to help you contrast PRIDE and HUMILITY and put them into perspective for yourself. Really take a look at the way your life was different during each of these times.

Looking back, as we remember times when we were prideful and caught up in what the world thought of us, or the way others looked at us – it was exhausting. That's the best way we know how to put it. It's tiring to live your life to appear to be something great in the eyes of the world, and none of it matters. Our parents taught us to live our lives so that our Father in Heaven would approve, not so that the people in the world would approve. Life in this manner is so much more meaningful, so much simpler.

When we do things to help others and are truly focused on doing good, the work is effortless. When we are practicing Humility, we are at peace.

What are your thoughts and impressions now about the gift of HUMILITY?

Has anything changed or come into your awareness now that you didn't notice before?
Jot down your thoughts after 30 days of reflection:

_____

_____

_____

_____

_____

_____

_____

_____

_____

_____

_____

_____

_____

_____

_____

"But the meek shall inherit the earth; and shall delight themselves in the abundance of peace."
~ Psalms 37:11 ~

CONCLUSION:

Humility is a special gift. If we want to improve in other areas of our life, Humility is a necessary part of that. In order for us to be compassionate and forgiving, we need to look closely at ourselves and see where we could be better at becoming more Humble. If we want to see the good in others and focus on the positive aspects in our lives, we need to become Humble.

The opposite of Humility is pride. So, if we choose not to work on becoming more Humble, we are inadvertently choosing pride. Pride can't be stopped if we don't work to overcome it – we will be overly critical of others and of ourselves – we will find fault with the people in our lives.

Humility is one of those things that requires a lot of work, and it requires many experiences in order to finally see that we are dependent on our Savior, Jesus Christ. If we can all work to do the things that will ultimately bring us to that place of Humility, our lives will be filled with an overwhelming sense of wanting to constantly improve.

DAILY REFLECTION

Each chapter is meant to be read slowly,
Absorbing the deeper essence behind the words and stories.

This allows for continual reflection,
Prayer and listening for answers,
Which opens the door to
Greater insight and awareness of
The Gift of Honesty.

If we devote one month of the year,
To learning and living the Gift of Honesty,
Our awareness of the precious Gift of Honesty,
Will be spiritually heightened,
And our daily existence will emulate this awareness.

As we make this shift to mindful attentiveness to the Gift of Honesty,
We will be less likely to take for granted, Honesty.
We will have developed a habit,
Which becomes part of who we are.

As we develop a new habit each month,
Based on a different Gift each month,
A Gift that Jesus came to earth to give each one of us,
We will become more like Jesus in the way we live.
As this happens,
We will be living a more Christlike life, every day.
As we do this,
We are expressing our deepest gratitude to Jesus
And our Heavenly Father.

As we share the 12 Gifts with others,
We cannot help but bring the same love and peace
To our own hearts and spirits.

9

The *Gift* of

HONESTY
AND
INTEGRITY

We said early on in this book that we wanted to choose the gifts given to us by our Savior, Jesus Christ, that have life-altering abilities. If anything can make the life of a person meaningful, it is the ability to have Honesty and Integrity. Those two gifts make all the difference in relationships, in business, in our relationship with our Savior, and in daily living.

Keep in mind it is our desire that each of us practice the gifts on a regular basis throughout life, so we may become more like Jesus Christ. And Honesty and Integrity are no exception.

Integrity is one of those characteristics you either have, or you don't. There is no middle ground. You can't be Honest some of the time or tell half-truths and then expect people to think you have Integrity. This is why being completely Honest and full of Integrity are so important. If you feel you fall short – don't worry. Honesty and Integrity can become ingrained in each of us if we are willing to do what it takes.

Why did we choose HONESTY AND INTEGRITY as the ninth gift?

"Let us walk honestly, as in the day; not in rioting and drunkenness, not in chambering and wantonness, not in strife and envying."
~ *Romans 13:13* ~

"But have renounced the hidden things of dishonesty, not walking in craftiness, nor handling the word of God deceitfully; but by manifestation of the truth commending ourselves to every man's conscience in the sight of God."
~ *2 Corinthians 4:2* ~

As we discussed the gifts we wanted to include in this special book about Jesus Christ and trying to become like him, we chose Honesty and Integrity as our ninth gift because of Jesus' example in being Honest in everything He said and did, and His ability to have Integrity in every situation.

Without Honesty and Integrity, we would all be lost. There would be no trust, no faithfulness, no truth among the population of the world.

We believe Integrity is just about the most important quality each of us can possess. If a person has integrity, he is:

honest,	strong,	faithful,
solid,	trustworthy,	respectful,
kind,	forthcoming,	and a joy to be around.

When I, Janeen, think of a man who has great Integrity, I think of my father. He is a Patriarch in his church, and he is highly respected by all who know him. He is the kind of man you want to be associated with. He is the kind of man you want to be your father so he can help you know what to do in any situation, and he can watch over you and your children.

People come to him for advice, they trust him with their burdens, they know he is non-judgmental and kind, they know he is honest, and they respect his ability to help people put their lives in order.

A man who has great Integrity is not always popular.

Jesus Christ suffered at the hands of His enemies because they didn't want to face the fact that they weren't living a righteous life. They wanted to be able to do what they wanted without feeling guilt. They didn't like it that someone was trying to teach them to change their ways.

Sometimes we can be like that when we get off track. Sometimes people who aren't doing everything they should will look at the man with Integrity and feel guilt. They may throw blame his way because they are not like him. They may judge him and try to make him feel insignificant because he is not worldly.

The man who can stand up to that is truly great.

But let's back up just a bit. We are all human and, therefore, we will do things sometimes that are dishonest. We will do things that hurt other people. We don't necessarily do these things intentionally. Sometimes we find ourselves in a situation we don't know how to handle or get out of, and we do things we wouldn't normally do.

But it doesn't do us a lot of good to walk around feeling guilty about those things. We would propose that if you are thinking you might need to change a few things – begin working on them. Use your "guilt" to do something positive. Take a look at the things in your life you'd like to change and start chipping away at them. God looks to us to make the effort. He wants us to progress throughout our lives in a positive direction. Sometimes, we get caught up in the notion we need to fix everything all at once. It becomes overwhelming to us and then we get discouraged and wind up doing nothing. So, as you read this chapter, think about making small changes, if needed. Just start somewhere and improve one little thing. And then keep going. Don't worry about what others think of you – do what's right for YOU.

Integrity Is doing the right thing even when no one is watching.
~ C.S. Lewis ~

"Providing for honest things, not only in the sight of the Lord, but also in the sight of men."
~ 2 Corinthians 8:21 ~

When we think about Honesty and Integrity, we might also contemplate closely-related words that help us embrace a deeper meaning of Honesty and Integrity. These words could include: FAITHFULNESS, TRUTHFULNESS, SELF-RESPECT, LOYALTY, MORALITY, TRUSTWORTHINESS, VIRTUE, HONOR, SINCERITY, UPRIGHTNESS

The following story is an example of how doing something that's against our grain can affect us. This happened to me many, many years ago, but I still remember it, and it has had a significant impact on the way I have chosen to live my life. I have not been completely Honest at all times, but I have tried to continually do better.

I CAN'T LIVE WITH 90%
by Janeen

When I was five years old, my family was transferred to a small town where my dad became the manager of a division of a large company. It was the summer before I was entering kindergarten, and I was so excited. I was too young to be scared, and too naive to be worried about making friends.

We moved into a small motel for the summer while our house was being built, and I thought it was a great adventure. We eventually moved into our new home, and I started school. I made friends easily, and the next few years of elementary school were good. I was popular, and I was an excellent student. I had a reputation to live up to, and that became the most important thing to me.

But by the time I reached sixth grade, my popularity was slipping because I thought I was pretty awesome, and my friends began to grow tired of my "perfection." I was feeling kind of lonely because my friends weren't hanging around me as much, but my grades were still at the top of my list as far as priorities. Well, one day, I took a spelling test. I had never missed a spelling word in my entire school career up to this point, so you can imagine my disappointment when my test was returned and I had spelled one of the words wrong. And now that I've thrown that out there – I sure hope we don't have any misspelled words in this book – how embarrassing! If you find any errors, make sure you make a note, and let us know.

I remember looking at my test in utter shock. I couldn't take my eyes off of the 90% staring me in the face, and I simply could not accept it. Without even thinking, I took out my big eraser and changed my answer. I erased the 90% and made it 100%. I turned my test back into my teacher to be recorded.

What happened next cut me to the core, and I have never forgotten it.

The teacher called me to his desk and called me out. He kindly mentioned my test score did not match what he remembered giving me. Let's see – and I think he probably noticed the big eraser mark and my own handwritten 100 staring him in the face. But I denied knowing what he was even talking about. In the end, he gave me the 100% and let me keep my perfect spelling test streak. But my conscience never recovered.

I didn't know how to fix it after that. I never went back to tell the teacher I had been dishonest – he already knew. And because I didn't fix it, I still carry that twinge of guilt around for having lied about something so insignificant.

That was a big lesson for me. I have worked hard since that point to be Honest in the things I do. I have slipped up at times, like we all have, but that feeling of knowing I did something dishonest made me realize I never wanted to feel that way again.

And as far as my slipping popularity – well, after realizing I needed to adjust my attitude, I began to show kindness to people without expecting their friendship in return. I lost my sense of entitlement and became my genuine self. It has been a true blessing in my life to learn to love people of all kinds and receive their love and acceptance back.

The spelling test might sound like a small thing, but in hindsight, I wish I would have let my teacher know what I did, and asked him to change my grade back to 90%. If I had, I wouldn't still be thinking about it to this day. Such a small, insignificant thing, but yet so powerful.

"Recompense to no man evil for evil. Provide
things honest in the sight of all men."
~ *Romans 12:17* ~

"Pray for us: for we trust we have a good
conscience, in all things willing to live honestly."
~ *Hebrews 13:18* ~

**As we consider the gift of Honesty and Integrity and what
it truly means, we came up with a few questions we'd like
you to contemplate and carefully answer. Really think about
these questions before you answer them:**

Have you had an experience where you didn't tell the complete
truth to someone and you are still feeling uneasy about it? Write
about the experience.

_____

_____

_____

_____

_____

Have you ever been lied to or deceived by someone you love?
How did you react and what was the outcome?

_____

_____

_____

_____

_____

What does it mean to have Integrity?

_____

_____

_____

_____

_____

Think about a person you know who you trust completely. What are the qualities they posses and how do they treat you?

_____

_____

_____

_____

_____

If you could change one thing about yourself that would increase the way you feel about your own Integrity, what would it be?

_____

_____

_____

_____

_____

How do you teach your own children to have Integrity? How do you teach them to be Honest?

_____

_____

_____

_____

_____

There are many ways in which we can be dishonest. And if we stop and evaluate the harm that is done – to ourselves, to those we love, and even sometimes to innocent bystanders who we don't know – we can begin to understand why Honesty is such a huge and important gift.

It can be very tempting sometimes to distort the truth, even if we don't tell an outright lie. Our motivation for doing so can seem harmless. Maybe we don't want to hurt someone's feelings by telling the truth, or maybe we are trying to save face.

But think about the best relationships you have. The people who mean the most to us are the ones who are completely Honest with us. Even when the truth hurts, it is better to hear it than be deceived, for a time, by a lie or a half-truth. We all appreciate being told the truth – no matter how blunt it can seem. In the end, the truth always comes out. It is better to tell it up front than live a lie because so many bad things can happen when truth is revealed:

- Relationships end because lies have been told and carried on;
- Jobs are lost over dishonest actions;
- Reputations are destroyed over a lack of Integrity;
- Friends are lost when we gossip behind their backs;
- Businesses crumble because of lying and stealing;
- Good things come to an end because someone lacked Integrity

Jesus is our ultimate example. He had Integrity even though His actions did not always make Him popular. He told people the truth, and He did it with a sense of compassion and love. That is the key. Learning to tell people the truth is easier when we realize we can be forthcoming without being hurtful. Hiding the truth from people is never the answer. When it finally comes out, so many people can be affected.

As you keep this in mind, make it your GOAL this month as
you ponder the Gift of Honesty and Integrity to think about
an area where you could be more honest and
work to change something.

Think of someone you know who has Integrity
and watch them closely – what do you want to emulate?

Come up with your own GOAL that you personally want to
set as a way to improve in the area of Honesty and Integrity.

What are your thoughts and impressions about the gift of
HONESTY AND INTEGRITY? We would like you to begin
thinking deeply about this gift.

As you begin reading this chapter, write down a few thoughts
you have as you contemplate the gift of Honesty and Integrity.
We will ask this question again at the end of the chapter after you
have completed your study of the gift of Honesty and Integrity.

_____

_____

_____

_____

_____

_____

_____

_____

_____

_____

_____

What did Jesus say about HONESTY AND INTEGRITY?

*"But that on the good ground are they, which
in an honest and good heart, having heard the
word, keep it, and bring forth fruit and patience."*
~ Luke 8:15 ~

*"God forbid that I should justify you: till I
die I will not remove mine integrity from me."*
~ Job 27:5 ~

*Wrong is wrong,
Even if everyone is doing it,
Right is right, even if no one is doing it.*
~ William Penn ~

Honesty and Integrity were a clear choice as we were deciding on which gifts to include. Think about the people you are close to. If people don't possess these qualities, most of us tend not to develop lasting relationships with them. And, if we find out later that they are lacking in Integrity, or they have lied to us, how is it possible to carry on a healthy relationship?

Jesus taught that these gifts of Honesty and Integrity are essential to a happy life. Think about the Ten Commandments –

Thou shalt have no other gods before me;
Thou shalt not make unto thee any graven image;
Thou shalt not take the name of the Lord thy God in vain;
Remember the sabbath day, to keep it holy;
Honour thy father and thy mother;
Thou shalt not kill;
Thou shalt not commit adultery;
Thou shalt not steal;
Thou shalt not bear false witness against thy neighbour;
Thou shalt not covet.

How many of these have to do with Integrity?

If a person possesses pure Integrity, would that person kill someone? Would he commit adultery or steal or gossip about his neighbor? Would his language be offensive? Would he want to possess things that didn't belong to him?

If a person were Honest in every sense, would he have a difficult time keeping these commandments?

Keep in mind none of us is perfect. We all make mistakes, and we tend to break a commandment from time to time because we are human. What we are striving for here is to become better. We want to practice these gifts so we can eventually have the kind of Integrity that will earn us the complete trust of the people around us.

We like to think the Ten Commandments were given to us as a way to help us live, not only a righteous life, but a life of Integrity. They provide a path for us to follow, a guideline to help us be good people.

We are told that we were all born with the gift of the Holy Spirit – the ability to know right from wrong. But without laws and rules to help us, it would be too easy for each of us to begin to justify the things we do and become confused about what we should and shouldn't be doing. For us, it is the accountability that reigns us in when we want to choose something we know might not be right.

Do we always make the right decision? That would be a resounding NO!

None of us make the right decisions ALL of the time. It goes back to our free agency. And we believe we were given the freedom to make our own choices so we could grow and learn from them.

I, Janeen, was teaching a Sunday School class not too long ago, and the discussion led to the question, "Is it right for us to pray to our Heavenly Father over every little decision we have to make?"

I had expressed interest over an acquaintance of mine who tends to believe the Spirit guides her in every single decision –

- which hosting company to use,
- which hosting company to change to,
- which hosting company to finally settle on...
- but wait, now I'm being led to this one over here.

I am being a bit facetious here, but is it right for us to go to the Lord with every decision we have to make? Or is it required of us to use our God-given brains to make our own decisions and learn from our mistakes? Heavenly Father is there to guide us, to help us do the things that will lead to a happier life, but I think he expects us to put ourselves out there and be self sufficient in many ways too.

Now, we would never assume to say what is right or wrong for each particular person. Only YOU know what is right for you, what works for you. Some of us need a little more help than others, and, from time to time, those who are strong might need extra help if they are struggling.

Learn to know what it is you need to keep you on the path to Integrity.

Stories to help us reflect on the Gift of HONESTY AND INTEGRITY:

We love reading and hearing stories about people who did the Honest thing, or people who have huge amounts of Integrity. We all know people who have truly been blessed with this gift, and we look up to them as a guiding light in our own lives.

As we listen to the stories of others, we learn from their example, and we can often find truth for ourselves. That's why we have included so many stories in our book, so that we could each be taught and impressed by things that could help us solidify the gifts into our minds.

As you read these stories, think about people you know who you would like to be more like. What qualities do they have that you'd like to possess? We want to help you learn from some of the lessons we've learned in our own lives. And we'd like to learn from you as well. Think about and jot down some of your own stories for future reference. We will provide a place for you to share yours with others.

"I BEGAN THIS PROJECT TO MAKE A DIFFERENCE"
by Janeen

I became involved with three business partners a few years ago when they brought me onboard with their project and asked me to hang in there with them while we worked on getting funding.

I liked these guys right away. They were excited about the project they had been working on for a short time, and after two years of running a pilot, they were successful in getting it into 10,000 locations across the United States. That meant they needed a lot of money in order to expand. I fell in love with the idea and came on board without hesitation.

About three years in, they were approached by a group back in New York who wanted to offer a very, very large some of money to buy the project. It was such a tempting offer that the guys flew back for a meeting to see what it would mean for us. They had never intended to sell, but this was just too good to say no to without at least some serious consideration.

We had turned down investment money several times before this because there was always something that just wasn't quite right in the end. But we really wanted this one to be different.

As the meeting commenced, the investors talked about how much they loved the project and congratulated my partners on a really great idea and business model. They were ready to write the check. And let me just say here, had we taken the money, we could have all walked away and retired at that point.

But as they began to discuss the way in which they wanted to change the project, which is geared toward helping teenagers do great things, my partners were completely taken aback. These investors wanted to turn our wonderful, positive, change-the-world kind of project into a distasteful, obscene display that would entice teenagers and advertisers in great numbers, no doubt.

My partners thanked the investors for their time and interest, turned the money down, walked out of their offices and flew home.

When I asked our founder what made him say no, he said, "I began this project to make a difference in the world. No amount of money is going to stop what we started. I know this is what we are supposed to be doing."

I had always respected my partners, and I knew I was working with a great group of guys, but this sealed it for me. I have been hanging in there with them ever since, and after eight years of searching, we finally found the right investor with exactly the right circumstances for this project.

Patience and faith played a great part in this whole entire process, and I believe the Honesty and Integrity of these great men was what led us to the investor we found in the end. We were greatly blessed for our patience. But I know this investor would never have even given us the time of day had he not seen the Integrity of these great men I am proud to call my business partners.

LIVING EACH DAY WITH A CLEAR INTENTION, MAKES A HUGE DIFFERENCE
by Elizabeth

This is a story about my personal growth as I changed some habits of how I go about the beginning of each day, along with changes I made in the planning and preparation to my work schedule. These changes have created many more opportunities for me to live my truth and have more connected relationships. These changes also allowed me to feel the Spirit of Jesus with me more frequently, as I go about my daily activities.

In the past, I have gone through periods of time in my life where I have over-scheduled my days with too many things to do, and I said "Yes" to invitations and activities because they all seemed worthy and wonderful. I recall those time periods where I might begin each day by writing down the list of all the things I needed to do and accomplish that day. Just writing the list created anxiety in me because I knew it would be a race to get it all done and, as usual, at the end of the day, there would be about five things that would have to roll over to the next day. That is not a satisfying feeling, and even though I did accomplish many things, I typically felt disappointed because I did not get the last five things done. This is a form of setting ourselves up for failure.

Living such a fast-paced life diminished the quality of many of my experiences because I was not one-hundred-percent engaged in the moment. My mind was already moving on to the next responsibility, or where I needed to go next. As you can imagine, just reading this creates stress and anxiety. I was typically in a hurry, and when we live like that, it's inevitable we will forget things. This caused me to have to make up excuses about why I was late, or why I didn't bring the items I had agreed to bring, and other excuses. I developed a pattern of telling little white lies to justify my frantic behavior.

When I think about my own experiences, it makes me realize that many of us are living this very same way. Consider the fact we get in our cars feeling all hurried and frantic, and then we drive around desperate to get wherever we're going. NOT SAFE! Everyone has a day, here and there, when we are in a hurry, but when people are habitually late – we are putting everyone else at risk. We often hear about people driving under the influence of drugs or alcohol, drowsy driving and using electronic devices. But we don't often hear about people driving under the influence of STRESS or people who RUN LATE CONSTANTLY! People who have habits of running late tend to be discourteous drivers. They are in such a hurry to make up for time they cut other people off, weave in and out of traffic, speed and put everyone else at risk because of their tardiness. These patterns of erratic driving contribute to accidents more than we probably realize.

I am sharing this story because living this type of lifestyle of over-scheduling creates confusion and stress. I'm sure it contributed to how frequently I was getting sick. My body could feel the stress, and I ignored the quiet promptings to slow down and rest a little. We've all heard the saying, "Slow down and don't forget to smell the flowers." It's hard to smell the roses when you are running past them.

Here is an example of how fast my mental processes were going. I was a runner for decades, including many 10K races, marathons and a triathlon. I vividly recall times when I was running and noticed others walking in small groups or alone, and I remember thinking to myself, "That's sad that they are walking. They could cover so many more miles if they would just pick up their pace and learn to run!" Wow! What frantic thinking!

I am now one of those walkers, often with a friend or two, enjoying meaningful conversations, and not at all concerned with how many miles we've covered. I now know what it means to be engaged in the moment, fully present, and I feel more connected to the people I am conversing with. I look forward to these walks, and they are not a means to the end – they ARE the process.

We live in a world that seems to move faster and faster over time, simply due to so many advances in technology, which allow us to have instant connections with people all over the world. These advances are amazing and so beneficial, but we need to always strive for a balance in our lives. The human connection of face-to-face conversations seems to have weakened due to our ability to connect with so many different devices.

Here's how I made the mental, emotional, physical and spiritual shift of being more HONEST to myself, to Jesus and to others: First, I just paid attention and noticed how stressed I felt on the inside and how often I was hurrying to events. Second, I had a real ah-hah moment when I noticed two people whom I worked with and how different they both were.

One of them, Nancy, had developed habits of always being on time, and made it a practice to arrive at least fifteen minutes early to all of her appointments. She brought her briefcase with her so she always had things to do if she chose to pull out some work. She was typically calm, centered, in the moment, relaxed and ready with a few funny things to say that usually made me laugh, and she was always prepared for the meeting. I realized I wanted what Nancy had. (This reminds me of that famous line in the movie, "When Harry Met Sally," when the woman in the restaurant says, "I'll have what she's having!" So I asked Nancy about how she gets herself together enough to always be early. But before I get to Nancy's story, I want to contrast this with the other person, Peter.

If Nancy is a 10 on the scale of INTEGRITY and Peter is a 1, I would put myself at about a 5.

Where would you rate yourself? Are you satisfied with this?

I had many meetings with both Nancy and Peter as we worked on several projects together. Peter was late to over ninety percent of the meetings he attended, and he would always send a text (probably while driving) explaining why he was running late and would give his new estimated time of arrival. By the time Peter arrived at the meeting, he was out of breath, frazzled, apologetic, and then had to play catch up with us.

Some of our meetings were in a restaurant, and at the beginning of these patterns, we would politely wait for Peter before ordering our lunch. Eventually, we didn't wait for him because it would cause us to be late for our next appointments when we accommodated Peter's tardiness. So then Peter would have to get the menu and place his order, and all of this interrupted the flow of our meeting. We would also have to repeat things to Peter we had already talked about. Then he would leave to use the restroom. It became very frustrating. Eventually, Nancy and I worked on the project alone. We graciously and honestly explained to Peter why we were doing this and, of course, Peter was upset. However, Peter acknowledged his shortcomings and tried to explain how hectic his schedule was and how much pressure he had in his life. Nancy and I were both empathetic to Peter, but that frantic pace was not conducive to the goals we had set for the project. Peter was busy justifying and rationalizing his behavior, as opposed to correcting it.

Back to Nancy and what motivated her to have the professional and responsible habits she had developed – She was very blunt about it. She began her day with prayer and meditation. She visualized herself moving through her day with ease, calmness and focus. She saw herself making real connections with everyone she met with. She was a spiritual person, and she said that she made a point of living her life in a Christ-like manner. She prayed to Jesus to be a vessel for his love, compassion and Integrity. Nancy was a successful businesswoman who had many irons in the fire, and many people had great respect for her and recognized her many talents.

Clearly, the difference between Nancy and Peter was obvious, and their patterns created their outcomes. My own style was somewhere in the middle between Nancy and Peter. But just by paying attention to the differences in their extreme behavior patterns, I found great motivation to change my own patterns. I began doing what Nancy did each morning with prayer, meditation and visualization. It really helped. Now I arrive early about ninety percent of the time. I pray on my way to meetings, asking Jesus to help me bring my best self, and let the Holy Spirit inspire me with wisdom and sincere connections with others. It works!

It begins with being Honest with yourself, with God, and with the reality about not scheduling too many things. Living like this, at least for me, begins with intention. This lifestyle of Honesty and Integrity does not happen by accident. It happens on purpose. Make it your purpose and intention also and, I promise, you will feel and notice a huge difference in your stress level, and you will feel a greater sense of peace.

Here's a typical prayer that I start each day with, but it always changes. Perhaps this will get you started, and then you can start your own prayers.

"Lord, thank you for all of the opportunities I have today

to be a vessel for living the Spirit of Jesus.

Please help me to be the best I can be today.

Remind me to stay in the moment

when I am interacting with people,

and to allow your LOVE to come through me.

I ask that the Holy Spirit inspire me

with promptings when needed,

and that I will be open to listening.

Thank you for the peace I feel

as I mindfully walk with Jesus throughout my day.

I ask for your protection as I drive to my meetings,

and for your guidance to help me support my intention

of staying calm and arriving early.

I ask these things In the name of Jesus Christ, Amen."

As you've read these stories, hopefully you have remembered many of your own stories that have helped you cherish the gifts of Honesty and Integrity. Think of a person who has been a great example to you in this area.

Pull out a nice card and begin writing a note to that person. Let them know what a wonderful influence they have been for you. Once you have completed the note, mail it. Letting people know they have had an impact on the way we live our lives can truly make a difference in their life and fill us with gratitude as we express our appreciation.

Here is a sample affirmation to say each day, to reinforce the commitment to living each day mindfully, while appreciating the gift of Honesty and Integrity:

AFFIRMATION: I am a person of high Integrity. Each day, I will think before I speak and make sure what I say is true. I will be Honest with the people in my life and save them from the betrayal of lies and half-truths. I will strive to have more Integrity each and every day.

"The just man walketh in his integrity:
his children are blessed after him."
~ *Proverbs 20:7* ~

Applying the gift of HONESTY AND INTEGRITY:

There is almost nothing as important as Integrity. Being Honest with people will help you in all other areas of your life. It will also sharpen many of the other gifts we have talked about in this book. Think about it. If you have Integrity, it is easier to have compassion, easier to be at peace, easier to love others, easier to forgive, easier to feel a connection to the Holy Spirit. Honesty and Integrity are anchors, no doubt.

So, here is our list of 75 ideas to help start the process of appreciating the gift of Honesty and Integrity – ways we can all begin thinking about, feeling and acting on it. Remember that this is what forms the habit. This is why our intention is to have you focus on one gift each month – for 30 days – before moving onto the next one. We want you to begin to instill new habits into your life, and begin a whole new thought process about each gift.

So take our starter list and add to it as you think of things that are personal to you.

- Make a promise to someone – and keep it
- When the cashier makes a mistake – point it out and make it right
- Make a decision to tell the truth ALWAYS
- Remember that leaving out information is the same as telling a lie
- Teach your children to be honest
- Do something kind for someone and don't tell anyone about it
- Make sure your wife always knows where you are
- Know who you are and stay true to that
- Stand up for your beliefs
- When you make a mistake – own it

- Pray that you can have integrity
- Put yourself in the presence of people who have integrity
- Be authentic
- Be straightforward with people
- If you believe in something – stand alone if you have to
- Keep your commitments
- Stay loyal to the people you love
- Have the courage to make tough decisions
- Listen to the needs of others
- Give of yourself – even when it's hard
- When you speak – make sure what you say is true
- Always do the right thing
- Don't cheat your employer
- Think of others before yourself
- Stick to your guns when you make a decision
- Point out to your child how proud you are when they choose the right
- Expect your teenagers to be respectful
- If someone tells you an untruth, give them a chance to explain
- Express your thoughts if they are different from someone you are speaking with
- Be true to yourself and who you are
- Strive to become a better version of yourself each day
- If you find someone's wallet – return it
- Let those you love know how much you appreciate their honesty
- Make sure the things you say about people are true
- Practice what you preach
- Don't do things for selfish reasons
- Get outside yourself and serve others
- Say you're sorry when you mess up
- Don't spend money you don't have
- Try hard never to hurt your husband's feelings

- Let your kids see what integrity is through your example
- When you say you'll do something – do it without complaining
- Don't engage in behavior that forces you to lie about it
- If you are carrying guilt around – do what it takes to unload it
- Always make sure your family comes first
- Dress in a professional and modest manner
- Avoid the appearance of evil
- Don't go to places that would put your integrity in question
- Live your life as though the Savior were standing by your side
- Express your gratitude to your Heavenly Father
- Search the scriptures for verses about honesty and integrity
- Let someone go ahead of you in line
- Pay for someone's meal when they realize they left their wallet home
- Don't hang around with people who have different morals than you do
- Hang a picture of the Savior in your home
- Find quotes about integrity and save them
- Don't go to bed angry at your spouse
- Tell someone you appreciate their honesty
- Be home when you said you would be
- Choose friends who make good choices
- Do something thoughtful for your significant other every single day
- Be helpful
- Inspire others to want to be better
- Think of one thing you need to change about your behavior – then change it
- Look into your wife's eyes when you talk to her

- Think about the choices you make before you make them
- Plan ahead how you will react in certain situations
- Tell people how much you appreciate them
- Be faithful
- Live the ten commandments 70
- Don't do something you would tell others not to do
- Never live by a double standard
- Develop a close relationship with your Savior
- Do the right thing when you are alone
- Pray for those who may be struggling with honesty or integrity

Now choose a few items from the list that you think you can do immediately. And DO THEM.

Begin practicing this gift of Honesty and Integrity right away and be deliberate about the things you choose to do. Make it your intention to improve in this area of Integrity in a big way. It will improve every other area of your life.

Knowing what's right
doesn't mean much
unless you do what's right
~ Franklin Roosevelt ~

We thought of the following activity to help in this important area of Honesty. We want you to begin to appreciate the gift of Honesty and Integrity through the experiences you have each and every day. So complete the following activity and write about it in your journal.

Make a list of three people you may have hurt because of something you did or said.

Write in your journal what your experience was with each person.

Ask yourself if you made restitution with each of these individuals and, if not, think of a way you could make things right at this point.

- Do you need to call them or pay them a visit?

- Would a simple note or email clear the air?

- Could you simply decide to treat people differently from this point forward?

- Do you need to pray and ask for Heavenly Father's forgiveness?

- Do what you need to do in order to Honestly and sincerely make things right.

Now put it behind you and move on.

The point of this exercise is to get you thinking about being Honest in everything you do. It will hopefully help each of us realize that living a life of Integrity is the easiest way to be at peace throughout your life.

"And if thou wilt walk before me, as David thy father walked, in integrity of heart, and in uprightness, to do according to all that I have commanded thee, and wilt keep my statutes and my judgments: Then I will establish the throne of thy kingdom upon Israel for ever, as I promised to David thy father, saying, There shall not fail thee a man upon the throne of Israel."
~ Kings 9:4-5 ~

We have all been surprised and saddened at times when we hear about people who have done things that are not right – either people in the news that we don't know personally, or people who are our friends and neighbors – and it hurts us.

Even though it feels like such a shock or a betrayal when we hear of these things, it's important for us to keep in mind that sometimes people get caught up in things that take them to places they weren't planning on going. Sometimes the lies keep getting bigger because a person doesn't know how to stop the original lie.

It's not for us to judge why. Maybe our job is to have compassion and let God figure things out. We are all on our own path in this life, and sometimes, the things we do lead us to a decision to do things better. So do what you can to live a life of Integrity. We believe part of having Integrity is allowing others to make their own mistakes.

What are your thoughts and impressions now about the gift of HONESTY AND INTEGRITY?

Has anything changed or come into your awareness that wasn't there before?
Jot down your thoughts now after 30 days of reflection:

_____

_____

_____

_____

_____

_____

_____

_____

_____

_____

_____

_____

_____

_____

_____

_____

"Thou shalt not bear false witness against thy neighbour."
~ Exodus 20:16 ~

CONCLUSION:

Honesty and Integrity are some of the greatest gifts we have been blessed with. So many other things in life will fall into place if we can master these these two things. When we meet people who speak the truth, we want to be around them. We feel safe when we are with them, and we want to be a part of their lives in some way.

The best relationships are based on trust, and we can only trust people who are Honest with us. If they cannot be Honest, nothing else matters. We have both had experiences where we let people go from our lives because they lied. Sometimes people lie about big, important things. But sometimes people lie about the little things. We believe there is no difference. Dishonesty is dishonesty, and people who feel a need to stretch the truth – no matter how far – are difficult to trust.

The good news is... we believe that people who have a tough time with Integrity can learn the necessary skills for turning it around. If we can engage ourselves in doing things in our lives that promote Honesty and Integrity, and if we practice these gifts on a regular basis, we will come closer to being like Jesus Christ in everything we do.

DAILY REFLECTION

(Repetition is what creates new habit. Read this page daily as a reminder.)

Each chapter is meant to be read slowly,
Absorbing the deeper essence behind the words and stories.

This allows for continual reflection,
Prayer and listening for answers,
Which opens the door to
Greater insight and awareness of
The Gift of Gratitude.

If we devote one month of the year,
To learning and living the Gift of Gratitude,
Our awareness of the precious Gift of Gratitude,
Will be spiritually heightened,
And our daily existence will emulate this awareness.

As we make this shift to mindful attentiveness to the Gift of Gratitude,
We will be less likely to take for granted, Gratitude.
We will have developed a habit,
Which becomes part of who we are.

As we develop a new habit each month,
Based on a different Gift each month,
A Gift that Jesus came to earth to give each one of us,
We will become more like Jesus in the way we live.
As this happens,
We will be living a more Christlike life, every day.
As we do this,
We are expressing our deepest gratitude to Jesus
And our Heavenly Father.

As we share the 12 Gifts with others,
We cannot help but bring the same love and peace
To our own hearts and spirits.

10

The *Gift* of

GRATITUDE

G ratitude is a big word these days. We hear it everywhere we go. A lot of people are keeping "Gratitude Journals" as a way of bringing good things into their lives. Many of us believe when we express Gratitude, we are blessed. We chose Gratitude as one of the gifts because it is something that makes our lives run smoother. Expressing appreciation in any form allows positive vibes to come our way. When we are Grateful, God can see that we appreciate what He does for us.

We encourage you to express Gratitude every single day of your life. The more Grateful we are, the happier we will become. It's a chance to stop and realize just how blessed we truly are – no matter what our circumstances. We will always have God's love, and that, in and of itself, is something to rejoice over. As you read this chapter on Gratitude, keep in mind that our constant attention and effort is required throughout our lives if we want to become more like Jesus Christ.

Why did we choose GRATITUDE as the tenth gift?

"Offer unto God thanksgiving; and
pay thy vows unto the most High."
~ Psalms 50:14 ~

Gratitude is the key to living a joyous, happy life. We believe, if we are Grateful, we won't want more than we have – we will be thankful for what we do have. What we have becomes enough. Gratitude can turn our house into a home and acceptance into love. When we let our Heavenly Father know how Grateful we are, He provides us with more --

- more opportunities;
- more friends;
- more joy;
- more blessings;
- more talents;
- more resources;
- more contentment.

It has been said by many that if you want to find happiness, find Gratitude. Gratitude gives us the ability to be happy no matter what our circumstances. Have you ever heard people talk about their travels to a third world country? You will often hear stories of extreme poverty – of people who have nothing but each other or of people who don't know where their next meal is coming from – and yet, they are happy. Why? Is it because they have to rely on each other and on the Lord? Is it because they have no worries beyond what they are going to eat that day? Is it because they truly understand what's important?

It often makes us ponder.

We have a friend who is constantly working on getting care packages sent to Zimbabwe. She has experienced, first-hand, the joy in a mom's eyes from receiving a blanket to wrap a baby in, or a dress for a little girl who has no nice clothes to wear, or a hygiene kit for a teenager who is struggling to maintain her dignity.

She often talks about how these people are so Grateful when they receive gifts of necessities that we take for granted every single day of our lives. Their hearts are tender. Their Gratitude is genuine. It is a blessing to feel such Gratitude. It can change a person's life in many ways.

We are so blessed as a whole that we sometimes wonder if we often have no real sense of what true Gratitude is. It is sometimes maybe more of a challenge for some of us to have Gratitude which is why we need to practice it and be more aware of it.

Practice makes it easier for us to form a habit. And a habit of expressing Gratitude is something we could probably work on a little more.

"Let us come before his presence with thanksgiving,
and make a joyful noise unto him with psalms."
~ Psalms 95:2 ~

"A grateful heart is a magnet for miracles."
~ Anonymous ~

When we think about Gratitude, we might also contemplate closely-related words that help us embrace a deeper meaning of Gratitude. These words might include: ACKNOWLEDGMENT, APPRECIATION, GRATEFULNESS, INDEBTEDNESS, PRAISE, THANKFULNESS

I am sharing the following story because when people are full of Gratitude, it makes me Grateful that I know them. This particular friend has always felt blessed just to be alive. She is truly an inspiration.

A NEW BABY
by Janeen

I have a good friend who lives quite far away from me now, but we stay in touch through phone calls and emails. She comes to visit me when she's in town, and she always remembers my birthday, even though I am not nearly as good about that. I look forward to her cheerful phone calls every November.

We met when we were in college, and I fell in love with her instantly. Whenever she is engaged in a conversation, she takes the opportunity to tell people how blessed she is, and how much she loves her Heavenly Father. It is not strange in any way – it is who she is. And everything she says comes from the heart. She never misses an opportunity to let people know how wonderful life is, no matter what might be going on at the time. She is truly inspirational to people of all walks of life, and in so many precious ways.

Rachelle comes from a large family, and she has a large family of her own – seven children. When her last child was born, she called me to express her deepest joy and Gratitude about how wonderful it was to have another baby. She has her hands full, and yet, she wasn't overwhelmed at all by the birth of this new little life – she was extremely Grateful that she was able to have another child after the age of 40. Most women in her position would be stressed out working, caring for a husband and six children, and then having a new baby arrive in the mix. But not Rachelle. She looked at it as an opportunity to have even more love and joy in her life.

Rachelle is one of those special people I truly admire. Her family is her life. It's what matters most, and her time is spent caring for them and working hard to do special things for them to make them happy. She is selfless and joyful, and her sense of peace comes from within because she is able to constantly give all that she has to her family and to the Lord.

I am Grateful to know people like Rachelle. Having her in my life has been a true blessing for me.

"Enter into his gates with thanksgiving, and into his courts with praise: be thankful unto him, and bless his name."
~ Psalms 100:4 ~

"Giving thanks always for all things unto God and the Father in the name of our Lord Jesus Christ."
~ Ephesians 5:20 ~

As we ponder the gift of Gratitude and what it actually means to each of us, we thought it would be helpful to give you some questions to answer so you could really think through what Gratitude means to you. Give these questions some deep thought before you answer:

What fills your heart of a deep sense of appreciation?

_____

_____

_____

_____

_____

What are you thankful for?

_____

_____

_____

_____

_____

If you could do something to change someone's circumstances, what would you do?

_____

_____

_____

_____

_____

Who is the one person you feel the biggest sense of Gratitude toward? Why?

_____

_____

_____

_____

_____

What are you Grateful to Heavenly Father for?

_____

_____

_____

_____

What and who are you truly blessed with?

_____

_____

_____

_____

_____

_____

_____

_____

_____

Think for a moment about ALL the things you are Grateful for. It won't take long to come up with a very lengthy list. Gratitude is a feeling of appreciation for the blessings that have come to us. An attitude of Gratitude is more likely to make us happy. When we feel that thankfulness in our hearts – and, even better, when we express our thankfulness out loud – to family, friends, and especially our Father in Heaven, we will feel uplifted.

It's pretty difficult to be mean, bitter or resentful when we are feeling and expressing Gratitude. There are so many things to be Grateful for and so many people to be Grateful to. A lot of people – family, friends, teachers, neighbors, co-workers – add wonderful elements to our lives. Stop and think just how lonely you would be without all those wonderful people in your life.

Looking for the silver lining in every situation is one way to be Grateful. There is almost always a positive aspect that comes from everything we experience. Another way is to look for the good in people. Everyone has their quirks, but everyone also has great things about them. Giving up some of what we have to those who are in need is a direct expression of the Gratitude we feel. Acknowledging our Heavenly Father in all things and thanking Him for what He blesses us with are also ways to show our Gratitude.

When we feel Gratitude in our hearts and express Gratitude for all things, we don't leave much time to be negative or angry. The next time you feel resentment or bitterness or any negative emotion, try taking a step back and realizing how blessed you are. See if it turns things around for you.

With that in mind, make it your GOAL this month as you ponder the gift of Gratitude to begin a "gratitude journal."

And use your journal to write about something you need to put down on paper in order to work it through.

Come up with your own GOAL that you want to set that will allow you to improve in some area of your life.

What are your thoughts and impressions about the gift of GRATITUDE?

As you begin reading this chapter, write down a few thoughts you have as you contemplate the gift of Gratitude. We will ask this question again at the end of the chapter after you have completed your study of the gift of Gratitude.

_____

_____

_____

_____

_____

_____

_____

_____

_____

_____

_____

_____

What did Jesus say about GRATITUDE?

"Sing unto the Lord with thanksgiving;
sing praise upon the harp unto our God."
~ Psalms 147:7 ~

"Being enriched in every thing to all bountifulness,
which causeth through us thanksgiving to God."
~ 2 Corinthians 9:11 ~

The 12 GIFTS would not be complete without the gift of Gratitude. I, Janeen, had a good friend give me a "Gratitude Journal" once. I have done my best to keep notes and remember each and every day to be Grateful and express it – not only to my Heavenly Father – but out loud to my family and friends. Having that attitude of gratefulness brings blessings to us, and I think it helps us be more aware of the blessings we receive.

But everything that happens in our lives isn't necessarily positive. We mentioned earlier that finding the silver lining is helpful. And maybe you are the type of person who can always find the silver lining, or look for the good in a really bad situation, but maybe you will agree that it isn't a bad thing to acknowledge the negative things in our lives too and write about them so you can deal with them and let them go.

I actually have a section in my "Gratitude Journal" that is filled up with a heartbreaking experience I had. I wrote every day in detail – what I was feeling, what I was thinking, if I had made any progress in recovering, what I had learned... And I believe, in the end, putting those things down on paper actually brought me to Gratitude because I realized what had happened needed to happen. I came to a place of awareness, a place of calmness, a place of freedom from the prison I had been in.

For me, the Gratitude came after the intense pain. And I realize now how sweet it is!

"When you are grateful, fear
disappears & abundance appears"
~ Anthony Robbins ~

Stories to help us reflect on the Gift of GRATITUDE:

Stories of Gratitude are inspirational. When we can get outside of ourselves and realize that everything we have was given to us by God, it is humbling and inspiring. We love to listen to people who are truly Grateful, and as you read some of the stories we share here, you will think of your own experiences with Gratitude and you will recall people in your life who have shared inspirational stories of their personal Gratitude.

We hope as you read our personal stories, you will learn something from the lessons we have learned. We hope you will begin to notice all that you have to be Grateful for. We had this experience as we wrote this book. The more stories we remembered, the more Gratitude we began to feel. We are hoping the same will be true for you as you read and ponder.

"I'M NOT GOING ON THE FAMILY TRIP THIS YEAR"
by Janeen

I know a woman, Tracy, who was my neighbor many years ago. We were close in age and shared many similar experiences, so we became life-long friends.

She was married when I first met her and had two small children, a son and a daughter.

Every year around the holidays, her family rented a place on a beautiful island where the entire family would gather for a week to enjoy the company of each other, and talk about the events of the past year.

This particular year, her husband came to her the night before they were to leave for their annual trip and said, "I have a chance to go to the east coast with a friend to see a football game, so I'm not going on your family trip this year." Tracy was disappointed, but understood. She went ahead and left on her trip as planned with the children and the rest of her family. But little did she know how drastically her life was about to change.

She returned home to an empty house.

When she called her husband to find out when he was planning to return, she discovered he had not been at a football game at all, but with a woman he had met over the internet. He gave up the family trip so he could fly back to meet this woman for the very first time. He informed Tracy he would not be returning home – ever.

You can imagine how devastated Tracy must have felt. Her life was turned upside down within a matter of a moment. Shortly after, she was diagnosed with cancer.

When her life went spiraling out of control, Tracy took action. She went to school and earned her degree. She was able to land a wonderful job and buy and darling house where she finished raising her children.

I have known Tracy for many years now. Her children are grown. Her cancer was taken care of with surgery. She has not remarried at this point. And she has the most positive outlook on life that I have ever witnessed. Whenever we get together, she talks about how Grateful she is that her life took the turn it did. She has so much more in her life now than she every thought she could have. She is polite to her former husband and his wife, and she speaks kindly of them to her children.

Tracy is one of the most Grateful, inspirational people I have ever met. Her Gratitude is what ultimately turned her life around – Gratitude for the people in her life, for the opportunities that came her way, for the resolution of her health issues, for her education. She is happy, and she is at peace.

"THIS PLAYER KNELT IN PRAYER"
by Elizabeth

Several years ago I had the opportunity to experience how positivity, hope and Gratitude all came together for one high school, as their school won two state championship titles for their men's football team and basketball team that year. My daughter was a student at this high school, and I was an active parent, attending many games, and I felt the strong school spirit. It was in the air, and everyone could feel it. My story will be about an unexpected special privilege, immediately after the team won the football state championship. I remember it vividly because it touched my heart and soul.

I will share this special story because it reminds me that every person is an individual person to our Heavenly Father, and He knows that every one of us had made mistakes, but we all have the Gift of Jesus Christ to help us admit, repent and accept forgiveness. Some people are determined to hold onto a strong resentment towards a person who made a mistake, or maybe a series of mistakes. Some of these folks do not fully embrace how God can forgive them and allow them to succeed. But hope, change and forgiveness are all a part of our Heavenly Father's plan. We are all given the chance to grow, learn, and improve our lives. This is why Jesus came to earth, because He knew that we were all imperfect without our connection to Jesus Christ. We learn from our choices, make amends, and we move forward with the hope of Jesus and how He loves us. We are all offered the same Hope and Faith in our Savior. We can all trust in this amazing gift. The story of this young man has many lessons in it, because he had overcome so many challenges in his life. He choose a positive path, and it was clear to many, that this involved a spiritual path for him.

The gifts that I will be discussing involve his faith, and then his pure Gratitude.

High School Football At Its Best

So here is the story of a young man in his senior year of high school. During this particular school year, I had a teenage son and daughter, and our entire community was rallying around the local high school football team because they were undefeated and heading into the state championships. It was exciting for everyone.

This high school senior was a very talented athlete, both in football and basketball. My guess is that this student could have been successful in either sport in the professional leagues. But he did not have an easy childhood, and he struggled with issues and challenges, as many teens do. Yet, he had a strong determination to focus his talents and goals towards success. He was fortunate because other families, friends and leaders all recognized that this young man had gifts and talents, and he was very likable. He was also motivated for good. Perhaps he was a little rough around the edges in the way he expressed himself, but he was a young man growing up, and that process of growth takes time. It's always a little harder when a person is talented because many others seem to be paying attention to all aspects of their life. Strength, focus, discipline and awareness all contributed to his ability to overcome obstacles, pursue his goals and find a positive path. Our community is very proud of this young man.

The Final Game

Allow me to set the stage for this amazing, final game on a wonderful Friday night at a well known University Football Stadium – big lights and all the rest. It was a beautiful autumn evening, and we all knew that the top two teams in this league were going to play their hearts out, and they did. It was an exciting game for everyone to watch, and more so for the players!

I arrived a bit late after picking up my son's friends, who all played football. Before I realized it, they had front row seats on the far right side on our side of the stadium. They later explained, "We wanted to be close to the field!" and I understood. So we all sat there for five minutes and then the kids all got up and ran around the stadium. So there I was, sitting in the front row, sort of alone (the middle section was full, but I was on the extreme right side) and wondering what I should do. Then some of the junior varsity football players recognized me and came over and sat with me. They explained the game, play by play, and shared their excitement. We all became friends that night, and each time I saw them at school, they went out of their way to say hi to me. The game was so close, and everyone was on the edge on their seat.

I was completely captivated by the game. It went back and forth so many times. Eventually, it went into overtime, then double overtime, and then triple overtime. Nail biting for sure. Sure I wanted our team to win, just like the other side, but I always feel sad for the losing team. (I always pray for the team and the players who needs the win the most. I've learned that God does not get involved in choosing a winner. He lets it play out on the field, but He does teach life lessons through the game, and we can all learn through this.)

Back to this particular game that I will always remember. After TRIPLE overtime, it was clear that there were two powerful plays that created an opportunity for our high school team to win, and they both involved this one talented and focused player. This player created the win opportunities for his team. (I will not reveal his name because this is his private story to tell, if he chooses to share it. Obviously, those who read this, and know our school will figure it out, but again, he can share his story in his own time. I think he has an amazing story to share with others from all walks of life.)

I Am Sharing This Story For A Reason

After this amazing winning play, for a state championship title, after triple overtime, everyone knows that this was a spectacular game. My heart went out to the losing team with compassion and appreciation, and then my heart shifted to the team who won the game. All of the kids sitting amongst me, had all ran to the field or somewhere, and there I was sitting alone again. I felt fortunate that I could witness, so close up on the front row, an amazing game. There was so much heart, effort and hope put into this game. I felt some sadness for the losing team, as I saw them walk slowly off the field.

And then, as spectators were leaving the stadium, this star player that I spoke about, came running over to the far right side of the field where he probably thought there were no cameras, and he was alone. This player knelt in prayer, and he was obviously giving Gratitude. None of us know what he was thinking or praying, but this player was overwhelmed with Gratitude and joy. He was the only player that I saw who ran away from the pile of players jumping around with joy. It was a huge pile of players celebrating a victory, and congratulations to all of them!!

Since I was still sitting alone in the front row, when this star player came running over to fall on his knees and clearly offer his Gratitude, I felt that I was also experiencing a gift. The gift I experienced was watching a child of God transform himself into a person who had a connection to our Heavenly Father. He allowed his teammates to have their moments of joy. The team mates all screamed and jumped around, and it appeared that he was so at peace with this. His prayers and dreams were quiet and focused. It seemed like he just wanted to show his Gratitude. While all of his teammates were jumping around and so happy, this other player, who was THE reason for the win, was kneeling on his knees, clearly saying "Thank You" and he was very humbled by the events just minutes before. This player did his best to find the most private area of the stadium, and this is why he fell on his knees, on the sideline where I was sitting.

My gift was being fortunate enough to watch this amazing heartfelt game, and then being on the front row to feel, absorb and watch an expression of pure Gratitude. I was able to witness the display of pure Gratitude just feet away from my front row seat. My heart was truly humbled and Grateful. This player went on to become a star player for a prominent university, and he is now on a key player on an NFL football team. He has worked hard to achieve his goals, and from my personal front row observation, he was/is Grateful. If he ends up reading this story about his story, I just want to share a few words with him. "We love and appreciate you, and your efforts. Stay close to the truth you know in your heart. You are loved by many, but the greatest love is from Jesus. Gratitude always keeps us humble, and mindful of how we care for others. Thank you for being a wonderful example to so many younger kids. Our family wishes you all the best. Go forth in hope and love!!"

Words Of Encouragement

After I rounded up the kids and we left the stadium that night, we crossed paths with the team players who lost the game. After triple overtime, during a state championship title, what can you say to the players who lost? I found some positive words of encouragement, and maybe silly things that only a grandmother can get away with saying, and a few of them actually smiled as they climbed onto their departing bus. A triple-overtime loss takes time to get over. It's a game – It's not about you. Please always remember this all of you players, the game or outcome does not define you!

It's not about winning or losing, but how you play and live the game of life. Let love be your compass, and your heart and spirit will grow and embrace the lessons it needs to learn. Trust it. You will be surprised at how your heart and soul can shift, when you focus on love. The people you share your love with, will always remember, and will forever be affected from your exchange of kindness. Love is never wasted. Share it, wisely, with guidance from above. When you live like this, your heart will overflow with Gratitude.

LIFE CAN CHANGE IN AN INSTANT
by Janeen

My dad is one of the finest examples I know of a person who shows Gratitude at every turn. He shows Gratitude to Heavenly Father and Jesus Christ by praying constantly, reading scriptures daily, and giving service to others.

He is continually doing things for others and never expects anything in return. I have watched him over the course of my life spend endless hours listening to those who are hurting and trying to find answers. He visits his neighbors when they are sick, and takes gifts to those who are getting married, graduating, or celebrating an important event. He will always give of his time, no matter how busy he is, if someone is in need.

He is so Grateful for everything he has in his own life – he is anxious to give back to others and help them learn lessons of Gratitude for themselves.

Dad has been friends with his next-door neighbors for about 35 years. Over the years, they have been through a lot together. Dad has helped them with their family struggles, invited them to family parties, supported them in their business endeavors, and always been kind to them. They, in return, have helped my dad when mom was sick, brought gifts at holidays, checked in on the things when needed, and stayed connected as though they were family.

A couple of years ago, a serious illness required that Ben's leg be amputated. Not an easy thing as this couple spent all of their free time climbing some of the highest mountains in the world. The decision to amputate was devastating for both him and his wife, but their attitudes about the whole experience have been incredible. My dad counseled him, walked with him, sat with him and talked with him.

He stepped outside of himself and became this man's comforter, and spent many hours answering questions about life. Through the entire experience, Ben put all of his faith in his Savior, Jesus Christ. He is a humble man today, full of Gratitude for his life, his Savior and his friends.

It is not happy people who are thankful, It is thankful people who are happy.   ~

Anonymous ~

"Do ye thus requite the Lord, O foolish people and unwise? is not he thy father that hath bought thee? hath he not made thee, and established thee?"
~ Deuteronomy 32:6 ~

"SURPRISE"
by Janeen

As I have pondered on my own experiences with Gratitude, a particular time in my life came to mind.

I recently spent four years as a leader over the youth in my church. These girls were my life during that time. I devoted a significant amount of time and effort, along with the other leaders, to creating experiences that would have a real impact on their lives.

During the time I was serving, I happened to have my 50th birthday. That particular day happened to be an activity night, and we had planned to get together as usual. I received a phone call about a half hour before we were to meet from one of the other leaders. She asked me to swing by her house so we could talk before going over to the activity. She sounded pretty urgent, so I thought there was a problem and headed over with a little bit of anxiety wondering what was happening.

As I walked into her house, I noticed several of the girls and leaders were there. But I was so focused on the reason I thought I was there that it took me several seconds to realize the girls and leaders were throwing me a 50th birthday party!

I stood there in shock for a few moments and then began to cry. Those tears were tears of Gratitude. These girls and leaders loved me so much, and they wanted to give something back to me. I was in awe of the work they had gone to and the thoughtful gift they had created for me. I will never forget that moment.

I realized at that time true Gratitude comes from the heart. The girls were showing their Gratitude for me by doing something special to show their love. And I had shown Gratitude to them by serving them and helping them grown and learn.

Gratitude is a wonderful thing. It opens up our hearts and fills us with joy. It makes everything in life better. One of the things we taught the girls over the years was to keep a "Gratitude Journal" - a place to right down one thing every day they are Grateful for. Expressing Gratitude is like giving a gift – to ourselves, to others, and to our Savior.

Living in Gratitude

G **Giving without expectation**
R **Receiving with thanks**
A **Always looking for the gift**
T **Taking nothing for granted**
I **Initiating random acts of kindness**
T **Treating all as equals**
U **Understanding the needs of others**
D **Developing humility**
E **Experiencing free joy**

www.facebook.com/wonderlandsteatray

We hope as you've read over some of our stories, you have remembered many of your own stories – stories of people who have had a direct influence on you because of their Grateful attitudes. Think of one person who has really made a difference – someone who is truly an example to you of showing Gratitude.

Write in your journal about this person. Think about the way they behave, the things they do, the way they treat people, the attitudes they have, and write it down. Consider what changes you would like to make in yourself that would allow you to express Gratitude in the way this person does. Make yourself a list of some of the things you would like to do differently.

Here is a sample affirmation to say each day, to reinforce the commitment to living each day mindfully, while appreciating the gift of Gratitude:

AFFIRMATION: I will be mindful each day of the blessings in my life. I am Grateful for the people, opportunities, necessities that fill my life with joy and comfort. i will express my Gratitude on a daily basis to my Father in Heaven, my family, my friends. I am Grateful.

*"Then thine heart be lifted up, and thou forget
the Lord thy God, which brought thee forth out of
the land of Egypt, from the house of bondage."*
~ Deuteronomy 8:14 ~

Applying the gift of
GRATITUDE:

Gratitude is a life-changing gift. Learning to feel and express our Gratitude can make all the difference in the course our lives take. We want you to be deliberate about the way you practice Gratitude in your life so you can literally feel the blessings growing.

So here are our 75 ideas that are intended to help each of us begin appreciating the gift of Gratitude – ways we can begin thinking about, feeling and acting on this gift.
Remember to think of some of your own ideas that will get you on the path of some serious reflection about the gift of Gratitude.

Here's our list to get you started:

- Think of your greatest accomplishment and thank God for it
- Realize what your talents are
- Thank Heavenly Father for all that you have whenever you pray
- Make a list of the people who inspire you
- Think of what you love about your job
- Be thankful for your good health
- Realize all the opportunities that have come your way
- Tell your family how much you love them
- Realize God's hand in everything you do
- Open your eyes each day to the beauties of the world
- Think of the ways you are blessed
- Thank your husband for the amazing things he brings to your life
- Thank your wife for making your life more comfortable
- Realize how wonderful it is to have friends
- Thank your neighbors for the nice things they do
- Think about what you have learned from the challenges in your life
- Be grateful for each and every day you are alive
- Take the time to make other people feel happy
- Enjoy nature in any way you can
- Avoid gossip and look for the good in people
- Be happy that you have a house to clean
- Realize that doing the laundry means you have clothes to wear
- Say a blessing on the food you have to eat
- Learn to love yourself with all of your imperfections
- Be grateful for your relationships – one of the few things we take with us when we die
- Be thankful for parents who care about you
- Always say "thank you"
- Try to see the good in every situation

- Remember, the more you are grateful – the more you will be given to be grateful for
- Take the time to slow down and breathe
- Stop and smell the roses
- Don't let yourself get so busy that you are stressed
- Think of something every day to be thankful for
- Don't let what others think of you bring your own self worth down
- Practice being still
- Avoid negative people
- Love yourself
- Believe in the people you love
- Use positive affirmations on a daily basis
- Be grateful for the trials you DON'T have
- Do the things you love
- Talk to your children about what gratitude means
- Give the clothes you don't wear to a charity
- Ask others what they are grateful for
- Express your appreciation to those who help you
- Remind yourself how strong you are
- Be content with your life
- Know that gratitude has the power to change everything
- Be kind to others
- Be grateful for the little things in your life
- Get involved with a non-profit or volunteer
- Don't complain to your friends
- Meditate daily
- Connect with family members and re-connect with old friends
- Sit quietly each day and think of the things you are grateful for
- Appreciate your spouse and express it often
- Realize that being thankful attracts other things to be thankful for
- Help others feel good about themselves
- Surround yourself with grateful people

- Say thank you to someone who does something for you
- If someone is mean to you – keep smiling
- Think positive thoughts
- See the good in everything
- Love your life
- Increase your talents
- Realize that you can CHOOSE to be grateful
- Create an attitude of "I have enough"
- Be optimistic
- Don't make excuses – just get out there and do it
- Forgive everyone who has wronged you
- Let go of your past and be excited about your future
- Dream big and believe you can accomplish your goals
- Take care of your body and your health
- Con't compare yourself to others – be happy with who you are
- Slow down and take it all in

Now, choose a few items from the above list that you'd like to do immediately. And DO THEM.

Gratitude is a gift that requires a lot of positive energy. Get out of your comfort zone and do some things you've never done before. Before long, you will be feeling Gratitude like never before. And, in the meantime, remember to be thankful for the things you are already very aware of – your health, your food, your shelter – whatever it is for you that makes your life good.

"Be happy with what you have
while working for what you want."
~ Helen Keller ~

"Talk about your blessings more
than you talk about your burdens."
~ Anonymous ~

We'd like you to work on the following activity to increase your awareness of Gratitude and what a special gift it is in each of our lives. Write about it in your journal.

Think about the things you are Grateful for right now, and write them down.

Think about the people you are Grateful for and write about why you are Grateful for them.

Think about the difficulties you are currently having and write them down.

Now, find the silver lining in each of those difficulties and write them down.

Think about how your Grateful attitude affects you and write about it.

Consider ways you can express your Gratitude to Heavenly Father and write them down.

The point of this exercise is to help you realize how much you have to be Grateful for, and to turn negatives into positives, where possible. Get yourself in tune with an attitude of Gratitude and you will increase your happiness dramatically.

Gratitude is a precious gift. In our opinion, it is a life-changing gift. Think deeply about Gratitude, and see what you can do to start feeling thankful for everything you have. Begin to realize how blessed we all truly are. And take the time to express your Gratitude to God and to yourself and others. Gratitude is contagious, so start sharing.

The more you are in a state of gratitude, the more you will attract things to be grateful for.   ~
Anonymous ~

What are your thoughts and impressions now about the gift of GRATITUDE?

Has anything changed or come into your awareness that wasn't there before?

Jot down your thoughts now after 30 days of reflection:

_____

_____

_____

_____

_____

_____

_____

_____

_____

_____

_____

_____

_____

_____

_____

_____

"Will a man rob God? Yet ye have robbed me. But ye say,
Wherein have we robbed thee? In tithes and offerings."
~ Malachi 3:8 ~

CONCLUSION:

Gratitude is one of those rare, life-altering gifts that can change attitudes, create abundance and literally change lives. Learning to be Grateful is one of the most wonderful things we can experience in this life.

Gratitude, not only for the things we are blessed with, but the the PEOPLE we are blessed to have in our lives, is something we should express on a daily basis. When we are Grateful, we are happier, more humble, move loving, more caring, less stressed, healthier, the list goes on...

Expressing our Gratitude to our Father in Heaven through prayer, by the way we live, in everything we do and say, will lead us to more things to be Grateful for. We believe that when we are Grateful, more things, more opportunities, more amazing people come our way. It's like, we reap what we sow. In the area of Gratitude, when we are Grateful, we will receive even more to be Grateful for.

How wonderful to reach the end of our journey here in this life and be filled with gratefulness for the life we have lived.

DAILY REFLECTION

(Repetition is what creates new habit. Read this page daily as a reminder.)

Each chapter is meant to be read slowly,
Absorbing the deeper essence behind the words and stories.

This allows for continual reflection,
Prayer and listening for answers,
Which opens the door to
Greater insight and awareness of
The Gift of Peace and Joy.

If we devote one month of the year,
To learning and living the Gift of Peace and Joy,
Our awareness of the precious Gift of Peace and Joy,
Will be spiritually heightened,
And our daily existence will emulate this awareness.

As we make this shift to mindful attentiveness to the Gift of Peace and
Joy,
We will be less likely to take for granted,
The beauty, the power, and the mystique of Peace and Joy.
We will have developed a habit,
Which becomes part of who we are.

As we develop a new habit each month,
Based on a different Gift each month,
A Gift that Jesus came to earth to give each one of us,
We will become more like Jesus in the way we live.
As this happens,
We will be living a more Christlike life, every day.
As we do this,
We are expressing our deepest gratitude to Jesus
And our Heavenly Father.

As we share the 12 Gifts with others,
We cannot help but bring the same love and peace
To our own hearts and spirits.

11

The *Gift* of

PEACE AND JOY

---

12 GIFTS is ultimately a book about Jesus Christ. But it's also a book celebrating Christmas. The intent is to practice each of the 12 Gifts for 30 days so that by the end of the year – at Christmas – we can each give the GIFT of a better, more Christ-like self to Jesus Christ.

So, it only makes sense then that we include Peace and Joy as the eleventh gift, right before we offer our love back to our Savior. We always think about having Peace and Joy during the holidays, but we believe it is possible to experience these gifts all year round. If you are like us, you LOVE November and December because there is such a special feeling during that time of year. We are much more focused on our Savior, Jesus Christ. And we are getting ready to spend the holidays with those we love. It can mean many different things – some of us decorate, send cards, cook wonderful food to share, give gifts. Others may attend church, read scriptures, drive around to see Christmas lights, play with the kids in the snow – but whatever our holiday traditions, we are each busy doing the things that remind us of Christmas.

And then January rolls around and we're back in the rat race. Sometimes we feel a little depressed because the holidays are over, the decorations are coming down, the family isn't around as much, it's cold – and we let our hearts turn to work again and sometimes allow ourselves to lose those wonderful gifts of Peace and Joy.

But it is possible to have these gifts with us all year long when we turn to our Savior and rely on Him always – not just sometimes – and especially not just during Christmas.

Why did we choose PEACE AND JOY as the eleventh gift?

"And the angel said unto them, Fear not: for, behold, I bring you good tidings of great joy, which shall be to all people."
~ Luke 2:10 ~

Think about PEACE for a moment.

What is it exactly?

Does being at Peace mean we are completely free from all disturbance, turmoil, sadness, stress, heartache, pain and suffering?

Does having Joy mean we are in a state of constant bliss?

We think not. Don't you think it would be impossible to live constantly in that state in this life? Of course it would be. We think if we lived with continual Peace and Joy, we would be already living in heaven.

So what does it really mean to be at Peace and have Joy in this life? It is possible to be at Peace even when we are stressed over things like money, our kids, our jobs, whatever it might be. It is possible to have Joy after suffering a broken heart, or being diagnosed with an illness, or going through a divorce, or losing a job, or any number of earthly trials we have to endure.

We found an anonymous quote while we were studying about this topic and it reads:

"Peace is not the absence of conflict,
but the presence of God no matter what the conflict."

We have discovered that truth for ourselves as we have searched for absolute Peace throughout our lives. The absence of conflict is impossible, but Peace is attainable as we align ourselves with God and live our lives in such a way that we can be at Peace with ourselves.

We think there are some secrets to finding Peace:

- Be kind always;
- Ask for forgiveness from those you have hurt;
- Think of others first and then yourself;
- Stay close to Heavenly Father;
- Take time to appreciate nature;
- Take time to enjoy your family;
- Live within your means;
- Practice patience and control your temper;
- Find ways to give.

Maybe you can think of other things that should be on this list. Add to it for yourself and your personal journey toward Peace.

It can be extremely difficult to be at Peace with ourselves if we are not at Peace with those close to us and at Peace with God.

"Finally, brethren, farewell, Be perfect, be of good comfort, be of one mind, live in peace; and the God of love and peace shall be with you."
~ 2 Corinthians 13:11 ~

When we think about Peace and Joy, we might also contemplate closely-related words that help us to embrace a deeper meaning of Peace and Joy. These words could include: LOVE, RECONCILIATION, HARMONY, AGREEMENT, GREAT HAPPINESS, BLISS, COMFORT

I chose to share the following story because I love this couple so much, and have been impressed by their willingness to offer Peace and Joy to their daughters amidst their own trial and hardship.

UNSELFISHNESS BRINGS PEACE
by Janeen

Peace is one of my favorite words – perhaps because I am constantly searching for it. It seems that just as I am about to declare that I am at Peace, something happens to take it back. Sound at all familiar? What is the secret to finding and keeping Peace?

There are so many things that can cause turmoil in our lives. It isn't just about the things we do or the choices we make. Sometimes the things OTHER people do and the choices OTHER people make, can disturb our sense of calm and turn our lives upside down. But we do have the ability to react in a way that will keep us settled.

I recently experienced a devastating event in my life, and, after all that I have been through up to this point, I made a conscious decision to treat this situation differently than I ever have before. After all, my way of dealing with hurt in the past has been to walk away and let the anger fester. And, as a result, I have closed off a couple of people who probably could have used a little bit of acceptance from me.

So this time:
- I decided to put my own hurt and anger aside.
- I did everything I could to understand the heartbreak this person has endured.
- I considered the ways in which I could be a positive influence.
- I spent my time talking through things with him and asking questions.
- I offered sincere advice from my heart.
- I expressed my love and heartfelt empathy for the pain this person is working through.
- I forgot about how I was feeling, and focused instead on the love and forgiveness this person needed from me.

In the end, our relationship was not only salvaged, but raised to a much higher level. And, because he feels loved, he is working diligently to fix his pain by doing proactive things.

I believe the ability to find Peace lies greatly in keeping our relationships positive, and our emotions in check. I have a couple of friends, Chad and Sarah, who are getting divorced. When I learned of their situation, I was devastated. They work together in their business, and they have two young daughters. They really do like each other and love the people around them. They seemed like the perfect family. But some troubling things brought them to the point of believing divorce is the answer for them. And so they made the decision to move forward and file the papers.

Divorce is a heartbreaking experience for all involved, but this particular couple has proven, with their actions, it doesn't have to be the end of the world.

They picked up their little family and moved them to another state where they could live separately, but raise their daughters together. They are nurturing their daughters and continue to work their business together. They continue to maintain a close friendship because they like each other, and they allow each other the freedom to pursue other relationships.

So far, the situation is working. The most important elements of this story are that Chad and Sarah's daughters are happy, and everyone is at Peace.

Sarah believes the only way to truly achieve Peace in a divorce situation is through unselfishness. Interesting thought – I believe the only way to truly achieve Peace in a MARRIAGE situation is through unselfishness. Something to ponder.

If we could all just learn to care about others more than we care about ourselves, the world would be a much more PEACEFUL place.

*"Glory to God in the highest, and on
earth peace, good will toward men."*
~ Luke 2:14 ~

*"Blessed are the peacemakers: for they
shall be called the children of God."*
~ Matthew 5:9 ~

We want to get you to contemplate the gifts of Peace and Joy and figure out ways to attain it for yourself. Answer the list of questions below and start to think about what you need to change in your own life:

What puts you in turmoil?

_____

_____

_____

_____

_____

What causes you to feel the most Joy?

_____

_____

_____

_____

_____

When you experience emotional pain or suffering, what makes you feel better?

_____

_____

_____

_____

_____

_____

When something is out of your control, what helps you to let it go?

_____

_____

_____

_____

_____

If someone asked you, "how can I find peace," what would you tell them?

_____

_____

_____

_____

_____

_____

_____

_____

Who are the people in your life that you feel troubled by, and what steps do you think you can you take to change those feelings for yourself?

_____

_____

_____

_____

_____

The older we both become, the more we realize that having Peace is almost a choice. Life wasn't meant to be Peaceful most of the time. We are in this life to suffer trials and learn from our mistakes. We can't very well expect Peace under those circumstances. But what we can do is CREATE Peace.

Think about some things that you could do to help you feel at Peace, even for a MOMENT, when you are going through a difficult time. What about things like:

- Meditating,
- Praying,
- Getting a couple of hours of extra sleep,
- Calling a close friend to chat,
- Sitting outside on a beautiful day,
- Cooking a wonderful meal for yourself,
- Wrapping up in a cozy blanket with a good book,
- Hanging out with your family.

These are just a few things we think of when we need to calm down and feel better.

Notice we used the word MOMENT above. While it is possible to momentarily feel at Peace – true, lasting Peace comes from above. It comes through our Savior, Jesus Christ and our ability to connect with the Spirit. True Peace comes from practicing the 12 Gifts and incorporating them into your life on a daily basis.

With these things in mind, make it your GOAL this month to make a list of some things you could do WITHOUT that would make it easier for you to feel at Peace.

And think of something that would bring Joy into your life right now – then work toward it.

We would like you to start thinking daily about having Peace in your life. What your thoughts and impressions are about the gift of PEACE AND JOY?

As you begin reading this chapter, write down a few thoughts you have as you contemplate this wonderful gift. We will ask this question again at the end of the chapter after you have completed your study of the gift of Peace and Joy.

_____

_____

_____

_____

_____

_____

_____

_____

_____

_____

What did Jesus say about PEACE AND JOY?

"And he arose, and rebuked the wind, and
said unto the sea, Peace, be still. And the
wind ceased, and there was a great calm."
~ Mark 4:39 ~

"Salt is good: but if the salt have lost his
saltness, wherewith will ye season it? Have salt
in yourselves, and have peace one with another."
~ Mark 9:50 ~

As we thought through what we would include in the 12 GIFTS, we knew we had to include Peace and Joy. After all, that is what we all long for in this life. We can't even count the number of times we have said, "I just need to be at Peace." Can you relate? We go through our lives with moments of Peace and spurts of Joy here and there, but what does it require to have Peace and Joy as a constant in our lives?

As we ponder that question, we think about the things that disturb our feelings of Peace. For us, some of those things might include:

- The actions of other people
- Our inability to let things go
- Our willingness to let others' moods affect us
- Self-inflicted stress business
- Too many responsibilities
- The inability to say no

I, Janeen, had a dear friend say to me one time, "Janeen, you are too busy. Life is about 'being' more than about 'doing.'"

Her words hit hard, and I realized there are times in my life when I allow myself to take on too much. I sometimes want to accomplish too many things, and then I begin to realize I am caught up in getting things done, and I am missing the JOY of just "being."

The times I am the happiest in my life are the times when I have enough free time to take walks, cook, enjoy my family, be with friends, sit out on my deck and eat breakfast for an hour if I want, and just breathe for heavens sake!

We have to prioritize and really put some thought into what's important to us.

- Do we need the big house?
- Do we need the expensive cars?
- Do we have to be traveling all the time?
- Is it necessary to eat out all the time?

Think about this...
- What if there were less house to clean?
- What if there was less yard to take care of?
- What if you had time to cook dinner every night?
- What if you could play with your kids every day?
- What if you had time to sit down and talk to your husband each evening?
- What if you could alleviate the stress?
- What if you had time to just sit and read once in awhile?
- What if you could relax in the bathtub when you felt like it?
- What if you had time to take the dogs for a walk?

There are a whole list of things you could probably come up with that you would rather be doing than working all of the time in order to pay the bills. Of course, we have to work. Work is good for us, and it is necessary to live. But maybe there are some things we could give up in order to allow that Peace and Joy to flow into our lives a bit more freely.

"To give light to them that sit in darkness and in the shadow of death, to guide our feet into the way of peace."
~ Luke 1:79 ~

Stories to help us reflect on the Gift of PEACE AND JOY:

When we think about Peace and Joy, it always brings thoughts of Christmas, as we're sure it does with each of you. But Peace and Joy can be attained throughout the year if we learn to do the things that will let them into our lives, AND if we learn to do WITHOUT the things that take our Peace and Joy away.

As you read the following stories, think of your own stories and reflect on the times when you have felt at Peace – what were you doing or NOT doing that allowed that blanket of serenity to cover you up and hold you tight.

LET GO AND TRUST

by Janeen

Throughout my life, there have been times when I longed for Peace. I know I am no different than any of you in this. When life gets stressful and events take their toll, we feel anxious and agitated and long for life to slow down.

We want to feel better.

We want to feel at Peace, but the question is – how do we achieve it?

I believe it is possible to be at Peace no matter what the circumstances of life. If we wait for all of our problems to go away, we will be waiting a lifetime to enjoy those highly anticipated feelings of Peace. We have to make a conscious choice to live in Peace rather than chaos - no matter what's going on at the time.

We have to CHOOSE Peace.

I have lived plenty of my life in unrest. When things haven't gone the way I planned or expected, I have allowed myself to feel angry or resentful or try to force my circumstances to change to the way I want them to be. It took me many years to finally realize that is no way to live.

What I have learned over the years is that forcing our lives to
- Fit a certain mold; or
- Achieve a certain status; or
- Feel a certain way; or
- Attract certain people
- Only sets us up for disappointment.

Heavenly Father has a plan for each one of us, and it took me several years to learn to trust and let go and allow Him to guide me through my life.

Does that mean we just sit back and let whatever is going to happen - happen? No, it means we work hard, we do all that we can to bring good things into our lives, and then we trust in our Lord and Savior to take us where we need to be.

One night about five years ago, I woke up with an idea that would not leave me alone. I decided right then that I would begin writing a book the very next day. It was to be a book about marriage. I wanted to let people know the things I wish I had done before I decided to end my marriage. I wanted to help others learn from my mistakes.

I began taking a few notes right then, and began writing the very next morning. I worked long and hard until I completed my book, Save Your Marriage in 30.

The book was not a bestseller, but it took me down a path that began to change my life.

First, to a non-profit company looking for people like me to share their stories and contribute on an even higher level. We began organizing support groups for people who had been divorced and needed to heal – which led me to Elizabeth Hickey, my dear friend and co-author of this book.

I was being led. And the journey is not over. I think of the paths that have crossed over mine during the past five years and the opportunities that have knocked on my door, and I can't help but see the miracle that began to occur in my life once I turned things over and allowed myself to be guided by the Holy Spirit.

*"His lord said unto him, Well done, thou good
and faithful servant: thou hast been faithful
over a few things, I will make thee ruler over
many things: enter thou into the joy of thy lord."*
~ Matthew 25:21 ~

THERE IS ALWAYS ROOM FOR PEACE AND JOY
by Elizabeth

We deliberately made the eleventh chapter PEACE AND JOY because it relates to the anticipation that many of us feel as were prepare for the Joy of the Christmas season. If you have decided to begin using the book in January, following one chapter per month, you will have reached Peace and Joy in November. Many of us think about having gratitude in November, which we can still do. However, whether we agree with the timing or not, the season of Christmas is present during the month of November. Also, we believe by practicing the previous 11 gifts throughout the year, the culmination of those 11 new habits in our daily lives will manifest a greater awareness of love.

As we have referenced throughout the book, we believe we come to earth to learn many lessons about living, sharing, caring and becoming more Christ-like. As we engage in the activities of our lives, we will have many opportunities to become wiser, more thoughtful, and more loving. Loving like Jesus is a worthy goal, but none of us will come close to be able to love like Jesus truly did, because our lives were not appointed for this role. Jesus knew his divine plan, and He accepted it. We know that our divine plans are to strive to be more like Jesus, and we can accept this. Just striving to live our lives which reflect love and the other gifts from Jesus, would surely please Him and our Heavenly Father.

Becoming perfect like Jesus is not really the goal of this book. The goal of developing these habits is to become more like Jesus. Loving others in a way that Jesus would have, is a beautiful way to live our lives. There is much more about love in the next chapter. My intention with writing the above paragraphs was to explain why we selected Peace and Joy for the eleventh chapter. I hope this explanation clarifies why we formatted it this way. However, all readers can certainly use this book in whatever manner suits your style. There is not one way to approach any of this. Readers are free to creatively design any type of path which works. I was diagnosed with ADD and dyslexia many years ago. Once I learned about these two issues, I finally understood why I skipped all around a book and could not read it from front cover to back cover. I would often pick up a book and begin by reading the last chapter, and then I would weave my way through the book, in a backwards direction. It worked for me! So whatever works for you, just plunge in and read. Mix it up!

One of the reasons Janeen and I worked so well together on this book is because we have completely different ways of going about things, yet our unique styles compliment one another. But if we tried to be roommates in college, we probably would have asked to be switched! Janeen starts from the beginning, and I begin from the end. How confusing would that be, unless you reached a point where you valued the talents and gifts of the other person. So use this book in any way that works for you and your loved ones/friends whom you might be sharing it with. There is no way to fail at this if you simply embrace the intention to become more Christ-like.

Clearly, I am long winded in sharing a story, and Janeen gets to the point. One of the goals of this chapter is to reflect on the gift of Joy. One way to do this is to reflect on the many differences amongst people and, instead of trying to conform one another to become more similar, we should celebrate the marvelous, unique talents each person has.

When we think about the gift of Joy, we often feel a sense of exuberance, energy and plain old enthusiasm! Joy is an expression of how our hearts feel when our emotions are overflowing with happiness and excitement. I spent many years working with children who have special needs, and one of the gifts these kids taught me is that every person is an individual. Something that excites one child, causing them to feel over the top Joy, might cause another child to want to take a nap. We are all individuals, and we all have unique experiences which prompt pure Joy and happiness. As we learn to value these things in ourselves, it is a beautiful gift to others to take a step back and appreciate the unique things in another which prompt expressions of pure Joy.

Whatever it is that causes you to find overwhelming Joy and happiness, we wish it for you during this festive season. If you haven't fully recognized what it is, or where the sources of your greatest moments of Joy are, we wish you a wonderful journey as you explore these wonderful wells of Joy and happiness. Some of us have concluded that it is wrong to feel Joy when others are suffering. There is always room for great Joy, and there is also plenty of room for empathy and sympathy.

I remember a time in my life when I felt guilty about expressing my full Joy and showing my happiness because many people of my generation frequently heard expressions about how many other people in the world were suffering. I wrongly assumed that if I felt Joy, I wasn't caring about the kids who were suffering. So I squashed my Joy. I recall hearing how the starving kids around the world would be so happy to have the dinner I had. When I was about ten years old, I remember hearing many variations of how so many other kids would love the dinner I had. I vividly recall a family dinner where I had heard this phrase one too many times, and I boldly said back to my parents, "Well let's send it to them then and they can eat it!" My siblings put down their forks and watched and waited. OOPS! Very WRONG thing to say, and even I knew it when the words were coming out of my mouth. But once it began, there was no turning back. Yikes!! No more dinner, no dessert, nothing. Off to bed I went to think about how mean I was being to all of the starving children. Of course, this blocked my ability to feel Joy for a long time. I felt like I was being insensitive to those who were suffering.

We can and should work past these issues by talking about them with our friends, family, loved ones and a counselor. if needed. I believe Jesus wants each and every person to feel great moments of Joy. It is in these moments where we are sending up great gratitude to heaven also. We are feeling and expressing the Joy of living true to who we are, recognizing our spiritual connection to God, Jesus and the Holy Spirit, and this awareness should bring us Joy. It is a beautiful thing to know and feel the truths in our lives. We can celebrate the beautiful Joy of our Savior's birth at Christmas time. It's wonderful to feel happiness. We are not being disrespectful to others when we express Joy.

However, sensitivity, compassion and tenderness for those who are actively grieving or suffering, is absolutely necessary. There are definite occasions in life where we do want to suppress our Joy, in respect for others. But we shouldn't have to suppress our Joy as we go through life. Paying attention to timing and being aware of the pain that others are feeling, is key to doing this.

PEACE IS LIKE A MAGIC WAND
by Elizabeth

When we hear the word Peace, many of us think about moments of beautiful tranquility, serenity and feelings of calmness. Peace is a desired and sought after state of being. Many of our greeting card messages use the word Peace in them when we are wishing others positive messages, comfort and sympathy. Nature also provides many stunning and amazing landscapes and images which are so breathtaking and beautiful, they fill us with overwhelming awe and feelings of great Peace as we submerse ourselves in these natural gifts.

One of the reasons we hear so many expressions of Peace and Joy during the Christmas season is because we are celebrating the birth of Jesus Christ, and all of the gifts he has provided to us. Peace and Joy are two of the most overwhelming emotional gifts that Jesus bestows upon us. I recall one of the first times in my life, as a twelve-year-old child, struggling with great emotional pain and turmoil after an abusive situation, I hid in our garage and prayed my heart out through a steady of tears, and then I felt this incredible deep sense of Peace sweep over me. It was the most beautiful feeling I had ever felt.

At twelve years old, the only way I could describe it to my best friend, Pam, was to say, "Imagine a magic wand that sweeps over you and makes all of your pain turn to gold." I still recall trying to explain it and find the words to describe what happened to me, but there were no words that could even came close to it. Pam said something like, "Wouldn't that be great if we could really have a magic wand that could do that? We could make so many things better in the world?" Pam was an optimist and an amazing and supportive friend, and she did the best she could as she shared encouraging words.

The thing about a supportive friend, as I look back at it now from an adult perspective, is that the friend doesn't need to have the right words, they just need to have the right attitude – one of acceptance, trust and hope. A great friend allows you to say whatever you need to express and, they don't judge you, they just listen like Pam did, and they help you find a glimmer of hope or a silver lining. They believe in you and they show it. I did not share the abuse story with Pam (just like most kids who are victims of abuse don't – partly because we are told not to, and we feel ashamed, but also because we are confused and don't know how to express it.)

I am sharing this story, not to focus on the story of abuse, but to relate the hope of feeling the gift from Jesus which we call Peace. It was the first time I had ever known such Peace, and it overwhelmed me. Recalling those moments in my garage, as I sat there bawling my eyes out, makes me cry again as I write this. It was such a sacred experience. (I share it with you because I want you to know that it is available to all of us.)

We never forget those type of moments because they are so profound. That was the first time I knew, for sure, that Jesus was real, and that His Peace was real, along with His love. It transformed me, and I just knew. There was no way to deny it because those peaceful feelings came over me while I was crying to Jesus and begging for His help. I was twelve, but it didn't matter what age I was – it was the most real thing I have ever felt.

I had always believed in Jesus because my family attended our local Catholic church every Sunday. I could feel the Peace in the church, and I liked going. On the few occasions when my family decided not to attend on Sunday, I would walk to church and sit in the back by myself because I liked the feeling of Peace in the church. It made me feel Peace inside no matter what else was going on in my life or in the world.

Now that I am an adult, with more decades of living experience, I will reveal a truth that has sustained my faith, hope and love in Jesus. When I described the feeling of Peace to my best friend, Pam, when I was twelve, I could only describe it as a magic wand of Peace being swept over me. That's how it felt. Now as an adult, in my prayers and in my mind, I call it a spiritual wand. I pray to be used for good in the world, and to reach out and care for others. As a social worker and mediator, I have many opportunities to do this. I ask Jesus to sweep His spiritual wand over others, using me to do it. And He does. When I know in my heart that Jesus is sweeping His spiritual wand and using me to love others, those indescribable feelings of Peace return again. They are so fulfilling, and they sustain me. Joy overflows in my heart when I know I am being used. It feels like heaven is tapping me on the head saying, "Thank You!" The saying about when we give to others, we are also giving to ourselves, is so true. When we are loving others and helping them, we feel the strongest sense of Peace. Play around with it – don't just accept my story. Try it for yourself. Pray to be used for good, and notice others around you. Listen for promptings. I believe and hope that you will also discover one of the greatest sources of Peace ever, which is living close to Jesus Christ.

"For where two or three are gathered together in my name, there am I in the midst of them."
~ Matthew 18:20 ~

Try to imagine the invisible, but very real power, of many people all coming to one beautiful and sacred place – a church to worship, to pray and to reflect upon Jesus. Of course, Jesus will be there! With all of the sincere intentions in the room gathered together in His Name, and according to scripture, "When two or three are gathered together in my name, there am I in the midst of them."

So if you are reading this, and perhaps you haven't been to church lately, find a church near you. And since this book is about Jesus and you are reading it, consider looking for a Christian church where they celebrate Jesus. As you sit amongst other people who are praying, try and imagine the invisible power of prayer going up to heaven. Imagine that Jesus is present amongst you, listening and sharing and caring. It's an amazing feeling! Sometimes I can't even recall the words that were spoken in church that day, but I can always remember the warm and PEACEFUL feelings I experienced. I wish the same for you. (The words are good too, so pay attention because sometimes the words will really inspire you!)

As we celebrate the Christmas season, we sincerely wish you, the reader or listener of this book, the warmest feelings of Peace. Once you feel Peace, the Joy just follows. So celebrate Jesus and His gifts to us, embrace them, feel them and let the Joy overflow! Jesus will be so pleased to have so many people truly remember the reason for this special season of Christmas. Enjoy it! Feel the Peace, Joy and love and share it! The more we share it, the more we get to feel it too!

GET INTO THE LIFEBOAT
by Janeen

Stop and think for a moment – how many times have you said out loud, or thought to yourself "I just want to have Peace in my life."

We've all said it. We all want it.

I have discovered that I don't think so much about it when I am feeling at Peace. It's when I'm not feeling at Peace – when I'm in turmoil or chaos – that's when I notice something is missing.

I was living in a very difficult marriage that had my stomach turning constantly over the course of ten years. I knew all was not well, and I prayed everyday to my Heavenly Father to help me understand and know what to do. I was able to find happiness in many other areas of my life, but never able to feel at Peace in my relationship with my husband.

One day, a phone call came that rocked my world. My husband had been involved in an extramarital affair for, not only the entire length of our marriage, but for several years before - during our courtship.

I was stunned.
I was shocked.
I was heartbroken.

I took the next five days to sort things out and gather information. I talked with an attorney, my parents, my bishop and my best friend. I tried to calm down before rushing to judgment or making any rash decisions. But now things began to add up. A lot of unanswered questions started to become clear. It was no surprise that I had felt so much turmoil between us. I didn't know why, but I knew things weren't right. The next 2 1/2 years were a trial of my faith. In the end, I left him.

I now know what it feels like to have true Peace in my life. Because of my decision to do the right thing for myself and my family, I have felt guidance and love from my Savior. I have felt the pure love of Christ and been blessed with joy and absolute Peace. Not only did my decision to leave bring Peace, but my decision to continue living a Christ-like life – one filled with service to others, prayer and forgiveness – has brought great Joy into my life.

Because of this experience, I have learned to trust my instincts and my gut. When something isn't feeling right – when something is nagging at you and you feel unsettled – listen. Stop and listen. Hear the whisperings of the Spirt and take them to heart.

A very dear friend of mine said something to me not long ago that has stayed with me and helped me to heal from this experience. As I related my story to him about the pain I had suffered and the difficult decision I made, he said,

"Janeen, you got off of the sinking ship and into the lifeboat!"

As I thought about what he said, I realized my lifeboat is my Savior, Jesus Christ.

Peace IS attainable. It requires aligning ourselves on the correct path and staying true to ourselves and close to the Spirit.

I truly did get into the lifeboat, and it has made all the difference.

"Rejoice, and be exceeding glad: for great
is your reward in heaven: for so persecuted
they the prophets which were before you."
~ Matthew 5:12 ~

Think of some things you can do to start to move toward true Peace your life. Not just for the moment, but for a lifetime – that Peace of mind that comes with living a Christ-like life – the kind that won't be rocked when something bad happens – the kind that settles in at your core and allows you to feel grief or pain or disappointment, but ultimately carries you back to that safe place.

Take some time to write these things down in your journal and begin incorporating them into your life. Choose things that will work for YOU. Only you know what you need and what you are able to do.

Here is a sample affirmation to say each day, to reinforce the commitment to living each day mindfully, while appreciating the gift of Peace and Joy:

AFFIRMATION: I am at Peace in my heart. There are many things that cause chaos and turmoil in my life, but I will rise above it and look to my Savior for true and lasting Peace. I will let my heart feel Joyful even when things are difficult. I will let others see my Joy and my Peace so they may realize it is possible to have these gifts at all times.

"Set peace of mind as your highest goal, and organize your life around it."
~ Brian Tracy ~

Applying the gift of PEACE AND JOY:

We have been anxious to get to our list about obtaining Peace and Joy. There are many, many things we can do, say, aspire to and work toward that could potentially bring us Peace and Joy.

Peace of mind, Peace with ourselves, Peace when we are at rest, Peace in our relationships with others. PEACE – what a beautiful word.

And feeling JOY as much as possible throughout our lives ought to be something we focus on each and every day. It's something we definitely want to incorporate more into our own lives. We are excited to work through this list and start thinking of the possibilities.

So be thinking of your own ideas too as you read through our list to get yourself thinking, feeling and acting in such a way that will make it easier to bring Joy into your own life and into the lives of your friends and family.

Here is our list to get you going:

- Go for a hike and enjoy the beautiful scenery
- Lay on the grass and find shapes in the clouds
- Sit on your porch at night and listen to the crickets
- Eat breakfast outside and enjoy the birds singing
- Sleep in a tent in your backyard with your kids and tell stories
- Take a nap with your puppies
- Take a nap with your husband :)
- Meditate every morning
- Work on your relationship with your Heavenly Father
- Hug your kids every day
- Find things that you can look forward to
- Live your life in the present

- Remember that life has a way of working things out
- Put your worries, your troubles and your stresses in God's hands
- Make sure your family always comes first
- Nourish your relationship with your spouse every day
- Let go of toxic friends who consume your energy
- Get yourself out of debt
- Be still and just listen at least once a day
- Surround yourself with happy, productive people
- Get organized – everything in its place
- Let go of the things you can't control
- Eat dinner at the table with your family
- Simplify
- Be excited about what could happen tomorrow
- Mend your relationships
- Accept yourself for who you are
- Go for a bike ride along a river or beautiful path
- Wrap up in a blanket and look at the stars
- Find something you truly enjoy and do it often
- Forgive those you have yet to forgive
- Forget about the hurt you have endured and look forward to a new life
- Don't ignore your problems – solve them
- Go to the park and have a picnic with someone you love
- Relax in the tub whenever you can
- Remember – the future is a gift
- Walk in the rain with an umbrella
- Fly a kite with your grandkids
- Realize that joy heals your spirit
- Build a snowman
- Make popcorn and watch a funny movie with your family
- Keep your home clean and quiet
- Listen to uplifting music
- Do the best you can – and keep in mind that everyone else is also doing the best they can

- Remember that peace comes from within – do what is required to obtain it
- Take care of your health – eat right and exercise
- Don't judge others – try to understand them instead
- Treat yourself with respect
- Speak kindly to those who treat you unfairly
- Let go of grudges
- Take a canoe out on a lake
- Get out of bed before the sun comes up and watch the sunrise
- Walk through a flower garden
- Recognize how blessed you are
- Make a decision to be happy no matter what's going on in your life
- Laugh with someone every day
- Joy is created by YOU – not your circumstances – don't forget that
- Try to look for something good in every day
- Try to look for something good in every person you meet
- Choose to be joyful
- Talk about the joys in your life with your friends
- Enjoy the journey
- Swim in the ocean
- Walk on the beach in bare feet
- Hold a baby
- Talk to Heavenly Father whenever you can
- Live a life of integrity
- Always tell the truth
- Put your trust in the Lord
- Have compassion
- Be useful to others
- Express concern when you can see that someone is hurting
- Find out what brings you joy and go there a lot
- Talk about happy things with your wife
- Be appreciative

Choose a couple of items from this list that you'd like to get started on right away. And DO THEM.

Be deliberate about the things you practice that will bring you greater Peace and Joy so that you can form new habits and continue to experience these things in a greater way.

We'd like you to think about some things that have gone on in your life now, so take a break from your reading and complete the following activity. Fill a couple of pages in your journal if you can.

Think back on a time when you were feeling like your life was out of control. What was going on?
- *Maybe you suffered the loss of a loved one*
- *Maybe you lost your job*
- *Maybe you received some terrible news*
- *Maybe you have been dealing with an illness*
- *Maybe you were going through a divorce*

Answer these questions:
- What were the circumstances that made you feel unsettled?
- Describe what you were going through emotionally.
- How were you treating people at the time – your family, your friends, people you didn't know?
- What ultimately did it take to get you back to a place of Peace?
- Or, maybe you're still struggling with getting back – in that case, what would it take for you to feel Peace again?
- What steps would you tell someone else to take if they were struggling to feel at Peace?
- What are the things that get you feeling stressed out and off track?

The point of this activity is to get you looking deep inside yourself to find out what things get you off track – Is it your relationships with people? Is it having no control over things that happen to you? Is it a lack of faith that things will work out? Get to the bottom of it, and figure out what YOU need to do to have PEACE in your heart.

Life can change in an instant. We can be going along, feeling like we have the world by the tail, when all of a sudden, there is a tragic accident, or we get news of a death in the family, or any number of events that are earth shattering and can change our lives forever.

We have come to realize that these things are necessary for us to grow. Sometimes our lives change for the better. Sometimes we experience things we needed to experience. Do you believe that God throws things your way to make you stronger? Do you think He wants to give you a wake-up call sometimes? Do you think He is trying to get you to see something you didn't see before?

God wants us to be happy. But He also wants us to grow. If we can figure out a way to do both – we can be at Peace. Happiness doesn't necessarily come by getting everything we want. Sometimes the things we think we want can make us unhappy in the end. And worrying about things that are out of our control is another sure-fire way to destroy any chance of having Peace.

Lord if it's not your will, let it slip through my
grasp and give me the peace not to worry about it.
~ *Tony A Gaskins Jr.* ~

The key, we believe, is to find that balance between getting what we want, and giving what others need.

A good friend of mine recently started dating someone who experienced a tragic death in their family. She wanted to attend the funeral and show her support for him, thinking her presence would calm him. But he told her he wanted to spend the time with his kids and his family – that it would not be an appropriate time for her to meet the rest of the family. She had to dig way down deep to accept the fact that he was right. She felt hurt and rejected, but ultimately, he appreciated her for understanding.

Sometimes giving others what THEY need is a way to obtain that life-long Peace that we talked about early in this chapter. By allowing the people we love to tell us what they would like from us – and then honoring that request – we build trust and respect. And everyone feels a sense of Peace.

What are your thoughts and impressions now about the gift of PEACE AND JOY?

Has anything changed or come into your awareness that wasn't there before?
Jot down your thoughts now after 30 days of reflection:

_____

_____

_____

_____

_____

_____

_____

_____

_____

_____

_____

_____

_____

_____

_____

*"These things have I spoken unto you, that my joy
might remain in you, and that your joy might be full."
~ John 15:11 ~*

CONCLUSION:

Peace and Joy are gifts we can experience all year long, not just at Christmas-time. We believe feeling Peace has a lot to do with the way we treat others. If we are kind, loving, understanding and respectful of those we love, AND those we don't know, we have fewer reasons to be in turmoil.

When we look back on our lives, it seems the lack of Peace tends to come when we are at odds with people. We all know people who have very difficult relationships – with family members, with neighbors, with their spouse – and it is very hard to feel at Peace when those circumstances exist. It is much harder to have a good relationship with our Savior, too, when we aren't getting along with those around us.

We want each of us to work hard to do the things that will bring Peace and Joy into our lives throughout the year. Work on your relationships first. When you have Peace in those areas, you will experience a greater sense of Joy and happiness.

DAILY REFLECTION

(Repetition is what creates new habit. Read this page daily as a reminder.)

Each chapter is meant to be read slowly,
Absorbing the deeper essence behind the words and stories.

This allows for continual reflection,
Prayer and listening for answers,
Which opens the door to
Greater insight and awareness of
The Gift of Love.

If we devote one month of the year,
To learning and living the Gift of Love,
Our awareness of the precious Gift of Love,
Will be spiritually heightened,
And our daily existence will emulate this awareness.

As we make this shift to mindful attentiveness to the Gift of Love,
We will be less likely to take for granted, Love.
We will have developed a habit,
Which becomes part of who we are.

As we develop a new habit each month,
Based on a different Gift each month,
A Gift that Jesus came to earth to give each one of us,
We will become more like Jesus in the way we live.
As this happens,
We will be living a more Christlike life, every day.
As we do this,
We are expressing our deepest gratitude to Jesus
And our Heavenly Father.

As we share the 12 Gifts with others,
We cannot help but bring the same love and peace
To our own hearts and spirits.

——— 12 ———

The *Gift* of

LOVE

I couldn't wait to talk about Love as our twelfth gift. Jesus has taught us to Love one another – no matter our differences. Learning to Love is one of the most wonderful, yet one of the most difficult things we will ever do while here on this earth. And having a Christ-like Love for everyone we meet is the ultimate gift we can give to ourselves.

Imagine how much easier and how much more fulfilling our lives would be if we could express Love rather than resentment – rather than judgment – rather than rejection. It's so easy to Love the people who are like us. But what about all the people who are NOT like us? What then?

Heavenly Father made us all different for a reason. If we all looked the same, thought the same, dressed the same, enjoyed the same things – how boring the world would be. But, not only that, it would be easy to get along and Love one another. Heavenly Father wants us to prove ourselves. He wants to know we can set aside our differences and, not only get along, but truly learn to Love each other.

Love is required in order to sincerely practice the eleven other gifts we have shared with you in our book. Can you imagine having Peace in your life if you don't Love people? Can you imagine Forgiving someone if you don't have Love in your heart? Can you imagine showing Gratitude to your Savior if you don't Love Him? Ultimately, it all comes down to Love.

By reading and working through this book, you are showing your Love for Jesus Christ by proving to Him you want to live a more Christ-like life. Your gift to Him now is greater Love and a greater commitment to becoming more like Him.

Why did we choose LOVE as the twelfth gift?

"But love ye your enemies, and do good, and lend, hoping for nothing again; and your reward shall be great, and ye shall be the children of the Highest: for he is kind unto the unthankful and to the evil."
~ Luke 6:35 ~

"For if ye love them which love you, what thank have ye? for sinners also love those that love them."
~ Luke 6:32 ~

In wrapping up our list of the 12 GIFTS we received from our Savior, Jesus Christ, we are ending with Love because, as you can see, Love is the all-encompassing, all-embracing gift that ties everything else together. Without Love, we would not be able to enjoy or share all of the other gifts we have talked about in this book.

Love is the first and great commandment. Of each of us it is required to Love everyone. As co-authors of this book, we have discussed, many times, the belief that we were put on this earth to learn to Love. It sounds so easy, but can be so difficult at times.

- How do we LOVE the person who betrays us?
- How do we LOVE the individual who treats us unkindly or unfairly?
- How do we LOVE the one who lies to us, cheats us, or steals from us?
- How do we LOVE someone who hurts our children?
- How do we LOVE a person who is selfish?

As difficult as it can sometimes be, it is not for us to question why or how. We are commanded to Love, and sometimes it requires digging deep within ourselves to look for –

- that last bit of compassion,
- that tiny bit of tolerance,
- that last ounce of self control,
- that last bit of acceptance.

We are all children of our Father in Heaven. He Loves each of us the same. He expects nothing less from us.

"A new commandment I give unto you, That ye love one another; as I have loved you, that ye also love one another."
~ John 13:34 ~

"By this shall all men know that ye are my disciples, if ye have love one to another."
~ John 13:35 ~

When we think about Love, we might also contemplate closely-related words that help us to embrace a deeper meaning of Love. These words could include:

DEVOTION, EMOTION, CHERISHING, RESPECT, ALLEGIANCE, APPRECIATION, KINDNESS

I am sharing the following story because I the woman in this story is one of the greatest examples of Love that I know in my life.

"WE DO WHAT NEEDS TO BE DONE"
by Janeen

I know a woman who is kind, generous, loving and selfless. Her name is Mandy, and she recently went through a serious illness. She has two young children and works from home.

A neighbor of hers had been struggling in many ways in her own life. She had three young children, and would often ask Mandy to watch her children and help her out with things. One morning, Mandy learned the news that her neighbor had tragically taken her own life. The sadness was all-encompassing. The thought of a grieving husband and three small children left alone to figure out why and how to put the pieces back together, was overwhelming.

Mandy showed great strength that day in caring for things that needed to be done and helping the family in any way she could. But the true test of her Love has come in the past several months as she has taken the girls into her home at any time of the day or night when they needed to be comforted, fed, or simply needed a place to feel safe. She has become their second mom in a way. She thinks nothing of taking care of three more children or being there emotionally for them. She plans to continue helping with the girls for as long as it takes. She is truly blessed with the gift of Love.

As we contemplate the gift of Love and what it means on many different levels, let's think about what Love really involves. Think about the following questions and answer after you have really put some deep thought into them:

What does it mean to Love your children or your close family?

_____

_____

_____

_____

_____

When you Love those who are different than you – how does that look?
How do you feel?
How do you treat them?

_____

_____

_____

_____

_____

When you "fall" in Love you feel wonderful. But when you come back to reality and settle into truly Loving your spouse, what is required of you?

_____

_____

_____

_____

_____

What does it mean to Love your Savior, Jesus Christ? What are your actions?

_____

_____

_____

_____

_____

If someone tells you they Love you – what do you expect from them?

_____

_____

_____

_____

_____

How do you show Love to those who have hurt you?

_____

_____

_____

_____

_____

THE 12 GIFTS ARE WRAPPED UP WITH LOVE. We want to quote a passage out of one of our favorite books, "Peace Be Unto Thy Soul" by Joseph L. Bishop. He talks about how to increase your Love and, by so doing, change your world. He talks in his book about people who overcome grief, and how a new appreciation for life emerges from the fact that they conquered such a huge mountain. They tend to have a spiritual shift to those things that matter most. Here is what he says:

"God has commanded us to love Him and our neighbors as ourselves because all things good flow into and out of Love."

- Recognize that you cannot truly Love without having charity.
- You cannot truly Love without being kind.
- You cannot truly Love without being humble.
- You cannot truly Love without being appreciative of your blessings.

But it works both ways.

- You cannot truly have charity for others and not have Love.
- You cannot genuinely be kind to others and not have Love.
- You cannot truly be humble and not have Love.
- You cannot be appreciative and not have Love.

This takes place because, again, all things are circumscribed into one great whole. And that whole is Love – the subject of the greatest commandment of all."

When we really take this to heart and stop and think it through, we believe that Love is the answer. It's the answer to just about every problem or dilemma we may experience. Think about it. Think about the struggles you've had in your life.

What was it that brought you to that place where you were able to:

- be at peace,
- forgive someone,
- feel connected to the Holy Spirit,
- feel compassion for someone else,
- be strong enough to be an example to others,
- experience humility,
- be honest in your relationships with others,
- feel gratitude,
- have hope in the future,
- or have faith in your Savior?

It was Love.

There is great power in Love. It is no coincidence that the first commandment is to Love the Lord. We believe if we can truly learn to love our Savior, our fellow men and ourselves, we can collectively make this world a better place.

Make it your GOAL this month as you ponder the gift of Love to contemplate the things that matter most to you in your life.

Choose someone in your life you could be more kind toward and work on that relationship.

Choose a GOAL that is in line with something you want to increase for yourself in the area of Love.

"Ye have heard that it hath been said, Thou shalt "love thy neighbour, and hate thine enemy. But I say unto you, "Love your enemies, bless them that curse you, do good to them that hate you, and pray for them which despitefully use you, and persecute you."
~ Matthew 5: 43-44 ~

What are your thoughts and impressions about the gift of LOVE?

As you begin reading this chapter, write down a few thoughts you have as you contemplate the gift of Love. We will ask this question again at the end of the chapter after you have completed your study of the gift of Love.

_____

_____

_____

_____

_____

_____

_____

_____

_____

_____

_____

_____

_____

_____

_____

_____

_____

_____

What did Jesus say about LOVE?

"And thou shalt love the Lord thy God with all thy heart, and with all thy soul, and with all thy mind, and with all thy strength: this is the first commandment."
~ Mark 12: 30 ~

When we Love someone, we give of ourselves to them. We sacrifice our comfort to make sure our children are taken care of. We give up things we want to make sure our family has what they need. We give up our time, our money and our own desires to make sure those we Love are happy.

Jesus Christ Loves each one of us. He Loved us so much that He sacrificed His own life that we may have everlasting life. He devoted His entire existence on this earth to us – to provide us with a Savior, to teach us how to be happy and to have the possibility of eternal life.

Our Savior Loved us so much He died for us.

And He doesn't ask for much in return. He asks us to keep His commandments and Love one another. Showing Him how much we Love Him by working to become more like Him is the greatest gift we can give back.

"And the second is like, namely this, Thous shalt love thy neighbour as thyself. There is none other commandment greater than these."
~ Mark 12:31 ~

Stories to help us reflect on the Gift of LOVE:

There are many stories in each of our lives that show us how Love can change lives and help people. We are sharing some of our favorite stories of Love here, and we hope you will reflect on some of your own stories as you read them.

Love is the most wonderful gift we have been blessed with. Life is so much more meaningful when we Love. The relationships we form with people we Love will go with us when this life is over. And the more people we know, the more we can Love. We have found it to be true that getting to know people we don't think we could ever Love, often changes things. It has been said that, "if you don't particularly like a person, you probably don't know them." Most people have good things to offer, and if we take the time to get to know someone, we most certainly will learn to Love them to some degree.

We hope you can gain greater insight into your own relationships with those you Love as you read the following stories.

"HE WAS GONE"
by Janeen

Last week marked the one-year anniversary of the death of my dear friend's son.

I was on vacation in Hawaii when I received the phone call. One of our mutual friends called to tell me that one of our friend's children had passed away, but she didn't know which one. There were police cars and emergency vehicles all around their house, and neighbors were standing outside waiting to hear the news.

My heart sunk. I knew it was her oldest son - a troubled young man who had lived a life of addiction for the past ten years. He had slipped into a coma when he was a teenager that lasted for three months, and nothing short of a miracle brought him out of it. What seemed like a blessing at the time, turned out to be a test of faith and enduring Love.

He came out of that coma only to live another ten years of torture, not only to himself, but to his family. My friend often told me stories of the tragic life he lived. He was not the same person coming out of the coma. When he woke up, his family knew his life would be changed forever, that he would never go near drugs again after that experience, but the opposite became true. He landed in and out of jail, in and out of drug rehab, and in and out of the emergency room many times over those next ten years.

Life for his family was so difficult, and yet – they loved him unconditionally. I watched in awe as my friend put up with unspeakable things day in and day out. She knew in her heart that one day he would simply leave this life, most likely from an overdose, and he did. That morning as she related the story to me, she had been on about her business.

"I had gotten up to go into my office to work and spent the day doing the things I always do. I left in the afternoon to go to the store to get groceries, and returned home to make dinner. I prepared the food and set the table, and when I called everyone up to the dinner table, I asked if anyone had seen their brother. My heart stopped as I realized he had come home from a job interview that morning and gone to his room. No one had seen him come out. His dad ran downstairs and broke through the locked door to find him, lying peacefully on his bed. He was gone. I lost my head for a few minutes. I was devastated. Even though I had prepared myself for this moment... I was NOT prepared. We had been through this scenario so many times before, but we had always called the ambulance in time to save his life."

She called me the next day to let me know of his death, and to talk through her pain and and grief and sadness and... relief. She was at peace. She knew it was for the best and that her son was now in a place of Love and peace. She knew he was at rest and had been blessed to leave his suffering behind. She could feel his presence and knew that he was truly sorry for the pain he had caused - not only his family - but himself. But still, they would miss him so much. They would feel the pain of this loss for a lifetime.

She spoke of the deep Love all of our kind friends and neighbors showed to her and her family during this time. She was so very grateful that everyone gathered around her and displayed a true Christ-like Love for, not only her family, but her son who had been so difficult. She continues to speak of how that Love saved her and has made her son's death bearable. The Love of people who care and who love unconditionally is a true gift.

The irony to me is that she doesn't see how her own ability to Love unconditionally is what brought that Love in great abundance back to her. She blessed the life of her son, and she continues to bless the lives of those she comes in contact with, and she will always have love coming her way because of it.

JACK AND TILLIE
by Elizabeth

Each of us should be lucky enough to be welcomed into the homes of happy and loving families, as we are growing up. Noticing other families gives a child perspective and appreciation for the various qualities that other people have, along with an awareness of how other families live. I'm sharing a very personal story of my childhood, and how an amazing family taught me so many life lessons.

Jack and Tillie were the parents of my best, life-long friend Pam. I met Pam in fourth grade when my family had moved to a small town in upstate New York. I felt insecure about the move, new town, and new people for many reasons. I was shy, anxious, and worried about acceptance. However, the first day in my new school, I saw Pam in my class, with her smiling happy face, I instantly felt a sense of joy that I had not known before. Pam was pretty, kind, smart, and had a sense of confidence that allowed her to move freely amongst the other students. I noticed that everyone liked Pam, and it was genuine. She was real, and she allowed others to be real. She really liked people, you could feel it.

True to her nature, Pam reached out and befriended me, the quiet new girl. She invited me to her house after school, so we walked there one day after school, and I had an amazing awakening. I had a glimpse of a stress free, happy family home for the first time. As I walked into Pam's home, I immediately felt joy, laughter, and kindness. In fairness, my family had financial problems, and we dealt with the stress from this. It's hard to be joyful and fun, when there are worries about not having enough money. My family had six kids, and my parents had many different jobs, with whispers about money and bills. It's just a different atmosphere. Every family has issues and challenges, and often these matters are kept private. In my adult years, I eventually learned that even Pam's joyful family had their share of losses and challenges. Most families do. But many challenges are kept quiet, so it's easy to assume that it's only our family dealing with sadness, pain and worries.

They Loved Me Like Their Own

However, the point of sharing this story is that I learned some of the most valuable lessons of my childhood from Pam's parents, Jack and Tillie. Jack was a respected executive in a big company, and he emulated every day in hid daily life the characteristics of why he had been promoted. He understood the importance of giving each person his undivided attention when he was engaged in a conversation, or when he asked the person how they were. He listened with interest and joy. As he listened, he always seemed to be smiling a little bit, because it was just his way. If he was focused on you at any given moment, you instantly felt Loved by the way he was paying attention to you, and by the kindness on his face. He Loved people and it showed. He adored and loved his family so much, and each person in their family knew it. They also had six children, and Tillie was such a happy mother, with an amazing sense of humor. She always knew how to make someone smile and laugh.

We all attended the same church in our small town, St. Mary's Catholic Church, and I always noticed their family on Sunday. There was a sense of joy and peace amongst them. Many of the kids inherited their mother's wit and sense of humor, so there were jokes, teasing, and lots of laughter in the air. It was shared with a Love and kindness for each other. I felt so lucky to be in their presence, and absorb the happy vibes in their home. They didn't have financial stress like my family did, so they weren't burdened with bills. In fact, they were financially comfortable enough that they installed one of the first "built in pools" in our village. Most of us had never seen a curvy slide that entered the pool. Their kindness and open hearts, welcomed the entire neighborhood to swim and hang out. Tillie was always running into her kitchen, getting lemonade and other drinks to make sure no one became dehydrated. Jack would arrive home about six, and he would always come out to the pool, still dressed in his business suit, and share his warm smile with all. He enjoyed seeing the smiles on the twenty or thirty people having fun. It was wholesome, good fun, and that's why he had the pool built. People like Jack, do many things to bring people together. Even though I rarely saw him swim, he probably had more joy and satisfaction from that pool than anyone else.

"I Still Love You"

When Pam and I became teenagers, we tested the rules and boundaries a bit. One night, we lied about where we were going, and the friend who was driving the car we were in, (and were NOT supposed to be in), drove too fast, and we ended up in a car accident. It was so frightening, and so wrong that we even went into this car. We knew that this person drove fast. I know that we had guardian angels watching over us. We were bruised up, but we were all okay. The car was totaled. The police called our parents to come and get us. Pam's father, Jack, picked both of us up. I can still remember the look on his face. He was so grateful that we were not harmed in the accident. He hugged us both, and we both felt Loved. What a comfort. We were scared, and we both knew we were wrong for getting in that car. Then he looked deeply into both of our faces, and he slowly said the most devastating thing to us. He said, "I am so disappointed in both of you. I trusted you to make good choices, and to not lie to me. I was so worried and so sad about this. But I still Love you." After that, Pam and I both cried very hard. That was the most powerful thing he could say to teach us a lesson. We both had so much admiration, appreciation and Love for this amazing human being, Jack, Pam's Dad, and we were both so upset because we disappointed him. He had trusted us, shown us his love and kindness, and we had let him down. Pam and I were so sad from this. I remember every detail of it because it taught me one of the greatest lessons in my life. Jack taught me to be a better person and to pay attention to what made him so great. I concluded that it was his faith and Love in Jesus Christ.

Throughout all the years of spending lots of time with this great family, including vacations, ski trips and more, I never once heard Jack raise his voice. He earned so much more respect and admiration by everyone, at home and at the office, by the way he cared about others. He did it by living his life, according to his faith and his connection to Jesus. Upon his retirement, he and Tillie spent many hours (and years) serving others, and their church. I cannot even begin to count how many thousands of lives they both impacted because of their Loving and generous hearts. They were both wonderful gifts on earth, and they made others feel Loved. Their hearts were humble, and they did not seek recognition. They taught with Love and example. They never preached to me, and I never heard them preach to others. Their actions and Love caught people's attention and created curiosity. Now that they are in heaven, I think they would smile, if I shared their story, but only if by sharing, it could inspire more good. They knew the meaning of, "Love one another, as I have Loved you." Thank you Jack and Tillie for loving me, and showing me how great it is to "Love one another."

Kindness and Love Are Never Wasted

This story is a powerful reminder for the many families who notice a child needing a little more Love and hope, and wondering if it's going to make a difference. Just know that it does. It did for me. Jack and Tillie were like a compass for Love, and they set my directions on a positive course for hope and really good expectations. Kindness and Love are never wasted on others. It really makes a difference.

We've all heard the saying, "It takes a village to raise a child", and we lived in a small town, and those who lived near the heart of the town, lived in the "village." Many others lived in or on the outskirts of town, in the mountains, farmland, or by the river. It's a great town. But the village helped raise many kids from all areas of the town.

You won't ever regret helping, but you might regret not reaching out, if you felt the prompting, and talked yourself out of it. (It happens. We all let logic and other excuses get in our head, and we skip the window of opportunity. Then later, we ponder it again, and we wonder. Pray, ask, and listen. You will know what to do, for you.)

The more I learned about Jack and Tillie, especially as a young adult, I kept their principles in my heart, mind and soul. They lived their lives in a Christ-like manner, doing lots of charity work, sharing joy, showing compassion, Loving others, and I noticed that everyone always felt their Love when they were in the presence of Jack and Tillie. They were active in their local Catholic church when I met them, and they stayed devoted and active until their earthly departure. They chose joy and Love each day, and they extended it to everyone. Yet underneath all of that joy, their peace came from their strong faith and their belief in Jesus Christ. They didn't try to persuade others to come to their point of view, but within seconds, you knew, without a doubt, that you were in the presence of Love and acceptance.

I am so grateful that I was invited to spend many hours in their home, and even go on family vacations with them. Those times in my life were a true gift. They showed me so many other possibilities, and a different way of living. During my adult years, I recognized what a profound impact they each had upon me as I shaped my values, dreams, and my belief in Jesus Christ. I wrote them a long letter, similar to what I am writing now, and I thanked them. I cried as I wrote it, because I knew without a doubt, that I would not be as kind and Loving as I strive to be every day, without their beautiful example of what true Christ like love looks like in everyday life. They shaped who I am today, and they deserved to know this. After that, we stayed in touch through letters, and through Pam, before they each went to heaven to meet Jesus. When I heard the news of each of their passing over, I smiled at the thought of how wonderful it would be for these two beautiful loving individuals to meet Jesus. Based on my experiences, I imagined that Jesus gave them both a long and Loving embrace and said, "Thank you." Then I cried.

The Ripple Effect

I share this very personal and profound story in writing, because they truly changed my life. These memories have caused me to reach out to people, who are needing more Love and some hope, and to extend a bit of the love and guidance that I learned from Jack and Tillie. There is always a wonderful ripple effect from love and pure intentions. Thanks again, Pam, for reaching out to the shy, new girl in town, and for sharing your family with me. I Love you forever.

P.S. Just so you can imagine beautiful Pam a little more in your mind, she was voted "Polly Personality" by our senior class in high school. She was and is still kind to everyone. Love and kindness are never wasted. Heaven smiles when they see it happening. We can all be better examples of this, because you never know when you might just change a life for the better. Living this way, makes each of us feel closer to Jesus, and that is enough, but it creates a great feeling, and it's like a bonus gift. The more you Love, the more you bring it right back to your own heart. Amen.

"BE THERE FOR HER"
by Janeen

I became friends with someone recently who is an absolute joy to be around. Every time we're together, I find myself laughing hysterically and sharing experiences that we can both find humor in. She has added a great deal to my life.

Just a couple of weeks ago we had lunch together and spent three hours talking about business and life. During the course of our conversation, she made a comment that if she were to get divorced or lose her husband, she would not re-marry. I told her of course she would – she is only 50 years old and would be too young to stay single. Just eight days later I received a text from her in the middle of the night – "my husband passed away tonight" it read. I was shocked and devastated for her! I couldn't help but wonder after her comment a week earlier if she had received a premonition – a prompting from the spirit that her husband would not be on this earth very much longer.

A connection to the spirit is a wonderful thing to have. And if we are listening, I believe we can be guided in ways we do not even understand.

A few days later, a service was held for my friend's husband followed by a "celebration of his life" at their church. My friends and I talked about going but we kept making excuses about why we didn't need to be there. As I look back at some of the things we said – "It should just be her time with her family," "I would feel uncomfortable because I'm not familiar with these types of services," "I don't really have the time to be there," – all of our comments were about US not wanting to go out of our way or be put out.

In the end, one of my good friends convinced me that I should at least show up and let our friend know that I had taken the time to be there for HER. I did so, and I was so grateful that my friend had talked some sense into me. It was so wonderful to be able to see my friend, talk to her briefly and let her know I cared about her. It meant so much to her.

Loved Ones Help Us Transition

We recently saw a post come across Facebook that talked about a survey that had been conducted among patients in hospice care. The question asked of these people, who were close to death, was about whether they had been visited recently by loved ones who had passed on.

An overwhelming majority of these patients said they had experienced visions or dreams from people who had passed on. As Elizabeth and I talked about this, we understood that it makes a lot of sense that our loved ones are sent to help us through the transition, prepare us and help us feel comforted as we approach death. They may be helping us realize death is close without us even realizing that is what's happening. But perhaps it also creates a sense of longing to go home and be with those who have passed on before us.

I had an experience several years ago where my friend, Pam, passed away in her sleep at the age of 48. Her husband was away on business, and her daughters found her that morning. It was a devastating time, but the family came through it because of their Love for each other and their Love for their Savior, Jesus Christ. Several years earlier, Pam had given birth to a precious baby boy. This tiny infant died at birth, and she and her husband were devastated. They were never able to have more children after that, so she and her husband adopted three children over the next few years. At the time of her death, her children were teenagers.

What makes Pam's death remarkable is the fact that just a week before her death, she had shared a dream she had with a few close friends. She was standing out in an open area holding an infant in her arms. A distance away, on the other side of some kind of barrier, her husband and daughters were standing waving at Pam and the baby. She was obviously impressed enough by the dream to share it.

We believe, at this point, it was a premonition or indication of her impending death. Maybe that vision or dream prepared Pam for her departure and most likely helped her by creating a longing to be with her baby boy whom she had not had the opportunity to raise.

We probably all are familiar with similar stories and experiences of loved ones who have passed on. But we believe the visitation of spirits coming to take us home is an overwhelming proof of our Saviors Love for us all.

We hope as you've read these stories, you have felt Love and remembered the times people have shown Love to you. Take some time to think of a person who, at a difficult time in your life, showed Love and kindness to you in a way that made your life so much better.

Take out a beautiful card and write a note to that person, thanking them for showing you such great Love at a time when you desperately needed it. Mail or hand deliver it. Your Love for this person will increase, and they will also be filled with Love and charity.

Here is a sample affirmation to say each day, to reinforce the commitment to living each day mindfully, while appreciating the gift of Love:

AFFIRMATION: I am full of Love. I will give all the Love I have to those who are important in my life. But I will also look to find someone each day, who I may not know, who could benefit from the Love and kindness I have to share. I will Love others and help them Love in return.

Thou shalt love the Lord thy God with all they heart, and with all thy soul, and with all they strength, and with all thy mind; and thy neighbour as thyself."
~ Luke 10:25, 27 ~

Applying the gift of LOVE:

This list for Love was the most fun for us as we worked to come up with 75 ideas that will help us all begin appreciating the gift of Love – our hope is that these ideas will help us all begin thinking about Love, feeling Love, and acting on Love – showing our Love to others and to our Savior.

Remember, good habits are powerful, and it is our intention to instill in each of you the ability to think, feel and act in such a way as to change your behavior for the better.

So here is our list of ideas to get you on the road to Loving more sincerely and more deeply:

- Write a letter or a card to each family member expressing your Love
- Throw your arms around your children every day
- Take a meal into your sick neighbor
- Pet your puppies
- Talk to a person who looks sad
- Express gratitude to someone who helps you
- Offer to help someone in need
- Put a blanket over your sleeping husband
- Give a meal to a beggar
- Kiss your significant other on the neck
- Pray to your Heavenly Father each day and thank Him
- Look someone in the eye when they speak to you
- Put your arms around your mom and dad when you see them
- Speak kindly to your family members at all times
- Tell someone you love them
- Write down something you are grateful for each day
- Help a hurt animal
- Smile at someone every day

- Let your children know how great they make your life
- Offer to do an errand for your aging father
- Visit your parents often
- Give to the homeless
- Sing your kids to sleep
- Donate items to the poor
- Get outside yourself and look for the good in others
- Write a love poem to someone you care deeply about
- Brush your daughter's hair
- Make cookies for your children's friends
- Get to know someone you think you don't really care for
- Live the ten commandments
- Tell your children you love them every single day
- Help someone through a difficult time
- Apologize to someone you may have hurt
- Listen to people without judgment
- Talk to someone who may look like they need a friend
- Make a special dinner for your family
- Surprise your daughter with a cupcake
- Frequently touch your spouse – on the arm, the shoulder, the waist, anywhere
- Share a book about Jesus Christ with a friend
- Ask Heavenly Father for forgiveness
- Make time for those you Love
- Teach a child a new skill
- Call your son who's away at college every week
- Do yard work for your grandparents
- Make your husband his favorite meal and surprise him
- Offer to take your elderly neighbor to an appointment
- Offer to clean for someone who is sick
- Cuddle with your significant other under a blanket during a storm
- Tell each of your children something you Love about them every day
- Lend a listening ear to someone who is angry or upset

- Share your dessert with your wife
- Let your dad tell his favorite stories over and over
- Tell your wife she is beautiful
- Tell your husband he is handsome
- Notice when someone changes their hair or gets a new outfit
- Teach your daughter to do something you enjoy
- Find something nice about someone you don't particularly like and tell them
- Kiss your significant other when they are not expecting it
- Give your wife a small gift once in awhile – a token of your affection
- Plan a secret getaway for your anniversary
- Take a walk with someone you Love
- Dance with your wife when you are all alone
- Help your son or daughter with their homework when they are having a meltdown
- Send emoji hearts in your text messages
- Say "I Love You" often
- Leave a voice message early in the morning for your husband
- Set aside time each week to go on a date with your spouse
- Volunteer at a care center
- Surprise your wife by doing the dishes or vacuuming the house
- If someone you love is stressed, help them with some of their work
- Give your significant other a back rub
- Spend less time working and more time with your family
- Give kisses and hugs to your family members
- Support your spouse in the things he or she does
- Take care of yourself so you can be there for those who need you

Choose a few items from the list that sound fun to you. And DO THEM.

Remember, we are trying to form new habits, so be deliberate about doing new things and experiencing things that are outside of your comfort zone. Set aside some time each week to experience Love in a way you have not experienced it before.

We have given you activities throughout this book that will help you really think about things, try new things, appreciate the people in your life, and work to live a more Christ-like life. We want you to experience the gift of Love in new ways. So fill a couple of pages in your journal by completing the activity below.

Think about someone in your life who you Love more than anything in the world.

- What makes you Love that person so much?
- How do you show your Love back to that person?
- Are there things you could do that would convey your Love in deeper ways?
- What does this person do for you that makes you happy?
- What qualities does this person possess?

Now make a list of the things you would like to start doing for this person (and others) that will show your Love for them.

DO THE THINGS ON YOUR LIST – Take them one at a time, and try them. See what kind of response you get back.

The purpose of this exercise is to get you thinking about how to truly show Love for another person. Love isn't a feeling, it's an action. That's why we can show Love for everyone. It's about doing. So let's go and do.

"For small creatures such as we, the vastness is bearable only through love."
~ Carl Sagan ~

Love is not always about the things we say to someone. It is simply about showing up. Acts of Love don't require recognition and they don't require that we be made known. Love quietly seeks a way to show kindness. It doesn't announce, "I'm here!"

If we see someone hurting, we put our arm around them;
If we see weeds in our dad's yard, we pull them;
We show up at our kid's performances;
We show up for our husband's work party;
We show up for our friend's presentation;
We show up to an event that's important to our spouse;
We change our plans when a friend is in need.

Love is about being there for the people who matter to us and sometimes for the people who simply need our support.

We all remember the Sandy Hook Elementary shootings.

Six-year-old Emilie Parker was among the children killed in the tragic shooting in Newtown, Connecticut. Her father, Robbie Parker, spoke out about the tragedy and came home to Utah to hold a public memorial service where he released a flying lantern representing his daughter into the dark sky. About 1,000 people gathered that night to pay tribute to the Sandy Hook victims and to show their support for those left behind. Then, one by one, lanterns were released as the names of the teachers and students killed were read aloud.

This was an act of Love – simply showing up.

Robbie mentioned to the press that he had been asked a lot lately how he was doing. He jokingly said, "In my opinion, you need to come up with an alternate way to greet somebody."

We often say to people who are grieving, "How are you doing?" We say it because we don't know what else to say, but the answer is obvious. How could they be doing? What do we possibly expect them to say?

A friend told me a better question is, "How are you doing TODAY?" It is a much more thoughtful question. It is a way to show we really do care. It is a simple act of Love.

> *"Therefore doth my Father love me, because*
> *I lay down my life, that I might take it again.*
> *~ John 10:17 ~*

What are your thoughts and impressions now about the gift of LOVE?

Has anything changed or come into your awareness that wasn't there before?
Jot down your thoughts now after 30 days of reflection:

_____

_____

_____

_____

_____

_____

_____

_____

_____

_____

_____

_____

_____

_____

"For God so loved the world that He gave His only begotten Son, that whosoever believeth in Him should not perish, but have everlasting life."
~ *John 3:16* ~

Garth Brooks, after four nights of sold out concerts in Salt Lake City on November 1, 2015, said:

"It's All About Love…"

I was just putting the finishing touches on our final chapter, Love, and then walked into another room, and heard the local evening news. The television anchors could not say enough positive things about Garth Brooks, who had just completed a four-night tour in our city, (SLC, Utah), and had sold out all four nights, along with breaking other records.

But the icing on the cake was that he and his band, crew and more, hosted an athletic conference for kids the next morning before they left town. Our local news reported that Mr. Brooks gives back to every community where he holds a concert, and Garth was interviewed by the news about why he does this. We think we heard him say at least three times, "It's all about Love," and he was so sincere as he said this. He talked about his own childhood of growing up in a blended family, and how Love was the key to making things work. He clearly wants to give back, and he provides a free athletic clinic in every city where he holds a concert, to give Love back to the kids.

What a great story to end our final chapter about Love. Thank you, Garth Brooks, for putting the final touches on our last chapter, and stating it loud and clear, that, "It's All About Love!"

We hear you, we join you, and we thank you!!

CONCLUSION:

We have thought a lot about Love as we've worked on this book. There are many people around us and in our lives who are great examples of Love. But one person in particular comes to mind. He is a friend of ours who stayed in a marriage where he was cheated on, treated as a second-class citizen in his own home, taken advantage of at every turn, and finally tossed out with little to show for his years of hard, selfless work. Of course, there are always two sides to a story, but this man has moved on without bitterness in his heart. He is kind and takes responsibility where it is warranted. As we think about his story, we are impressed by his ability to Love unconditionally a person who –

- betrayed him,
- took advantage of his kind heart,
- and was motivated by selfishness to hurt him.

So what does it actually mean to Love your enemy?
Honestly, how does a person Love someone like that?
In watching our friend's example, we can tell you now that what we believe it means is this –

- Don't speak unkind words about them,
- Turn the other cheek when they try to hurt you,
- Give them the benefit of the doubt by realizing some outside force is causing them to behave in an unkind manner – childhood trauma, stress, unhappiness, etc.,
- Be patient, even when it's hard.

Loving your enemy does NOT mean this –

- You have to be their best friend,
- You are required to do whatever they say,
- You need to allow yourself to be manipulated by them,
- You have to spend time around them.

Learning to Love everyone sounds like a tall order, but it can be done if we understand what it DOES and DOES NOT mean. We will truly be blessed if we can work toward the goal of Loving, not only our friends, but our enemies as well.

Love pays attention to what is going on in the moment, and Love notices the feelings of others. Love will reflect on the best way to approach someone who is in conflict or struggling with an issue. Love is gentle, kind, and shares a tone of voice that conveys Love and concern. Love does not have to solve the problem, but Love can open the door for others to come through, and share their expertise to help solve a situation. So much about conveying Love depends on how the pureness of Love is shared. It is not an intellectual decision. It is a choice of the heart, while trusting in the Holy Spirit to guide us. Love is guided, and humble, and Love trusts the Lord to know how to share it. The more we do it, with Jesus by our side, the more we become confident in reaching out to others.

As we Love more, the spirit of Jesus will guide us towards those who need His Love, and we will become an instrument for His intentions. Of course, we must use wisdom and listen to promptings. There are situations that are not safe to enter into, and we must be clear as we pray and listen for discernment. We must listen for the whispers of the Holy Spirit before we act, especially in situations where there is potential danger. However, if we are in tune with the Holy Spirit, we will hear the correct message. Our job is to pay attention and listen, and to fine tune our instrument for discerning what we need to hear. When we do this, we will be guided in Love. There are times when we will be told to walk away, and we must trust this prompting. Acting upon Faith, our Love will be guided by the Holy Spirit. Pray and practice this faith, and it will be shown to you."

The pure Love of Jesus desires to support others in their spiritual journey and growth in Love. We are His instruments to convey His Love to others. When we are receptive, His Love will pass through our being, and touch the one who needs to feel it. We need to be finely tuned to hear and feel His Love so that we can share it with those who need to be reminded of His unconditional Love for us.

Affirmation about Love:

"There are times when it doesn't feel convenient to extend Love to someone, or it might feel forced. However, these are the times that I remind myself the most, that it was not convenient or easy for Jesus to extend His love to us, when He choose to go along with the divine plan, and be crucified for us. Whenever I think about His sacrifice, I let go of any excuse to follow through with showing Love. His sacrifice of Love is something that we will never endure, and it was in accordance with the divine plan. It was His gift to all of us. Therefore, I choose to honor the promptings of the Holy Spirit as I go forth in my life. Because this is how I show my Love to Jesus for the Gifts that He has shown me. If the Holy Spirit is prompting me, I will be given the energy and means to follow through."

The more we extend Love in our world, the more we feel Love and Peace in our hearts and soul. This seems to be a universal law. There is a ripple effect of Love in our world. It's beautiful and heart-warming. Even if you are skeptical, and doubt these suggestions, we sincerely believe that if you just practice a few of these Gifts in your life, you will find more Gifts that are undeniable, and you will be pleasantly surprised by how the Gifts shift your world. We wish you all the Gifts of our beautiful Savior Jesus Christ, and a very special and powerful relationship with Him, and the Holy Spirit, in accordance with our Heavenly Father's plan.

We hope you are experiencing a beautiful Christmas season, and feeling the Love of Jesus in your hearts and homes, as we reflect on why we celebrate Christmas. These reflections can have enormous impact upon our lives, as we embrace the Love and the Gifts from above.

We have written the "12 Gifts of Christ" as our gift to you. But this is not just a project just for the Christmas season. This is a book and a message to be used year-round, as we all work to develop habits in our daily living that reflect the gifts that Jesus came to teach us.

Now that you have taken the past 12 months to practice these gifts, your gift to Jesus Christ can be your deeper understanding of Love, your commitment to living a more Christ-like life, and your decision to be a greater example to those around you.

We hope this has book been an inspiration to you. Please share it with someone you already LOVE and... with someone you are learning to LOVE. And please go to our website 12giftsfromjesuschrist.org to learn more about how we can each apply the Gifts in our lives, and become more Christlike. These are ideas and ways to increase your individual growth.

Wishing you a Love-filled Christmas season, and beyond.

Much Love to you and your loved ones,

Merry Christmas!!

Janeen Golightly and Elizabeth Hickey

My name is Janeen Golightly. When Elizabeth asked me to help her write this book, I was thrilled. I thought, what a great idea – a fun, chunky little Christmas book that people will want to add to their collection. I mean, that's what I do every year – add another Christmas book to my stack that sits on my coffee table in the living room during the holidays. I read them when I buy them, and then I let them sit on the stack for years to come because they look so pretty and so festive – an added "decoration" to my holiday decor.

But a couple of months into this project, I began to realize – that's not what this book is. It's not a fun, chunky Christmas book, and it certainly isn't a decoration. This book quickly became something very meaningful to me.

As I began adding content, meaningful stories began to come to my memory. Not only that, but new stories began to unfold. Elizabeth and I often speak of how many things have happened to both of us during the writing of this very special book. My divorce, her buying and selling of houses, the death of her brother, the death of a mutual friend's husband, projects coming into our lives, friends causing troublesome issues, new people coming into our lives, children giving us grief, business troubles, and on and on. Many good things and many difficult things have consumed us as we have worked to finish this book.

We have often said, the adversary is working overtime to try and prevent us from putting these thoughts down on paper. But we have worked hard to overcome, and continued on despite efforts to discourage us, distract us and even stop us from writing this precious book.

12 Gifts From Jesus Christ has significant meaning to both of us. It has increased our awareness and knowledge of our Savior, Jesus Christ. It has propelled us to research, learn and focus on something that is extremely important in each of our lives. It has had life-changing implications and helped us not only be more aware of, but more focused on practicing the gifts in our own lives.

I myself have realized some things I want to change in my own life. I recently endured a brutal divorce that left me asking myself how I might possibly forgive, how I might actually move forward with hope, and how I could ever in a million years love and trust someone again.

12 Gifts From Jesus Christ has given me the answers to my very own questions. It has been a reminder to me that my answers ALL lie in my Savior, Jesus Christ.

It is my hope that you will use this book as a guideline for a better life, as a tool for meditation and thoughtful prayer, as a resource when you are having difficulty, and as a comfort when you don't know where to turn.

Hello, fellow human being, traveling along this planet. **My name is Elizabeth Hickey**, one of the co-authors of this book. First of all, thank you for being curious enough to even pick up this book. I have embarked upon the path of writing this book, partly because I believe we are all curious and interested in how other people live their lives. We all wonder about what makes other people thrive. In contrast, we are interested in the lives of others who struggle through many life situations. I obtained a master's degree in social work, and also took additional training courses in mediation because I care deeply about other people, and I wanted to dedicate my professional career to improving human situations and the lives of others. This book clearly fits into the same intentions and provides the freedom to openly share my spiritual beliefs, compared to staying with the professional code of conduct and ethics as a social worker and mediator.

This shared sense of wonder and interest in other people's lives propels many of us to read personal stories about how others live their daily lives. Stories connect us. We recognize ourselves as we listen to similar descriptions of how our paths intersect and how life weaves a tapestry of shared highs and lows. Most of us empathize with feelings of compassion for our fellow human being. When we hear a touching story, we allow the emotions to rise within us. This is how we sense that our shared humanity really matters. We simply care about another person's life challenges, sorrows and struggles. Our hearts and shared love reach out to humanity to make a connection. Without words, we simply care and love. We see this over and over when a natural disaster happens in other areas of the world. We each send the best assistance and aid that we can at the time. We do it because we care. I believe most of us are hard wired to share love and kindness. We seek that invisible connection to other human souls because we know we are much more alike than we are different. As we seek, mediate, pray and search for meaning about our existence, many of us are led to study the Bible for answers. We wonder about the existence of Jesus, and why He might have come to earth. I am far from being a biblical scholar, or an expert in any religion, and I could not make an accurate reference to most of the profound scriptures. But I do know something for sure. I have felt the love of Jesus, and I have accepted Jesus into my heart and soul.

As a young child, I attended church every Sunday, and I listened closely to lessons about prayer and how it worked. When I really needed Jesus in my life as a child, I prayed. Jesus was there. Once you know this, you cannot go back and pretend that you don't know. Jesus was real ever since that time, and He will always be real. Jesus is real for each and every person who truly seeks Him. Be like a child, and seek His comfort and guidance. Do it over and over, and have faith that your prayers will be answered. Perhaps not in the timing pattern you hope for, but with faith, love and hope, your prayers will be heard.

We invite you to practice living the "12 Gifts of Jesus Christ." As we focus our intentions of living more like Jesus did, we will grow our love for others and for Jesus. When we live more mindfully using these 12 Gifts as a guide, we cannot help but feel the ripple of love returning to us. When we live with love and Christ-like qualities, we are seeking to emulate the way Jesus lived, and this pleases Him. It is a humble and quiet experience. The more we love others, the more we become love, and then we extend this love to others and to the earth we live upon, that sustains us. I believe this love is built upon using the gifts that Jesus came to teach us. As we practice and create habits of living the gifts as a way of life, we cannot help but to become more Christ like in our own lives.

www.ingramcontent.com/pod-product-compliance
Lightning Source LLC
Chambersburg PA
CBHW021209090426
42740CB00006B/169